THE LEGISLATIVE

BRANCH OF THE FEDERAL GOVERNMENT

PURPOSE, PROCESS, AND PEOPLE

THE LEGISLATIVE
BRANCH OF THE FEDERAL GOVERNMENT
PURPOSE, PROCESS, AND PEOPLE

EDITED BY BRIAN DUIGNAN, SENIOR EDITOR, RELIGION AND PHILOSOPHY

Britannica®
Educational Publishing

IN ASSOCIATION WITH

ROSEN
EDUCATIONAL SERVICES

Published in 2010 by Britannica Educational Publishing
(a trademark of Encyclopædia Britannica, Inc.)
in association with Rosen Educational Services, LLC
29 East 21st Street, New York, NY 10010.

Distributed exclusively by Rosen Educational Services.
For a listing of additional Britannica Educational Publishing titles, call toll free (800) 237-9932.

First Edition

Britannica Educational Publishing
Michael I. Levy: Executive Editor
Marilyn L. Barton: Senior Coordinator, Production Control
Steven Bosco: Director, Editorial Technologies
Lisa S. Braucher: Senior Producer and Data Editor
Yvette Charboneau: Senior Copy Editor
Kathy Nakamura: Manager, Media Acquisition
Brian Duignan: Senior Editor, Religion and Philosophy

Rosen Educational Services
Hope Lourie Killcoyne: Senior Editor and Project Manager
Nelson Sá: Art Director
Matthew Cauli: Designer
Introduction by Richard Worth

Library of Congress Cataloging-in-Publication Data

The legislative branch of the federal government: purpose, process, and people / edited by Brian Duignan.
    p. cm.—(U.S. government: the separation of powers)
"In association with Britannica Educational Publishing, Rosen Educational Services."
ISBN 978-1-61530-027-3 (library binding)
1. United States. Congress. 2. Legislative power—United States. 3. Legislators—United States—History. 4. Legislators—United States—Biography. I. Duignan, Brian.
K1021.L45 2010
328.73—dc22

                                                                2009037871

Manufactured in the United States of America

Cover credit: © www.istockphoto.com/Dra Schwartz.

Photo credit: p. 8 (The United States Capitol at night) © www.istockphoto.com/Cheng Chang.

CONTENTS

Introduction

As Americans were fighting for their independence during the Revolutionary War, they were governed under a framework known as the Articles of Confederation. The central government consisted of a Congress with representatives from each of the thirteen states. But the authority of the Congress was restricted, with most of the power resting with the states them-selves. After independence from Great Britain had been secured by the Peace of Paris in 1783, many Americans realized that the Articles of Confederation were inade-quate to govern the new nation. A new federal form of government eventually was established by representa-tives of the states who convened at a Constitutional Convention in Philadelphia in 1787.

Under the Constitution of 1787 there are three branches of government: the legislature, the executive, and the judiciary. The powers of the federal government are divided among the three branches—with each one act-ing as a check and balance on the others. This prevents any single branch—such as the executive or the legisla-ture—from becoming too powerful. Given their colonial experience, Americans were wary of concentrating too much power in a single person or institution.

The authority of Congress is carefully spelled out in Article I of the Constitution. Among the primary powers of Congress is the exclusive authority to approve all legis-lation. This acts as a powerful check on the power of the president.

The framers of the Constitution created a bicameral legislature—that is, one with two houses. In the lower house, or House of Representatives, each state receives a specified number of representatives based on the size of its population. This apportionment ensures that the larger states, such as California and Texas, have more votes than the smaller states. This important provision was hammered out in the Constitutional Convention to ensure the support of the large states for the new framework of government. Each representative is elected directly by the people in a congressional district for a term of two years. The framers of the Constitution wanted frequent elections for House members so that they would be forced to pay close attention to the needs of the constituents in their districts or risk being turned out of office at election time. Currently there are 435 representatives from fifty states.

In contrast to the House of Representatives, the United States Senate has a smaller number of members and operates differently. Under the Constitution, each state has two senators; there are currently 100 senators. This allocation ensures that every state will have the same voice in the U.S. Senate. Delegates from the small states at the Constitutional Convention, such as New Jersey and Connecticut, wanted this measure so that they would not be overwhelmed by the larger states. Unlike representatives in the House, United States senators serve for a term of six years. The Founding Fathers believed that this would enable the Senate to become a more deliberative body— one that was not swayed by the changing tide of public opinion because the members did not need to stand for reelection every two years.

Under Article I, Section 3 of the Constitution, senators were elected by the legislature in each state. This insulated them even further from the whims of the voters. However, the Seventeenth Amendment, passed in 1913, changed the way that senators were elected. Instead of being elected indirectly—by voters casting ballots for state legislators who in turn selected a state's U.S. senators—they are elected directly by voters from an entire state. One-third of the U.S. Senate stands for reelection every two years.

During the 19th century, the Senate was dominated by stirring debates among men such as Henry Clay of Kentucky, Daniel Webster of Massachusetts, and John C. Calhoun of South Carolina, who delivered impassioned speeches about the future of states' rights and slavery. In 1858 Democrat Stephen A. Douglas of Missouri defended his Senate seat in a series of debates over slavery with Republican Abraham Lincoln. These debates helped propel Lincoln to election as president in 1860. Later in the century, senators Robert La Follette of Wisconsin and William Borah of Idaho dominated the floor of the Senate with speeches about curbing the power of big business and rooting out corruption in government.

Since the U.S. Senate's creation, many senators have run for the office of president of the United States. But only a few have been elected, including Warren Harding in 1920, John F. Kennedy in 1960, and Barack Obama in 2008. One former president, John Quincy Adams, who was defeated for reelection in 1828, later ran for the U.S. Congress from his home state in Massachusetts. He served in the House of Representatives from 1831 to 1848 — the only former president ever elected to Congress.

Although Article I of the Constitution states that Congress has the "power of the purse," it is specifically the House of Representatives where all bills involving finances must originate. Finance bills are generally considered by the powerful House Appropriations Committee before going to the entire House. The Appropriations Committee is one of many committees in the House that consider various types of bills. For example, the Agriculture Committee deals with issues that affect farmers, while the Committee on Homeland Security focuses on problems relating to the security of America's borders and transportation centres to prevent further terrorist attacks like the one that occurred on September 11, 2001.

The political party, either Democratic or Republican, having a majority of members in the House of Representatives controls each committee and selects its chairperson. In addition, the majority party also selects the all-important position of speaker of the House of Representatives. The speaker leads the majority party in the House and presides over the entire legislative body. When the president of the United States is a member of the other political party, the speaker sometimes takes on the role of leader of the opposition. In the 1980s, for example, when Republican Ronald Reagan was president, Democrat Thomas P. "Tip" O'Neill was speaker of the House and often acted as leader of the Democratic Party; in the mid-1990s, during the presidency of Democrat Bill Clinton, Republican New Gingrich played the same role for his party.

Instead of a speaker, as in the House, the vice president of the United States acts as the president of the Senate. However, this is a largely ceremonial position except when a tie vote occurs in the Senate and the vice president has the authority to cast the deciding vote. While revenue bills originate with the House, many other types of legislation may be proposed by the U.S. Senate. For example, Democratic Sen. Edward M. Kennedy of Massachusetts was a leader of many legislative attempts to provide health care coverage for millions of uninsured Americans.

The Senate also has the power to approve or reject the president's nominations to a variety of offices. For example, members of a president's cabinet must be approved by the Senate; and the Senate must approve nominations to the U.S. Supreme Court and lower federal courts, as well as ambassadors to foreign countries. These powers enable the Senate to act as a check and balance on the power of the president.

Both houses of Congress also act as a check on each other. For a bill to become law, it must be approved by the House and Senate and signed by the president. If members of the House and Senate pass different versions of a new law, then a conference committee with representatives from both houses must meet together, iron out the differences in the legislation, and return it to both houses for a final vote. If the legislation is approved by Congress but vetoed by the president, a two-thirds vote of the members of each house can override the president's veto, at which point the legislation becomes law.

In addition to these powers, Congress alone has the right to declare war. In 1917, for example, Pres. Woodrow Wilson came to Congress and asked its members to declare war against the Central Powers—Germany, Austria-Hungary, and Turkey. This declaration enabled the United States to join the Allies—Great Britain and France—a decision that led to Allied victory in WWI in 1918. Similarly, Pres. Franklin D. Roosevelt appeared before Congress in 1941 and asked for a declaration of war following the Japanese attack on the U.S. naval base at Pearl Harbor on December 7. Nevertheless, many presidents have committed the United States to foreign conflicts without ever asking for a declaration of war. In the 1960s, for instance, Pres. Lyndon B. Johnson vastly increased the size of U.S. forces fighting in Vietnam without a formal declaration of war by Congress. In 1973 Congress passed the War Powers Act, which required the president to consult with Congress before involving U.S. forces in hostilities abroad, but the law has been largely ignored by subsequent presidents.

Twice in the history of the United States, Congress has exerted a powerful check on the president through the impeachment process. Under the Constitution, the House of Representatives has the power to pass a resolution of impeachment if a majority of its members believe that the president has violated the law. The president is then tried in the United States Senate, with the chief justice of the U.S. Supreme Court presiding over the trial. A two-thirds majority of the Senate is necessary for the president's conviction and removal from office.

In 1868, Pres. Andrew Johnson was impeached when Congress believed that he had illegally fired Secretary of War Edwin Stanton. Johnson escaped removal from office, however, when the Senate fell a single vote short of convicting him. Nevertheless, following his impeachment, Congress became the dominant power in the federal government.

In 1974, Pres. Richard Nixon became the first president to resign the office after the House Judiciary Committee voted to recommend articles of impeachment against him for his role in the Watergate Scandal. In 1998, Pres. Bill Clinton became the second president to be impeached, by a House vote of 221-212. He was accused of lying to a grand jury and obstruction of justice in the investigation of his relationship with a White House intern. President Clinton was tried in the Senate in 1999, but he was acquitted.

Political commentators have pointed out that the impeachment of Pres. Clinton illustrated the increasing level of partisanship that had arisen between the executive and legislative branches of government. Clinton, a Democrat, was impeached by a Republican-controlled House of Representatives. In the past, relations between the Congress and the president were characterized by a greater spirit of cooperation and bipartisanship. For example, during the late 1940s, Republicans controlled the U.S. Senate while a Democrat, Harry Truman, was president of the United States. Nevertheless, Republican

Sen. Arthur Vandenberg—chairman of the Senate Committee on Foreign Affairs—was a strong supporter of President Truman's plan to rebuild Europe after World War II and establish the North American Treaty Organization as a bulwark against communism.

Much of this spirit of bipartisanship has disappeared, however. And, in 2009, when Pres. Barack Obama's proposals to rescue the failing American economy through billions of dollars in stimulus spending were passed by the Democrat-controlled Congress, they received very little support from Republicans.

Since the early 20th century, the power of Congress has declined relative to that of the president. Although it is unclear whether Congress will ever again be the dominant institution it was in the second half of the 19th century, it will continue to play an essential role in the federal government of the United States for as long as the present Constitution is in force. By exploring the pages of this book readers will gain a deeper understanding of this unique and dynamic institution.

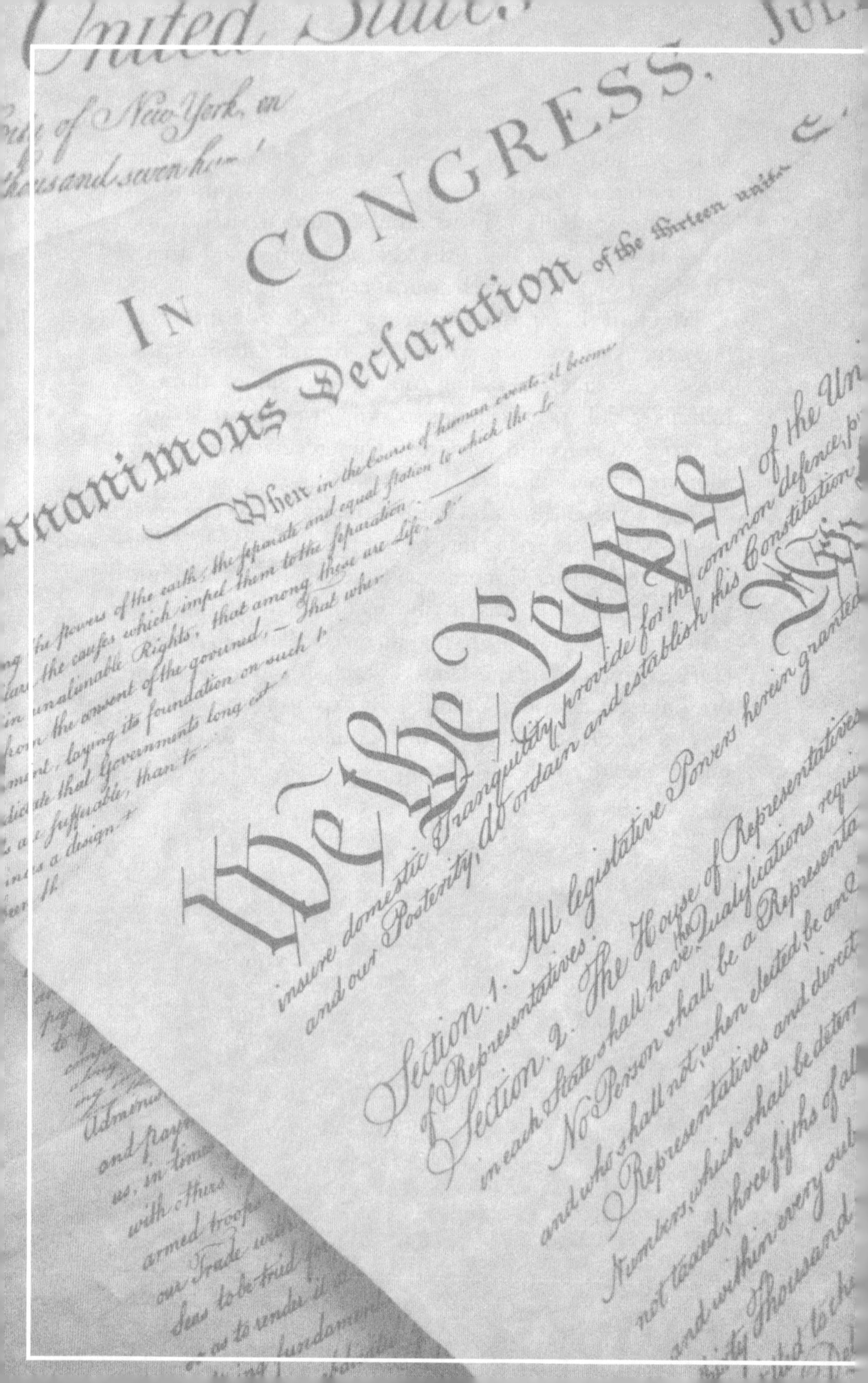
IN CONGRESS.
We the People

The Role of the Legislature

The characteristic function of all legislatures is the making of law. In most political systems, however, legislatures also have other tasks, such as selecting and criticizing the government, supervising administration, appropriating funds, ratifying treaties, impeaching officials of the executive and judicial branches of government, accepting or refusing executive nominations, determining election procedures, and conducting public hearings on petitions. Legislatures, then, are not simply lawmaking bodies. Neither do they monopolize the function of making law. In most systems the executive has a power of veto over legislation, and, even where this is lacking, the executive may exercise original or delegated powers of legislation. Judges, also, often share in the lawmaking process, through the interpretation and application of statutes or, as in the U.S. system, by means of judicial review of legislation. Similarly, administrative officials exercise quasi-legislative powers in making rules and deciding cases that come before administrative tribunals.

Legislatures differ strikingly in their size, the procedures they employ, the role of political parties in legislative action, and their vitality as representative bodies. In size, the British House of Commons is among the largest; the Icelandic lower house, the New Zealand House of Representatives, and the Senate of Nevada are among the smallest.

A legislature may be unicameral, with one chamber, or bicameral, with two chambers. Unicameral legislatures are typical in small countries with unitary systems of government—i.e., systems in which local or regional governments may exist but in which the central government retains ultimate sovereignty. Federal states, in which the central government shares sovereignty with local or regional governments, usually have bicameral legislatures, one house usually representing the main territorial subdivisions. The United States is a classic example of a federal system with a bicameral legislation; the U.S. Congress consists of a House of Representatives, whose members are elected from single-member districts of approximately equal population, and a Senate, consisting of two persons from each state elected by the voters of that state. The fact that all states are represented equally in the Senate regardless of their size reflects the federal character of the American union. The federal character of the Swiss constitution is likewise reflected in the makeup of the country's national legislature, which is bicameral.

A unitary system of government does not necessarily imply unicameralism. In fact, the legislatures of most countries with unitary systems are bicameral, though one chamber is usually more powerful than the other. The United Kingdom, for example, has a unitary system with a bicameral legislature, which consists of the House of Lords and the House of Commons. The Commons has become by far the more powerful of the two chambers, and the cabinet is politically responsible only to it. The Lords has no control over finances and only a modest suspensory veto with respect to other legislation (it may delay the implementation of legislation but not kill it). The parliaments of Italy, Japan, and France also are bicameral, though none of those countries has a federal form of government. Although in the United States all 50 states except Nebraska have bicameral legislatures, their governmental systems are unitary. In the 49 U.S. states with bicameral legislatures, the two houses have equal legislative authority, but the so-called upper houses—usually called senates—have the special function of confirming the governors' appointments.

The procedures of the U.S. House of Representatives, which derive from a manual of procedure written by Thomas Jefferson, are among the most elaborate of parliamentary rules, requiring study and careful observation over a considerable period before members become proficient in their manipulation. Voting procedures worldwide range from the formal procession of the division or teller vote in the British House of Commons to the electric voting methods employed in the California legislature and in some other American states. Another point of difference among legislatures concerns their presiding officers. These are sometimes officials who stand above party and, like the speaker of the British House of Commons, exercise a neutral function as parliamentary umpires; sometimes they are the leaders of the majority party and, like the speaker of the U.S. House of Representatives, major political figures; and sometimes they are officials who, like the vice president of the United States in his role as presiding officer of the Senate, exercise a vote to break ties and otherwise perform mainly ceremonial functions.

Legislative parties are of various types and play a number of roles or functions. In the U.S. House of Representatives, for example, the party is responsible for assigning members to all standing committees; the party leadership fills the major parliamentary offices, and the party membership on committees reflects the proportion of seats held by the party in the House as a whole. The congressional party, however, is not disciplined to the degree found in British and some other European legislative parties, and there are relatively few "party line" votes in which all the members of one party vote against all the members of the other party. In the House of Commons, party-line voting is general; indeed, it is very unusual to find members voting against their party leadership, and, when they do, they must reckon with the possibility of penalties such as the loss of their official status as party members.

THE LEGISLATURE OF THE UNITED STATES

The U.S. Congress, the legislative branch of the American federal system, was established under the Constitution of 1789 and is separated structurally from the executive and judicial branches of government. As noted previously, it consists of two houses: the Senate, in which each state, regardless of its size, is represented by two senators, and the

The United States Capitol in Washington, D.C., is the meeting place of the U.S. Congress. © Corbis

House of Representatives, to which members are elected on the basis of population. Among the express powers of Congress as defined in the Constitution are the power to lay and collect taxes, borrow money on the credit of the United States, regulate commerce, coin money, declare war, raise and support armies, and make all laws necessary for the execution of its powers.

THE CONTINENTAL AND CONFEDERATION CONGRESSES

The Congress established in 1789 was the successor of the Continental Congress, which met in 1774 and 1775–81, and of the Confederation Congress, which met under the Articles of Confederation (1781–89), the first constitution of the United States. The First Continental Congress was convened in Philadelphia in 1774 in response to the British Parliament's passage of the Intolerable (Coercive) Acts, which were intended as punishment for the Boston Tea Party and other acts of colonial defiance. Fifty-six deputies in a single chamber represented all the colonies except Georgia. Peyton Randolph of Virginia was unanimously elected president, thus establishing usage of that term as well as "Congress." Other delegates included Patrick Henry, George Washington, John and Samuel Adams, and John Jay. Meeting in secret session, the body adopted a declaration of personal rights, including life, liberty, property, assembly, and trial by jury, and denounced taxation without representation and the maintenance of the British army in the colonies without their consent.

Before the Second Continental Congress assembled in Philadelphia in 1775, hostilities had already broken out between Americans and British troops at Lexington and Concord, Mass. New members of the Second Congress

George Washington (centre) *surrounded by members of the Continental Congress.* Lithograph by Currier & Ives, c. 1876. Currier & Ives Collection, Library of Congress, Neg. No. LC-USZC2-3154

included Benjamin Franklin and Thomas Jefferson. John Hancock and John Jay were among those who served as president. The Congress "adopted" the New England military forces that had converged upon Boston and appointed Washington commander in chief of the American army. It also acted as the provisional government of the 13 colony-states, issuing and borrowing money, establishing a postal service, and creating a navy. On July 2, 1776, with New York abstaining, the Congress "unanimously" resolved that "these United Colonies are, and of right ought to be, free and independent states." Two days later, it solemnly approved this Declaration of Independence. The Congress also prepared the Articles of Confederation, which, after being sanctioned by all the states, became the first U.S. constitution in March 1781.

The Articles placed Congress on a constitutional basis, legalizing the powers it had exercised since 1775. This Confederation Congress continued to function until the new Congress, elected under the present Constitution, met in 1789.

PRIMARY DOCUMENT: A PROPOSAL FOR A CONTINENTAL CONGRESS

Early in May 1774 the Boston Committee of Correspondence sent a circular letter throughout the colonies urging a stoppage of trade with Britain. This appeal was met with a mixed response. In New York, a committee of fifty-one, dominated by merchants, drafted a reply on May 23. While this committee had no desire to halt trade, it was determined to maintain control of the anti-British sentiments of the populace. The reply, therefore, sympathized with Boston's situation but implied that only a Continental Congress could suitably handle the matter.

The alarming measures of the British Parliament relative to your ancient and respectable town, which has so long been the seat of freedom, fill the inhabitants of this city with inexpressible concern. As a sister colony, suffering in defense of the rights of America, we consider your injuries as a common cause, to the redress of which it is equally our duty and our interest to contribute. But what ought to be done in a situation so truly critical, while it employs the anxious thoughts of every generous mind, is very hard to be determined.

Our citizens have thought it necessary to appoint a large committee, consisting of fifty-one persons, to correspond with our sister colonies on this and every other matter of public moment, and at ten o'clock this forenoon we were first assembled. Your letter, enclosing the vote of the town of Boston, and the letter of your Committee of Correspondence were immediately taken into consideration.

While we think you justly entitled to the thanks of your sister colonies for asking their advice on a case of such extensive consequences, we lament our inability to relieve your anxiety by a decisive opinion. The cause is general, and concerns a whole continent, who are equally interested with you and us; and we foresee that no remedy can be of avail unless it proceeds from the joint act and approbation of all; from a virtuous and spirited union which may be expected while the feeble efforts of a few will only be attended with mischief and disappointment to themselves and triumph to the adversaries of our liberty.

Upon these reasons we conclude that a congress of deputies from the colonies in general is of the utmost moment; that it ought to be assembled without delay, and some unanimous resolution formed in this fatal emergency, not only respecting your deplorable circumstances, but for the security of our common rights.

We have nothing to add, but that we sincerely condole with you in your unexampled distress, and to request your speedy opinion of the proposed congress, that if it should meet with your approbation, we may exert our utmost endeavors to carry it into execution.

THE CONGRESS OF 1789

The Constitutional Convention (1787) was called by the Confederation Congress for the purpose of remedying certain defects in the Articles of Confederation. But the Virginia Plan, presented by the delegates from Virginia and often dubbed the large-state plan, went beyond revision and boldly proposed to introduce a new, national government in place of the existing confederation. The convention thus immediately faced the question of whether the United States was to be a country in the modern sense or would continue as a weak federation of autonomous and equal states represented in a single chamber, which was the principle embodied in the competing New Jersey Plan, presented by several small states (and hence has been referred to as the small-state plan). This decision was effectively made when a compromise plan for a bicameral legislature—one chamber with representation based on population and one with equal representation for all states—was approved in mid-June.

The Constitution, as it emerged after a summer of debate, embodied a much stronger principle of separation of powers than was generally to be found in the state constitutions. The chief executive was to be a single figure (a composite executive was discussed and rejected) and was to be elected by an electoral college, meeting in the states. This followed much debate over the Virginia Plan's preference for legislative election of the executive. The principal control on the chief executive, or president, against violation of the Constitution was the threat of impeachment (a criminal proceeding instituted by a legislative body against a public official). The Virginia Plan's proposal that representation be proportional to population in both houses was severely modified by the retention of equal representation for each state in the Senate. But the question of whether to count slaves in the population was abrasive. After some contention, antislavery forces gave way to a compromise by which three-fifths of the slaves would be counted as population for purposes of representation and direct taxation (for representation purposes "Indians not taxed" were excluded). Slave states would thus be perpetually overrepresented in national politics; provision was also added for a law permitting the recapture of fugitive slaves (though in deference to republican scruples the word "slaves" was not used).

Contemporary political theory expected the legislature to be the most powerful branch of government. Thus, to balance the system, the executive was given a veto, and a judicial system with powers of review was established. It was also implicit in the structure that the new federal judiciary would have power to veto any state laws that conflicted either with the Constitution or with federal statutes. States were forbidden to pass laws impairing obligations of contract—a measure aimed at encouraging capital—and the Congress could pass no ex post facto law (typically, a law that retroactively makes criminal an act that was not criminal when performed). But the Congress was endowed with the basic powers of a modern—and sovereign—government. The prospect of eventual enlargement of federal power appeared in the clause, giving the Congress powers to pass legislation "necessary and proper" for implementing the general purposes of the Constitution.

By June 1788 the Constitution had been ratified by nine states, as required by Article VII. After elections held late that year, the first Congress under the new Constitution convened in New York on March 4, 1789.

POWERS AND FUNCTIONS OF THE MODERN CONGRESS

Although the two chambers of Congress are separate, for the most part, they have an equal role in the enactment of legislation, and there are several aspects of the business of Congress that the Senate and the House of Representatives share and that require common action. Congress must assemble at least once a year and must agree on the date for convening and adjourning. The date for convening was set in the Constitution as the first Monday in December. However, in the Twentieth Amendment to the Constitution, the date was changed to January 3. The date for adjournment is voted on by the House and the Senate.

Congress must also convene in a joint session to count the electoral votes for the president and vice president. Although not required by the Constitution, joint sessions are also held when the president or some visiting dignitary addresses both houses.

Of common interest to both houses of Congress are also such matters as government printing, general accounting, and the congressional budget. Congress has established individual agencies to serve these specific interests. Other agencies, which are held directly responsible to Congress, include the Copyright Royalty Tribunal, the Botanic Garden, and the Library of Congress.

The term of Congress extends from each odd-numbered year to the next odd-numbered year. For its annual sessions, Congress developed the committee system to facilitate its consideration of the various items of business that arise. Each house of Congress has a number of standing (permanent) committees and select (special and temporary) committees Together the two chambers of Congress form joint committees to consider subjects of common interest. Moreover, because no act of Congress is valid unless both houses approve an identical document, conference committees are formed to adjust disputed versions of legislation.

At the beginning of a session, the president delivers a State of the Union address, which describes in broad terms the legislative program that the president would like Congress to consider. Later, the president submits an annual budget message and the report on the economy prepared by the president's Council of Economic Advisors. Inasmuch as congressional committees require a period of time for preparing legislation before it is presented for general consideration, the legislative output of Congress may be rather small in the early weeks of a session. Legislation not enacted at the end of a session retains its status in the following session of the same two-year Congress.

In terms of legislation, the president may be considered a functioning part of the congressional process. The president is expected to keep Congress informed of the need for new legislation, and government departments and agencies are required to send Congress periodic reports of their activities. The president also submits certain types of treaties and nominations for the approval of the Senate. One of the most important legislative functions of the president, however, is that of signing or vetoing proposed legislation. The president's veto may be overridden by a two-thirds vote of each chamber of Congress; nevertheless, the influence of the president's potential power may extend to the procedures of Congress. The possibility that a bill may be vetoed gives the president some influence in determining what legislation Congress will consider initially and what amendments will be acceptable. In addition to these legal and constitutional powers, the president has influence as the leader of a political party; party policy both in Congress and among the electorate may be molded by the president.

Although the U.S. Supreme Court has no direct relations with Congress, the Supreme Court's implied power to invalidate legislation that violates the Constitution is an even stronger restriction on the powers of Congress than the presidential veto. Supreme Court and federal court decisions on the constitutionality of legislation outline the constitutional framework within which Congress can act.

Congress is also affected by representative interest groups, though they are not part of the formal structure of Congress. Lobbyists on behalf of interest groups play a significant role in testifying before congressional hearings and in mobilizing public opinion on select issues. Lobbyists may "buttonhole" members of Congress in offices, hotels, or private homes. Letters may be written or telephone calls made to public officials, and campaigns may be organized for this purpose. Organizations may provide favoured candidates with money and services. Massive public-relations campaigns employing all the techniques of modern communication may be launched to influence public opinion. Extensive research into complex legislative proposals may be supplied to legislative committees by advocates of various and often conflicting interests. Substantial election campaign contributions or other assistance may be supplied to favoured legislators or executives. The persons who lobby in these ways may be full-time officials of a powerful trade or agricultural association or labour union, individual professional lobbyists with many clients who pay for their services, or ordinary citizens who take the time to state their hopes or grievances. Cities and states, consumer and environmental protection and other "public interest" groups, and various branches of the federal government also maintain staff lobbyists in the United States.

Many interest groups make use of political action committees (PACs) to solicit voluntary campaign contributions from individuals and then channel the resulting funds to candidates for elective offices in the federal government, primarily in the House of Representatives and the Senate. PACs rose to prominence after the Federal Election Campaign Act of 1971 set strict limits on the amount of money a particular corporation, union, or private individual could give to a candidate. By soliciting smaller contributions from a much larger number of individuals, PACs circumvent these limitations and manage to provide substantial funds for candidates.

Many of the activities of Congress are not directly concerned with enacting laws, but the ability of Congress to enact law is often the sanction that makes its other actions effective. The general legal theory under which Congress operates is that legal authority is delegated to the president or executive departments and agencies and that the latter, in turn, are legally responsible for their actions. Congress may review any actions performed by a delegated authority; and in some areas of delegated legislation, such as in proposals for governmental reorganization, Congress must indicate approval of specific plans before they go into effect. Congress may also retain the right to terminate legislation by joint action of both houses.

Congress exercises general legal control over the employment of government personnel. Political control may also be exercised, particularly through the Senate's power to advise and consent to nominations. Neither the Senate nor the House of Representatives has any direct constitutional power to nominate or otherwise select executive or judicial personnel (although in the unusual event that the electoral college fails to select a president and vice president, the two houses, respectively, are expected to do so). Furthermore, Congress does not customarily remove officials. Congress, however, does have the power of impeachment. In such proceedings the impeachment is made by the House of Representatives, and the case is tried before the Senate—a vote of two-thirds of the senators present is required for conviction.

The power to levy and collect taxes and to appropriate funds allows Congress considerable authority in fiscal matters. Although the president has the initial responsibility for determining the proposed level of appropriations, once estimates for the next fiscal year are submitted to Congress, a single budget bill is not enacted, but rather a number of appropriation bills for various departments and agencies are passed during the first six or seven months of a session.

In its nonlegislative capacity, Congress also has the power to initiate amendments to the Constitution, and it must determine whether the states should vote on a proposed amendment by state legislatures or by special state conventions.

Finally, Congress has the right to investigate any subject that affects its powers. Congressional investigating committees may call witnesses and require them to produce information. These committees may also be given the power that persons who deliberately block the legislative process may be charged with contempt of Congress and may be issued warrants for their arrests.

Since 1945 the activities and politics of the U.S. Congress have been reported in a group of periodicals called the *Congressional Quarterly* (*CQ*), published in Washington, D.C. *CQ* comprises a Weekly Report with a Quarterly Index, an annual Almanac, and a news service. In addition, various special volumes and series are published from time to time, reviewing significant government activities and special problems. In addition to news media, *CQ*'s users include libraries, lobbyists, and many government—including congressional—offices.

UNITED STATES CAPITOL

The Congress of the United States meets in the United States Capitol, one of the most familiar landmarks in Washington, D.C. It is situated on Capitol Hill at the eastern end of Pennsylvania Avenue. The Washington Monument and the Lincoln Memorial lie to the west, and the Supreme Court and the Library of Congress lie to the east. The Supreme Court held sessions in the Capitol until its own building was completed in 1935.

Pierre Charles L'Enfant, who had designed the basic plan of Washington, was also expected to design the Capitol. Claiming that the plan was "in his head," however, L'Enfant refused to submit drawings or work with local commissioners, and Pres. George Washington was forced to dismiss him. A plan by William Thornton, a versatile physician with no formal architectural training, was eventually accepted, though it was submitted months after the closure of a design competition held in 1792. Thomas Jefferson, who was then secretary of state, was impressed with Thornton's design, writing that it...

> *so captivated the eyes and judgment of all as to leave no doubt...of its preference over all which have been produced.... It is simple, noble, beautiful, excellently distributed and moderate in size.*

The cornerstone was laid by Washington on Sept. 18, 1793.

Because Thornton had no knowledge of building technology, the construction was initially supervised by the runner-up in the competition, Stephen Hallet. Hallet attempted to alter many of Thornton's plans and was quickly replaced, first by George Hadfield and later by James Hoban, the architect who designed the White House.

The north wing, containing the Senate chamber, was completed first, and Congress convened there in November 1800. The following year Jefferson became the first president to be inaugurated at the Capitol, a tradition that has been observed in all subsequent inaugurations. The remainder of the building was completed by Benjamin Latrobe, whom Jefferson appointed surveyor of public buildings in 1803. Latrobe followed Thornton's conception of the exterior closely but used his own designs for the interior. Perhaps Latrobe's best-known additions were the unique Corinthian-style columns, whose capitals depict tobacco leaves (symbolizing the nation's wealth) and corn cobs (symbolizing the country's bounty).

The south wing, containing the chamber of the House of Representatives, was completed in 1807. During the

War of 1812 the Capitol was looted and burned by British troops, though rain prevented the building's complete devastation. Latrobe began reconstruction in 1815 but resigned two years later. By 1827 his successor, the distinguished Boston architect Charles Bulfinch, had joined the two wings and built the first copper-sheathed dome, again adhering to Thornton's original design. In January 1832 the French historian Alexis de Tocqueville visited the Capitol and observed that it was "a magnificent palace," though he was less impressed with the sessions of Congress, writing that they were "frequently vague and perplexed" and that they seemed to "drag their slow length along rather than to advance towards a distinct object."

United States Capitol, Washington, D.C. Hisham Ibrahim/Getty Images

In order to provide more space for the increasing numbers of legislators from new states, in 1850 Congress approved a competition for a design to expand both wings of the Capitol. The winner, the Philadelphia architect Thomas Ustick Walter, finished the extension of the south wing in 1857 and the north wing in 1859. The new additions did not seem to alter the behaviour of the members, however. Aleksandr Lakier, a Russian visitor to the United States, wrote that everyone...

> *wears a black frock-coat or tails and sits where he pleases. Had I not felt regret for the nice new furniture and carpet in the House of Representatives, I would not even have noticed the rude, but perhaps comfortable, position of the feet raised by a*

*son of the plains above the head of his neighbor, and the nasty
habit many Americans have of chewing tobacco.*

The major architectural change to the Capitol during
Walter's tenure was the replacement of the old Bulfinch
dome with a 287-foot-high (87 metre) cast-iron dome,
which Walter modeled after the dome of St. Peter's Basilica
in Rome, designed by Michelangelo. At the onset of the
American Civil War, the dome remained unfinished, surrounded by scaffolding and cranes. In 1861 the Capitol was
used temporarily to bivouac federal soldiers who had been
hastily dispatched to protect Washington from an attack
by the Confederacy. These soldiers set up camp in the
House and Senate chambers and in the unfinished
Rotunda, occupying their free time by holding mock sessions of Congress and freely helping themselves to franked
stationery. At the insistence of Pres. Abraham Lincoln,
work on the dome continued, despite the war, as an important symbol of national unity. On Dec. 2, 1863, *Freedom*, a
bronze statue 19.5 feet (6 metres) high by Thomas
Crawford, was installed on top of the dome's crowning
cupola. Crawford's first drawings in the 1850s had adorned
the statue with a liberty cap—the symbol of freed slaves—
but after objections from Jefferson Davis, then the
secretary of war and later the president of the Confederacy,
the cap was replaced with a Roman helmet. (According to
records that surfaced in 2000, the workers who cast the
statue, as well as the worker who devised the method of
raising it, were slaves.) Constantino Brumidi's allegorical
fresco *Apotheosis of Washington* (1865), which depicts gods
and goddesses intermingled with George Washington and
other American heroes, adorns the ceiling's dome. In 1864
Congress established what would later be called National
Statuary Hall, where statues of two prominent figures
from each state were to be displayed. (All the statues were

to be displayed in National Statuary Hall, the original chamber of the House of Representatives; but by the 1930s engineers found that the weight of the many marble statues exceeded the floor's load-bearing capacity, thereby threatening its structure, and some statues were moved elsewhere.) After his assassination in April 1865, Lincoln became the first person to lie in state in the newly finished Rotunda, an honour since bestowed on some 30 people.

With the exception of various modernizations, including the installation of central heating, electricity, and elevators, no significant architectural alterations or additions were made until 1959–60, when the east front was extended 32.5 feet (10 metres) under the supervision of J. George Stewart. In December 2008 the 580,000-square-foot (53,884-square-metre) Capitol Visitor Center opened. Designed as an underground extension of the Capitol, it features exhibits about the building and Congress. The centre also provides shelter to visitors who previously had to wait in lines outdoors. Not including the Capitol Visitor Center, the building contains about 540 rooms and stands in a 131-acre (53-hectare) park.

LIBRARY OF CONGRESS

The Library of Congress is the de facto national library of the United States and the largest library in the world. In 2009 it had some 142 million items, and its collection was growing at a rate of about 2 million items a year. The Library of Congress serves members, committees, and staff of the Congress, other government agencies, libraries throughout the country and the world, and the scholars, researchers, artists, and scientists who use its resources. It is the national centre for library service to the blind and physically handicapped, and it offers many concerts, lectures, and exhibitions for the general public. Those outside the Washington, D.C., area have access to the library's growing electronic resources through the Library of Congress Web site.

The library was founded in 1800 with $5,000 appropriated by the Congress when the U.S. capital moved from Philadelphia, Penn., to Washington, D.C. It was housed within the new Capitol building, where it remained for nearly a century. However, on Aug. 24, 1814, during the War of 1812, the library's original collection of 3,000 volumes was destroyed when the British burned the Capitol as well as the White House. To rebuild the library's collection, Congress, on Jan. 30, 1815, approved the purchase of

Aerial view of the Thomas Jefferson Building, the oldest structure in the Library of Congress complex, Washington, D.C. In 1815 Congress created the Library of Congress from Jefferson's peronal library, which was said to be one of the finest in the United States. Photography by Carol M. Highsmith (digital file no. LC-DIG-highsm-03196)

former president Thomas Jefferson's personal library of 6,487 books for $23,950. On Christmas Eve 1851, another fire destroyed two-thirds of the collection. Many of the volumes have since been replaced.

Librarian of Congress Ainsworth Rand Spofford (1864–97) was the first to propose that the library be moved to a dedicated building. He also was instrumental in establishing the copyright law of 1870, which placed the Copyright Office in the Library of Congress and required anyone seeking a copyright to provide two copies of the work—books, pamphlets, maps, photographs, music, and prints—to the library.

Largely as a result of Spofford's vision, the library's burgeoning collection outgrew its space in the Capitol. In the early 21st century the Library of Congress complex on Capitol Hill included three buildings containing 21 public reading rooms. The Thomas Jefferson Building (originally called the Congressional Library, or Main Building) houses the Main Reading Room. Designed in Italian Renaissance style, it was completed in 1897 and magnificently restored 100 years later. The John Adams Building, completed in 1939, received its current name in 1980 to honour the president who in 1800 signed the act of Congress establishing the library. The Adams Building was built in Art Deco style and faced with white Georgia marble. The James Madison Memorial Building, modern in style, was dedicated in 1980. (That same year the Main Building was designated the Thomas Jefferson Building.) The Madison Building more than doubled the library's available Capitol Hill space. The continued growth of the collection in a wide variety of formats during the 1980s and 1990s necessitated the off-site relocation of some materials to storage facilities in Fort Meade, Md., and to the Packard Campus of the National Audio-Visual Conservation Center in Culpeper, Va.

*The African and Middle Eastern Reading Room in the Thomas Jefferson Building,
Library of Congress, Washington, D.C.* Photography by Carol M. Highsmith
(digital file no. LC-DIG-highsm-03194)

The vast majority of works in the library's collections
are received through the copyright deposit process mentioned above. Materials are also acquired through gifts,
purchases, and donations from private sources and other
government agencies (state, local, and federal), the library's
Cataloging in Publication program (a prepublication
arrangement with publishers), and exchanges with libraries in the United States and abroad. Those items that are
not selected for the library's collections or exchange programs are offered free to other federal agencies,

educational institutions, public libraries, or nonprofit, tax-exempt organizations.

The library's collections include more than 32 million cataloged books and other print materials, more than 63 million manuscripts, 5.3 million maps, 5.6 million pieces of sheet music, more than 3 million audio materials, and more than 14 million visual materials (comprising more than 12.5 million photographs and 1 million moving images). Approximately half of the library's book and serial collections are in languages other than English. Some 470 languages are represented. Particularly noteworthy are the library's preeminent collections in Arabic, Spanish, and Portuguese; the largest collections in many Slavic and Asian languages outside those geographic areas; the world's largest law library; and the largest rare-book collection in North America (some 750,000 volumes), including the most comprehensive collection of 15th-century books in the Western Hemisphere. The Manuscript Division holds the papers of 23 U.S. presidents, along with those of many other high-ranking government officials, of inventors such as Alexander Graham Bell and the Wright brothers, of social reformers such as Susan B. Anthony and Frederick Douglass, and of cultural figures such as Walt Whitman, Irving Berlin, and Martha Graham.

The Library of Congress provides direct research assistance to the U.S. Congress through the Congressional Research Service (originally the Legislative Reference Service), which was founded in 1914. Established in 1832, the Law Library provides Congress with comprehensive research on foreign, comparative, international, and U.S. law, drawing upon its collection of some 2.6 million volumes.

The Library of Congress is supported by direct appropriations from the Congress—as well as gifts and private

donations—and has been governed since 1800 by the Joint
Committee on the Library of Congress. Established in
1990, the James Madison Council—the library's first
private-sector advisory group—has supported the acquisition of hundreds of collection items (such as the 1507 map
by the German cartographer Martin Waldseemüller that
first used the word "America") and initiatives such as the
annual National Book Festival (launched in 2001). The
council's first chairman, John W. Kluge, also endowed a
major scholarly centre and a $1 million prize for lifetime
achievement in the humanities.

In addition to the Kluge Prize, the library sponsors
many privately endowed honours and awards recognizing
creativity and achievement in the humanities. These
include the poet laureate position, the Living Legend
medal, the Gershwin Prize for Popular Song, and the
National Ambassador for Young People's Literature,
through which the library honours those who have
advanced and embodied the ideals of individual creativity
with conviction, dedication, scholarship, and exuberance.

In 1994 the Library of Congress launched the National
Digital Library Program (NDLP), making freely available
on the Internet high-quality electronic versions of
American historical material from the library's special collections. By the end of the library's bicentennial year in
2000, more than five million items (manuscripts, films,
sound recordings, and photographs) had been mounted on
the library's American Memory Web site, which continued to expand rapidly. Also accessible on the Web site were
the library's exhibitions, bibliographic databases (online
public access catalog), a comprehensive legislative information system known as THOMAS, copyright
information, and a Global Gateway Web site for the
library's international collections and collaborative digital
libraries built with international partners.

Inspired by the success of the Global Gateway site, in 2005 Librarian of Congress James H. Billington proposed a project called the World Digital Library. Its goal was to make available to anyone with access to the Internet digitized texts and images of "unique and rare materials from libraries and other cultural institutions around the world." It was designed to be searchable in seven languages—Arabic, Chinese, English, French, Russian, and Spanish (official languages of the United Nations), as well as Portuguese. In 2007 the Library of Congress and UNESCO signed an agreement to build a World Digital Library Web site, which was launched in 2009 with approximately 1,200 digitized exhibits, including books, maps, and paintings. The library is also leading a collaborative effort mandated in 2000 by the Congress to preserve the country's digital assets.

Chapter 2 The House of Representatives

The House of Representatives is sometimes referred to as the "lower" house of Congress, in contrast to the Senate, which is the "upper" house. These terms, however, do not appear in the Constitution, and they are misleading in their suggestion that the legislative powers of the Senate are greater than those of the House. In fact, the House and the Senate share equal responsibility for lawmaking.

HISTORY AND FUNCTIONS

As conceived by the framers of the Constitution, the House was to represent the popular will, and its members were to be directly elected by the people. In contrast, members of the Senate were appointed by the states until the ratification of the Seventeenth Amendment (1913), which mandated the direct election of senators.

The constitutional requirements for eligibility for membership in the House of Representatives are a minimum age of 25 years, U.S. citizenship for at least seven years, and residency in the state from which the member is elected (a member need not reside in the constituency that he or she represents).

Each state is guaranteed at least one member of the House of Representatives. The allocation of seats is based on the population within the states, and membership is reapportioned every 10 years following the decennial census. House members are elected for two-year terms from single-member districts of approximately equal population.

In order to ensure that the populations of different districts remain approximately equal, legislative apportionment sometimes involves the redrawing of electoral districts or the creation of new ones. The authority to alter apportionment can be an important tool in maintaining the power of the incumbent political party. Constituencies can be defined, for example, in a way that concentrates the power of the opposition into relatively few districts and gives the ruling party narrow majorities in a large number of districts; the incumbent party is thereby awarded a disproportionately large share of seats. Using a different strategy, individual incumbents sometimes seek to influence the apportionment process to give themselves districts with no substantial opposition. The drawing of district boundaries in a way that gives an unfair advantage to one political party, a practice know as gerrymandering, is generally considered an abuse. U.S. courts, however, have tended to regard the practice as legal.

IN FOCUS: GERRYMANDERING

The term "gerrymandering" is derived from the name of Gov. Elbridge Gerry of Massachusetts, whose administration enacted a law in 1812 defining new state senatorial districts. The law consolidated the Federalist Party vote in a few districts and thus gave disproportionate representation to Democratic-Republicans. The outline of one of these districts was thought to resemble a salamander. A satirical cartoon by Elkanah Tisdale appeared in the *Boston Gazette*; it graphically transformed the districts into a fabulous animal, "The Gerry-mander," fixing the term in the popular imagination. Gerrymandering thus came to mean the drawing of electoral-district boundaries in a way that gives one party an unfair advantage over others.

Gerrymandering has been condemned because it violates two basic tenets of electoral apportionment—compactness and equality of size of constituencies. A U.S. Supreme Court ruling of 1964 stated that districts should be drawn to reflect substantial equality of population. However, using studies of regional voting behaviour, the majority parties in certain state legislatures continue to set district boundaries along partisan lines without regard for local boundaries or even contiguity. For example, in some states, representatives from rural and small town districts seek to limit the representation of more densely populated urban centres.

Sometimes gerrymandering is defended as the only means of securing any representation for minority groups. It is argued that violating local boundaries in drawing districts is preferable to denying a politically cohesive group any voice in state government.

During the last two decades of the 20th century, some state legislatures in the United States undertook what amounted to racial gerrymandering to preserve the integrity and power of special-interest blocs of voters in large cities and other regions and to increase minority representation. However, the Supreme Court subsequently invalidated several racially gerrymandered majority-minority congressional districts and ruled that race could not be the determining factor in the drawing of constituency boundaries.

During the first Congress (1789–91), there were 59 members of the House of Representatives. By 1912 membership had reached 435. Two additional representatives were added temporarily after the admission of Alaska and Hawaii as states in 1959, but at the next legislative apportionment membership returned to 435, the number authorized by a law enacted in 1941.

The Constitution vests certain exclusive powers in the House of Representatives, including the right to initiate impeachment proceedings. Impeachment has rarely been employed, however, largely because it is a lengthy, expensive, and politically charged process. The first president to be impeached was Andrew Johnson (1865–69), who was charged by the House of Representatives with attempting to remove the secretary of war in violation of the Tenure of Office Act; he was acquitted in the Senate by a single vote. In 1974 the Judiciary Committee of the House of

Representatives voted three articles of impeachment against Pres. Richard M. Nixon in connection with his role in the Watergate scandal, but he resigned before impeachment proceedings in the full House could begin. In December 1998 the House of Representatives voted to impeach Pres. Bill Clinton, charging him with perjury and obstruction of justice in investigations of his relationship with a White House intern, Monica Lewinsky. He was acquitted in the Senate.

A dominating element of House organization is the committee system, under which the membership is divided into specialized groups for purposes such as holding hearings, preparing bills for the consideration of the entire House, and regulating House procedure. A member of the majority party chairs each committee. Almost all bills are first referred to a committee, and ordinarily the full House cannot act on a bill until the committee has "reported" it for floor action. There are approximately 20 standing (permanent) committees, organized mainly around major policy areas, each having staffs, budgets, and subcommittees. They may hold hearings on questions of public interest, propose legislation that has not been formally introduced as a bill or resolution, and conduct investigations. Important standing committees include those on appropriations, on ways and means (which handles matters related to finance), and on rules. There are also select and special committees, which are usually appointed for a specific project and for a limited period. The committees also play an important role in the control exercised by Congress over governmental agencies. Cabinet officers and other officials are frequently summoned before the committees to explain policy.

The House has the constitutional right to originate bills of taxation and spending. Since 1921, however, the annual budget of the United States has been proposed by

the president and accepted or rejected, in whole or in part,
by the House. It is prepared under his direct authority by
the Office of Management and Budget (OMB). The process begins when the various departments and agencies
prepare their appropriation requests, based on expenditures required under existing law and those estimated
under new legislation to be proposed by the president.
The OMB carefully scrutinizes these requests. In case of
disagreement, cabinet officers negotiate directly with the
president, who is ultimately responsible.

The budget is submitted in January and normally
applies to appropriations for the fiscal year beginning July
1. These must normally be spent in the following two
years. For some items, such as construction or procurement of military hardware, appropriations are made to
cover expenditures for the whole construction period.

When the budget reaches the House of Representatives,
it is distributed among the subcommittees of the
Appropriations Committee. Each subcommittee is concerned with a particular organizational unit. There is
virtually no consideration of the budget as a whole by the
committee as a whole. Revenues fall under the jurisdiction
of the Ways and Means Committee and are considered
separately and possibly even at a different time from
Appropriations.

The organization and character of the House of
Representatives have evolved under the influence of political parties, which provide a means of controlling
proceedings and mobilizing the necessary majorities.
Party leaders, such as the speaker of the House and the
majority and minority leaders, play a central role in the
operations of the institution. However, party discipline
(i.e., the tendency of all members of a political party to
vote in the same way) has not always been strong, owing to
the fact that members, who must face reelection every

two years, often vote in the interests of their districts rather than their political party when the two diverge.

Article I, section 6, paragraph 2 of the U.S. Constitution prohibits members of Congress from holding offices in the executive branch of government—a chief distinction between parliamentary and congressional forms of government:

No Senator or representative shall, during the time for which he was elected, be appointed to any civil office under the authority of the United States, which shall have been created, or the emoluments whereof shall have been increased during such time; and no person holding any office shall be a member of either House during his ontinuance in office.

After the census of 1920, Northeastern and Midwestern states held 270 House seats and the South and West held 169. Thereafter, the balance between the two regions

IN FOCUS: THE HOUSE UN-AMERICAN ACTIVITIES COMMITTEE

The House Un-American Activities Committee (HUAC) was a standing committee of the U.S. House of Representatives, established in 1938 under Martin Dies as chairman, that conducted investigations through the 1940s and 1950s into the alleged communist activities and associations of American citizens. Those investigated included many artists and entertainers, including the writers Elia Kazan and Arthur Miller and the folk singer Pete Seeger. Richard Nixon was an active member of HUAC in the late 1940s. The committee's most celebrated case was perhaps that of Alger Hiss, a former State Department official accused of involvement in a Soviet espionage ring. HUAC's actions resulted in several contempt-of-Congress convictions and the "blacklisting" of many of those who refused to answer its questions. Highly controversial for its tactics, it was criticized for violating First Amendment rights. Its influence had waned by the 1960s. In 1969 it was renamed the Internal Security Committee, and in 1975 it was dissolved.

gradually shifted, and by the beginning of the 21st century the Northeast and Midwest accounted for only 183 seats, compared with the South and West's 252. Most notably, the number of representatives from New York declined from 45 in the 1930s to only 29 following the census of 2000, while the number from California increased from 11 to 53.

NOTABLE MEMBERS OF THE HOUSE OF REPRESENTATIVES

Partly because the House contains more members than the Senate, representatives typically receive far less national attention than senators do. Indeed, most representatives who are not part of the House leadership are almost unknown outside their home districts. For this reason relatively few members of the House have been considered potential candidates for the presidency. Nevertheless, in its long history the House has included some representatives who were (or came to be) politically powerful or who influenced national policies in significant ways. Others were known less for their role in the House than for their contributions to fields outside government, including scholarship, the military, science and exploration, business, and community service. Among all of these figures, the representatives discussed in the remainder of this chapter are particularly remarkable.

SELECT CURRENT AND RECENT MEMBERS

JOHN A. BOEHNER
(b. Nov. 17, 1949, Cincinnati, Ohio)

John Andrew Boehner is a politician who has served as a congressman from Ohio in the U.S. House of Representatives (1991–). A Republican, he served as majority leader (2006) and minority leader (2007–) and is perhaps best known for his role in the passage of the No Child Left Behind Act of 2001.

Boehner grew up in a large Roman Catholic family (he had 11 brothers and sisters) in southwestern Ohio. He attended an all-male high school in Cincinnati before earning a degree in business from Xavier University (1977). He then took a job at a plastics company, Nucite Sales, where he eventually became president. In 1984 he was elected to the Ohio House of Representatives and remained in office until his election to the U.S. House of Representatives in 1990.

As a junior member of the House, Boehner soon earned a reputation as a crusader against what he considered wasteful spending in the federal budget. Along with six fellow Republican congressmen, he formed the so-called "Gang of Seven" to fight congressional corruption; their activities included making public the names of representatives who had overdrafts at the House Bank. Boehner's anticorruption stance was questioned in 1995 after he handed out checks from tobacco lobbyists to fellow Republicans on the House floor. He came under close scrutiny again the following year when a tape of a conference call with Republican Speaker of the House Newt Gingrich was made public. In the call, Boehner, Gingrich, and other Republicans discussed how Gingrich's reputation could be salvaged in light of ethics charges against him. During his early years in office, Boehner also helped to draft the Republican Party's Contract with America, a 100-day agenda for the 104th Congress that included the goals of reducing crime and providing middle-class tax relief.

Shortly after the inauguration of Pres. George W. Bush in 2001, Boehner became chairman of the House Committee on Education and the Workforce (2001–07). In that role, he helped to introduce the No Child Left Behind Act, which was intended to bring accountability to public schools by requiring more standardized testing and by giving students at failing schools the option of attending other schools. President Bush signed the act into law in January 2002. Boehner also introduced the Pension Protection Act in 2006 (signed into law in August 2008), which helped to prevent large failures in the pension system resulting from unwise investments. Boehner was elected to serve as his party's majority leader in 2006 and served as minority leader since 2007. In that year he was a vocal supporter of a proposal to construct a 700-mile (1,130-km) fence along the U.S.-Mexico border to reduce illegal immigration.

ROY BLUNT

(b. Jan. 10, 1950, Niangua, Mo.)

Roy Blunt is a Republican politician who has served as a Republican representative from Missouri in the U.S. House of Representatives (1997–). In the House, Blunt was majority whip (2003–07), acting majority leader (2005–06), and minority whip (2007–09).

Blunt's father was a dairy farmer and a Missouri state representative. Blunt earned degrees in history from Southwest Baptist University (B.A., 1970) and Southwest Missouri State University (M.A., 1972). He worked as the clerk and chief election officer for Greene county, Mo., from 1973 to 1984, when he won election as Missouri secretary of state (1985–93), becoming the first Republican to hold the office in more than 50 years. After a failed gubernatorial campaign in 1992, he served as president (1993–96) of Southwest Baptist University before winning election to the U.S. House of Representatives in 1996.

In the House, Blunt rose quickly through the Republican ranks. He was elected chief deputy whip in

1999, only two years after entering Congress, and in 2003 he became majority whip. After Rep. Tom DeLay was indicted in 2005 on charges of conspiring to violate election laws in his home state of Texas, Blunt took over as acting majority leader until the position was filled by Rep. John Boehner in 2006. When Republicans lost their majority in the House after the 2006 elections, Blunt became minority whip.

Throughout his early years in the House, Blunt was a strong proponent of increasing domestic oil production, preserving the Second Amendment's guarantee of the right to bear arms, and lowering federal income taxes. In 2003 he supported legislation that allowed larger individual tax deductions for charitable giving. He sponsored the Combat Meth Act of 2006, which was intended to make it more difficult for methamphetamine producers to buy chemicals and drugs. In the same year, he supported an immigration bill that would have authorized the construction of a fence along the U.S.-Mexico border and the deployment of more border patrol agents.

ERIC CANTOR
(b. June 6, 1963, Richmond, Va.)

Eric Cantor is a Republican politician who has served as a representative from Virginia in the U.S. House of Representatives (2001–) and as House minority whip (2009–).

Cantor grew up in a Jewish family in Richmond, Va., where his father owned a successful real estate company. While a student at George Washington University in Washington, D.C. (B.A., 1985), he worked as an intern for Tom Bliley, a Republican representative from Virginia. He then earned a law degree (1988) from the College of

William and Mary and a master's degree (1989) in real estate development from Columbia University. He worked as a lawyer and real estate developer for his father's company before founding his own mortgage brokerage company. In 1991 he won election to the Virginia State House of Delegates, where he served until 2001. Along with his wife, Diana, Cantor started the Virginia College Savings Plan, an independent state agency that allowed parents to lock in current tuition prices for their children who would attend college in the future; Diana was the organization's first executive director. Cantor was also instrumental in finding a new building for the Virginia Holocaust Museum in Richmond.

After his election to the U.S. House of Representatives in 2000, Cantor was considered a rising star among House Republicans; he became chief deputy whip of the Republican caucus after only two years. He was the chief sponsor of the Tax Relief and Health Care Act (2006), which allowed individuals to set up tax-free savings accounts to pay for health care. At times displaying fierce partisanship, Cantor was a strong supporter of the Iraq War (2003) and the policies of Republican pres. George W. Bush (2001–09) and was a vocal critic of Democratic House Speaker Nancy Pelosi. Since his succession to minority whip in 2009, he has led the Republican opposition in the House to Democratic Pres. Barack Obama's economic stimulus plan. Cantor has also served as chairman of the Congressional Task Force on Terrorism and Unconventional Warfare.

JAMES E. CLYBURN
(b. July 21, 1940, Sumter, S.C.)

James Enos Clyburn is a Democratic politician who has served as a representative from South Carolina in the U.S.

House of Representatives (1993–). With his election as majority whip in 2006, he became the second African American and the first South Carolinian to hold that post.

Growing up in South Carolina during a time of intense racial discrimination and segregation, Clyburn became an active participant in the civil rights movement, as did other members of his family. He served as president of the local youth chapter of the National Association for the Advancement of Colored People (NAACP) and participated in many demonstrations, including a 1961 march on the South Carolina State House, for which he was jailed. He graduated from South Carolina State College the same year. While living in Charleston, S.C., Clyburn worked as a public school history teacher, an employment counselor, and a director of two local youth programs and a farmworkers' program before running a failed bid for the South Carolina House of Representatives in 1970. After his loss he was invited to work as an adviser to South Carolina Gov. John Carl West, and four years later he was appointed the state's human affairs commissioner (1974–92). In 1992 he won election to the U.S. House of Representatives, becoming the first African American since 1897 to serve as a U.S. representative from his state.

Clyburn has maintained a liberal voting record in Congress, especially on issues related to health care, education, and organized labour. He voted in favour of legislation to ban the "cruel, inhuman, or degrading" treatment of persons in U.S. military custody (2005), backed a successful effort to increase the federal minimum wage (2007), and supported a bill introduced to provide health insurance to all Americans (2009). He has also been a strong advocate for preserving Gullah culture in his home state.

Clyburn is the author of *Uncommon Ground: The Story of Briggs v. Elliott, South Carolina's Unsung Civil Rights Battle* (2004).

STENY H. HOYER

(b. June 14, 1939, New York, N.Y.)

Steny Hamilton Hoyer is a Democratic politician who has served as a representative from Maryland in the United States House of Representatives (1981–) and as House majority leader since 2007. In that year he became the longest-serving member of the House from Maryland.

Hoyer first became interested in politics when he heard John F. Kennedy give a campaign speech at the University of Maryland, College Park (B.A., 1963). He later attended law school at Georgetown University in Washington, D.C. (J.D., 1966), and, campaigning on a platform of fair housing, ran a successful bid for the Maryland state senate in 1966. In 1975, at age 35, he became the youngest person ever to hold the office of president of the state senate. Hoyer joined the U.S. House of Representatives in 1981 through a special election after Rep. Gladys Noon Spellman's seat was left vacant by illness; he subsequently won reelection.

Hoyer served as his party's caucus chairman from 1989 to 1995. He was defeated twice in elections for the post of party whip—by Rep. David Bonior in 1991 and by Rep. Nancy Pelosi in 2001. There was sometimes tension between Hoyer and Pelosi (who became speaker of the House in 2007), especially when she supported Rep. John Murtha in his unsuccessful bid against Hoyer to become majority leader in 2006.

In the House, Hoyer has earned a reputation as a moderate liberal. He was a strong supporter of the Americans with Disabilities Act (signed into law by Republican Pres. George H.W. Bush in 1990), which prohibited employers from discriminating against people with disabilities and mandated improvements in their access to educational facilities and public transportation. In 1990 Hoyer supported the Federal Employee Pay Comparability Act (FEPCA), which granted a 5 percent pay raise to federal employees. The law was passed after several federal agencies reported that they were constantly losing workers to the private sector, where pay was much higher. After the bitterly contested presidential election of 2000 and the controversial U.S. Supreme Court decision in *Bush* v. *Gore*, Hoyer supported the Help America Vote Act (2002), which sought to eliminate obstacles to voting and to guarantee that every provisional ballot (cast by a person whose eligibility to vote in a certain district is questioned) is counted. In 2009 Hoyer voted in favour of the Credit Cardholder's Bill of Rights, which was intended to protect consumers from allegedly deceptive or unfair practices by credit card companies.

DUNCAN HUNTER
(b. May 31, 1948, Riverside, Calif.)

Duncan Hunter was a Republican politician who served as a member of the U.S. House of Representatives (1981–2009) and who unsuccessfully pursued the 2008 Republican presidential nomination.

Hunter enlisted in the U.S. Army in 1969 after graduating from Western State University in San Diego the previous year. He served in the Vietnam War and used G.I. Bill funding to return to Western State, where he received a law degree in 1976. Upon graduation, Hunter established a private law practice in San Diego. In 1980 he ran for the U.S. House of Representatives in a heavily Democratic district and won an upset victory. Demographic shifts and personal popularity helped Hunter win reelections to Congress into the 21st century.

In the House, Hunter emphasized national security issues, including defense spending, and immigration. He

Duncan Hunter. Congressional Pictorial Directory of the 110th Congress

sponsored legislation in 1994 that led to the creation of a fence along parts of the border between California and Mexico and lobbied for its extension along the entire international border. Hunter served on the House Armed Services Committee throughout his congressional career, chairing it from 2003 to 2007. His 2008 presidential campaign focused on many of the same issues that characterized his term in the House, but he was unable to generate support beyond his core constituency in the Southwest. After a disappointing finish in the Nevada caucus in January 2008, he withdrew from the race.

DENNIS KUCINICH

(b. Oct. 8, 1946, Cleveland, Ohio)

Dennis Kucinich is a Democratic politician who has served as mayor of Cleveland (1977–79) and as a representative from Ohio in the U.S. House of Representatives (1997–). He unsuccessfully sought the Democratic nomination for president in 2004 and 2008.

Kucinich's family is Roman Catholic, and he is the oldest of seven children. He first ventured into politics while still a student at Cleveland State University, winning a seat on the Cleveland city council in 1969. In 1972 and 1974

Kucinich unsuccessfully ran for the U.S. House of Representatives, the first year as a Democratic candidate and the second as an independent. In 1974 he earned bachelor's and master's degrees in speech communications from Case Western Reserve University in Cleveland. He left the city council in 1975 and was elected mayor of Cleveland in 1977.

At age 31 Kucinich was the youngest mayor of a major U.S. city. In 1978 he fired the police chief after he publicly accused Kucinich of trying to force him to commit "unethical acts." The move

Dennis Kucinich. Congressional Pictorial Directory of the 110th Congress

helped precipitate a recall election, which Kucinich barely survived, winning by fewer than 300 votes. That same year the city defaulted on its debts when local banks called in their loans in an unsuccessful effort to seize control of the city-owned power company, Muny Light (now Cleveland Public Power). Cleveland became the first major U.S. city to default on its obligations since the Great Depression of the 1930s. Kucinich lost his reelection bid in 1979, and many assumed that his political career was over.

Kucinich returned to the city council (1981–82) and ran unsuccessfully for a number of offices over the next decade, including governor of Ohio (1986, as an independent) and U.S. congressman (1988, 1992). He was elected to the Ohio Senate in 1994 and held that office until his successful run for the U.S. House of Representatives in 1996. His presidential campaign platforms in both 2004 and 2008 emphasized early childhood education, opposition to the U.S.-led Iraq War, repeal of the USA PATRIOT Act (formally the Uniting and Strengthening America by Providing Appropriate Tools Required to Intercept and Obstruct Terrorism Act of 2001), the creation of a cabinet-level Department of Peace, and adherence to international treaties on climate change. After failing to garner much support for his 2008 presidential bid, Kucinich withdrew from the race in January of that year in order to focus on his congressional reelection campaign, which he won. Kucinich outlined his political views in *A Prayer for America* (2003).

Ron Paul

(b. Aug. 20, 1935, Pittsburgh, Pa.)

Ron Paul is a politician who has served as a Republican member of the U.S. House of Representatives (1976–77, 1979–85, 1997–) and who unsuccessfully ran as the 1988 Libertarian presidential candidate. He later sought the Republican nomination for president in 2008.

Paul grew up on his family's dairy farm just outside Pittsburgh. He earned a bachelor's degree in biology from Gettysburg College in 1957 and a medical degree from Duke University, in Durham, N.C., in 1961. He later served as a flight surgeon for the U.S. Air Force (1963–65) and the Air National Guard (1965–68). In 1968 Paul moved to Brazoria County, Texas, where he established a successful practice in obstetrics and gynecology.

Paul was inspired to enter politics in 1971 when Pres. Richard M. Nixon abolished the Bretton Woods exchange system. Paul believed that the abandonment of the last vestiges of the gold standard would lead to financial ruin for the United States. Though he was unsuccessful in his initial run for the U.S. House of Representatives in 1974, his opponent resigned before completing his term, and Paul won a special election to complete it. He lost the seat in the subsequent general election, only to regain it two years later. He chose not to seek reelection in 1984 and instead campaigned—unsuccessfully—for the Republican nomination for U.S. senator. He broke from the Republican Party to run as a Libertarian in the 1988 presidential election, ultimately winning more than

Ron Paul. U.S. Representative Ron Paul

430,000 votes. He returned to the U.S. House of Representatives as a Republican in 1997, though his votes have often been at variance with the majority of his party; for example, in the early 2000s he voted against authorizing the Iraq War and against the USA PATRIOT Act.

Paul's presidential campaign platform remained libertarian in spirit. It focused on free-market economics, a radical reduction in the size of government, increased privacy protections for individuals, and a reduction of U.S. participation in international organizations. Having claimed only a handful of delegates, he ended his bid for the White House in June 2008 and launched Campaign for Liberty, a political action committee. His views are outlined in *Freedom Under Siege* (1987), *A Foreign Policy of Freedom* (2007), and *The Revolution: A Manifesto* (2008).

NANCY PELOSI

(b. March 26, 1940, Baltimore, Md.)

Nancy Pelosi (née Nancy D'Alesandro) is a Democratic politician who in 2007 became the first woman to serve as speaker of the U.S. House of Representatives.

Pelosi, whose father was a politician and New Deal Democrat, studied political science at Trinity College in Washington, D.C., graduating with a bachelor's degree in 1962. The following year she married Paul Pelosi, and the couple moved to New York. Five children and six years later, the family settled in San Francisco, where Pelosi worked as a volunteer Democratic organizer. Earning a reputation as a highly effective fund-raiser, she rose through the ranks, serving on the Democratic National Committee and as chair of both the California Democratic Party (1981–83) and the host committee for the 1984 Democratic National Convention in San Francisco. Along the way, Pelosi befriended longtime U.S. Rep. Phil Burton. Burton died in 1983 and was succeeded by his wife, Sala, who, shortly before her death in 1987, urged Pelosi to run for the seat. She narrowly won a special election and was reelected in 1988 to a full term. Pelosi easily won subsequent elections in her overwhelmingly Democratic district.

In 2002 Pelosi was elected minority whip and—using what she referred to as her "mother of five" voice—began pushing for unity among the diverse factions within her party by embracing conservatives and moderates. Still, Pelosi continued to vote consistently in favour of such liberal causes as gun control and abortion rights, opposed welfare reform, and cast a vote against the Iraq War. Her criticism of Pres. George W. Bush could be harsh; she once characterized him as an "incompetent leader." Her critics in turn characterized her politics as "left coast," left-wing, and out of touch with most of the country.

Following the midterm elections in November 2006, the Democrats gained a majority in the House of Representatives. On Jan. 4, 2007, Pelosi was elected speaker of the House of the 110th Congress.

TOM TANCREDO
(b. Dec. 20, 1945, Denver, Colo.)

Tom Tancredo is a Republican politician who served as a member of the U.S. House of Representatives (1999–2009) and who unsuccessfully sought the Republican nomination for president in 2008.

Tancredo earned a bachelor's degree in political science from the University of Northern Colorado in 1968, and he worked as a junior high school civics teacher before entering politics. In 1976 he was elected to the Colorado House of Representatives, where he served two terms. In 1981 Tancredo was named a regional representative for the U.S. Department of Education, a post he held into the early 1990s.

In 1993 Tancredo returned to the private sector as the president of a libertarian think tank. He remained there until he launched his campaign for the U.S. House of Representatives in 1998. He

Tom Tancredo. U.S. Representative Tom Tancredo

entered Congress in 1999 on a platform that emphasized border control, budget reduction, and immigration reform. His views on security and border issues are outlined in his book *In Mortal Danger: The Battle for America's Border and Security* (2006). In the House he was an opponent of abortion rights and gun-control legislation. He focused on many of these issues in his campaign for the presidency in 2008. Although his tough stance on immigration resonated with many in the Republican Party, his poll numbers never exceeded single digits, and in December 2007 he withdrew from the race.

SELECT PAST MEMBERS

BELLA ABZUG

(b. July 24, 1920, New York, N.Y.—d. March 31, 1998, New York, N.Y.)

Bella Abzug (née Bella Savitsky) was a Democratic politician who served as a representative from New York in the U.S. House of Representatives (1971–77). She founded several liberal political organizations for women and was a prominent opponent of the Vietnam War.

The daughter of Russian-Jewish émigrés, Bella Savitsky attended Hunter College (B.A., 1942) and Columbia University Law School, where she specialized in labour law and became editor of the *Columbia Law Review*. She earned her L.L.B. in 1947 and was admitted to the New York bar the same year. In 1945 she married Martin M. Abzug.

Over the next 23 years Abzug divided her time between the practice of law—focusing mainly on civil rights and labour law—and work on behalf of various causes, especially those of peace and disarmament. Among those defended by Abzug were individuals charged in Sen. Joseph

McCarthy's anticommunist crusade. In 1961 Abzug founded Women Strike for Peace, and she chaired the organization from 1961 to 1970. In the late 1960s, as the growing involvement of the United States in the Vietnam War became a focus of public protest, she supported Sen. Eugene McCarthy's challenge to Democratic incumbent Pres. Lyndon B. Johnson.

Elected to the House of Representatives for New York City's 19th district in 1970, Abzug was a founder and chair of several of the country's first and foremost liberal political organizations for women. She supported the Equal Rights Amendment, a women's credit-rights bill, abortion rights, and child-care legislation. Her brash and flamboyant manner earned Abzug the nicknames "Battling Bella," "Hurricane Bella," and "Mother Courage," among others.

In 1971, with Gloria Steinem and Shirley Chisholm, Abzug cofounded the National Women's Political Caucus, which aimed at increasing the participation of women in government. She was reelected to the House in 1972 and 1974 from the redrawn 20th district but relinquished the seat in 1976 to run for the Senate; she was defeated by Daniel P. Moynihan. The following year Abzug lost a primary election for mayor of New York City and in 1978 she lost a special election for a vacated congressional seat.

After playing a prominent role at the National Women's Conference in Houston, Texas, in November 1977, Abzug was named cochairman of the National Advisory Committee on Women by Pres. Jimmy Carter. She was dismissed in January 1979 for openly criticizing the Carter administration.

Abzug returned to private law practice in 1980 but continued her political and public activities. She presided over Women USA, a grassroots political action organization, was a contributor to *Ms.* magazine, and worked as a

daily news commentator for the Cable News Network.
*Gender Gap: Bella Abzug's Guide to Political Power for
American Women* (cowritten with Mim Kelber) appeared in
1984. She was inducted into the National Women's Hall of
Fame in 1994.

CARL ALBERT

(b. May 10, 1908, McAlester, Okla. — d. Feb. 4, 2000, McAlester)

Carl Albert was a Democratic politician who served as a
representative from Oklahoma (1947–77) in the U.S. House
of Representatives and as speaker of the House (1971–76).
Because of his short stature (5 feet 4 inches [1.62 metres])
and the area of Oklahoma he represented, he was nicknamed the "Little Giant from Little Dixie."

Albert was the son of Ernest Albert, a poor coal miner
and cotton farmer from southeastern Oklahoma. He
received his early education in a two-room school but
went on to work his way through the University of
Oklahoma at Norman, where he graduated with a degree
in political science in 1931. He studied law at the University
of Oxford on a Rhodes scholarship and graduated in 1934.
After practicing as a lawyer and serving in the United
States Army (1941–46) during World War II, Albert won
election as a Democrat to the U.S. House of Representatives.
He became the Democratic whip in 1955 and speaker of
the House in 1971.

Albert served in the House during a turbulent period in
American history, one that included the Vietnam War
(1955–75), the assassination of Pres. John F. Kennedy (1963),
the heavily protested Democratic National Convention
held in Chicago (1968), and the resignation of Pres. Richard
Nixon (1974). He twice stood next in line for the presidency: in 1973 after Spiro Agnew resigned as vice president

and again in 1974 after Nixon's resignation. A New Deal Democrat who was an early opponent of civil rights legislation, he changed his views and supported Pres. Lyndon B. Johnson's Civil Rights Act of 1964. In the 1960s he drew criticism from the left wing of his party for supporting the Gulf of Tonkin Resolution, which authorized greater U.S. military involvement in the Vietnam War, and for not taking a stand against the war in subsequent years.

Instead of running for reelection in 1976, Albert chose to retire to his hometown of McAlester, Okla., where he remained for the rest of his life. *Little Giant: The Life and Times of Speaker Carl Albert*, an autobiography coauthored with Danney Goble, was published in 1990.

NATHANIEL P. BANKS
(b. Jan. 30, 1816, Waltham, Mass.—d. Sept. 1, 1894, Waltham)

Nathaniel Prentiss Banks was a politician and Union general during the American Civil War. From 1862 to 1864 he commanded Union forces at New Orleans.

Banks received only a common school education and at an early age began work as a bobbin boy in a cotton factory. He subsequently edited a weekly paper at Waltham, studied law, and, after being admitted to the bar, became active in politics. He served in the Massachusetts legislature (1849–53) and as president of the state constitutional convention in 1853. In that year he entered the U.S. Congress, holding the support of Democrats and Free-Soilers for a time, and later of the Know-Nothing Party. He joined the newly formed Republican Party in 1855, and in 1856, after a bitter and protracted contest, was elected speaker of the House of Representatives on the 133rd ballot. He served in Congress until elected governor of Massachusetts in 1858.

Although while governor he had been a strong advocate of peace, Banks was one of the earliest to offer his services to Pres. Abraham Lincoln, who in 1861 appointed him a major general of volunteers. He served in the campaigns of early 1862 in the Shenandoah Valley and later in the year was in command of the Department of the Gulf in New Orleans. Forces under his command laid siege to Port Hudson, La., which finally fell in July 1863. In 1863 and 1864 he organized a number of expeditions in Texas, but he proved unsuccessful as a tactician, and his Red River expedition (March–May 1864) ended in disaster.

After the war Banks reentered politics, serving several more terms in Congress and as U.S. marshal for Massachusetts (1879–88).

PHILIP P. BARBOUR

(b. May 25, 1783, Barboursville, Va.—d. Feb. 25, 1841, Washington, D.C.)

Philip Pendleton Barbour was a representative from Virginia in the U.S. House of Representatives (1815–23), speaker of the House (1821–23), and an associate justice of the U.S. Supreme Court (1836–41). He was known for his advocacy of states' rights and strict construction of the U.S. Constitution.

Barbour practiced law in Virginia from 1802 until he was elected to the state House of Delegates in 1812. Two years later he was sent to the House of Representatives, where he rose to speaker in 1821. After being defeated for the speakership by Henry Clay in 1823, he accepted an appointment to the General Court of Virginia (1825–27). Barbour opposed the nationalistic policies of Clay and John C. Calhoun, including the tariff, internal improvements, and the extension of federal jurisdiction by the Supreme Court, and he fought to protect Virginia from federal encroachments. In 1827 he briefly returned to Congress to continue this battle and in 1829 took the place of the ailing James Monroe as president of the Virginia constitutional convention.

In 1830 Pres. Andrew Jackson appointed Barbour a federal district judge in Virginia; and in 1836, when Roger B. Taney became the chief justice, Barbour succeeded Justice Gabriel Duvall on the U.S. Supreme Court. His only major opinion was in *City of New York* v. *Miln* (1837), which upheld states' jurisdiction over certain commercial activities. Barbour was part of the post—John Marshall majority, led by Taney, which began to shift the emphasis of the court away from nationalism and liberal construction. Although highly regarded for his scholarship, Barbour did not serve long enough to have a great influence on the court's direction.

BOB BARR

(b. Nov. 5, 1948, Iowa City, Iowa)

Bob Barr is a politician and attorney who served as a Republican member of the U.S. House of Representatives (1995–2003). He was the Libertarian Party's nominee for president in 2008.

Barr, whose father was a member of the U.S. Army Corps of Engineers, lived in various cities throughout the world, including Lima and Baghdad. In 1966 he graduated from the Community High School in Tehrān. He then studied at the University of Southern California, Los Angeles (B.A., 1970), and George Washington University, Washington, D.C. (M.A., 1972), before receiving his J.D. from Georgetown University, Washington, D.C. (1977). Between 1971 and 1978 he worked for the Central Intelligence Agency. Barr then moved to Georgia, where he practiced as a criminal defense lawyer until 1986, when he was appointed U.S. Attorney for the Northern District of Georgia by Pres. Ronald Reagan. He left the position in 1990 to become president of the Southeastern Legal Foundation, a conservative public-interest law firm (1990–91), and in 1992 he was unsuccessful in his bid for the U.S. Senate, losing narrowly in the primary.

In 1994 Barr ran for the U.S. House of Representatives and defeated the incumbent, six-term Democrat George Darden. As a freshman representative, he sponsored the Defense of Marriage Act (1996), which defined marriage as a legal union between one man and one woman, and he quickly became recognized as one of the most conservative members of the House. Barr later became a senior member of the House Judiciary Committee, where he helped lead the impeachment efforts against Pres. Bill Clinton in 1998–99. Barr was reelected to the House three times—in 1996, 1998, and 2000—but he lost the Republican primary in 2002 to John Linder.

In 2004 Barr founded Liberty Strategies LLC, a consulting firm based in Atlanta. Two years later he announced that he had joined the Libertarian Party, citing disillusionment with the Republican Party over the increasing size of government and the erosion of civil liberties under the administration of Pres. George W. Bush. He served as the Libertarian National Committee's regional representative for southeastern states, and in May 2008 Barr announced his bid for the Libertarian nomination for that year's presidential election. During the Libertarian National Convention on May 26, 2008, Barr endured six rounds of voting before finally being nominated as the party's candidate, with Wayne Allyn Root selected as his vice presidential candidate. Barr and Root received about 0.4 percent of the popular vote in the presidential election.

Barr is the author of *The Meaning of Is: The Squandered Impeachment and Wasted Legacy of William Jefferson Clinton* (2004).

JOHN BELL
(b. Feb. 15, 1797, near Nashville, Tenn.—d. Sept. 10, 1869, Dover, Tenn.)

John Bell was a politician and nominee for president on the eve of the American Civil War.

Bell entered the U.S. House of Representatives in 1827 and served there as a Democrat until 1841. He broke with Pres. Andrew Jackson in 1834 and supported Hugh Lawson White for president in 1836. After White's defeat Bell became a Whig and, in March 1841, as a reward for party services, was made secretary of war in Pres. William Henry Harrison's cabinet. A few months later, after the death of Pres. Harrison, he resigned in opposition to Pres. John Tyler's break with the Whigs.

After six years' retirement from political life, Bell was elected as a U.S. senator for Tennessee in 1847, serving in the Senate until 1859. Although a large slaveholder, Bell opposed efforts to expand slavery to the U.S. territories. He vigorously opposed Pres. James Knox Polk's Mexican War policy and voted against the Compromise of 1850, the Kansas-Nebraska Act (1854), and the attempt to admit Kansas as a slave state. Bell's temperate support of slavery combined with his vigorous defense of the Union brought him the presidential nomination on the Constitutional Union ticket in 1860, but he carried only Virginia, Kentucky, and Tennessee. He initially opposed secession; however, following Pres. Abraham Lincoln's call for troops, he openly advocated resistance and henceforth classed himself a rebel. Bell spent the war years in retirement in Georgia, returning to Tennessee in 1865.

JAMES G. BLAINE

(b. Jan. 31, 1830, West Brownsville, Pa. — d. Jan. 27, 1893,
Washington, D.C.)

James Gillespie Blaine was a leading Republican politician
and diplomat for 25 years (1868–93), who was particularly
influential in launching the Pan-American Movement
with Latin-American countries.

Blaine graduated from Washington (now Washington
and Jefferson) College in Washington, Pa., in 1847 and
then taught school for the next six years. He moved to
Augusta, Maine, in 1854 to become editor and part owner
of the *Kennebec Journal*, a crusading Republican newspaper. In 1856 he attended the first national convention of
the newly organized Republican
Party. He served in the Maine
state legislature from 1858
until his election to the U.S.
House of Representatives in
1862. After the Civil War, he
favoured a more moderate
Reconstruction policy than
the radicals of his party,
although he was a strong advocate of African American
suffrage.

In 1868 Blaine was elected
speaker of the House, where
his eloquence and leadership
won him a devoted body of
followers. He became known
as the "Plumed Knight," an
appellation given to him by
Col. Robert G. Ingersoll of

James G. Blaine. Library of
Congress, Washington, D.C.
(Digital File Number: cwpbh-
03708)

Illinois, who offered Blaine's name in nomination at the National Republican Convention of 1876. Blaine failed, however, to reply convincingly to charges that he had used his office for personal gain, and on the seventh ballot he lost the nomination to Rutherford B. Hayes.

Immediately after the election Blaine was appointed to the Senate to fill a vacancy, and he soon won election to a full term. In 1880 he again lost a bid for the presidential nomination, and, on the election of James A. Garfield, he resigned his Senate seat to become secretary of state. In this office he envisaged a system of inter-American arbitration to relieve tensions and strengthen the Monroe Doctrine, and in 1881 he revived the idea—conceived earlier in the century—of calling an inter-American conference to consider an arbitration plan designed to prevent wars in the Western Hemisphere. This idea marked the beginning of the Pan-American Movement. The assassination of President Garfield (1881), however, brought Blaine's resignation, and his Pan-American Conference was shelved by his successor.

Blaine finally won nomination for the presidency in 1884, only to lose by an extremely narrow margin to the Democratic candidate, Grover Cleveland, after an especially virulent campaign. By 1889 the Republicans were back in power, and Blaine again became secretary of state. As such, he assumed the chairmanship of the first Pan-American Conference, which had been authorized by Congress the previous year. The recommendation of separately negotiated reciprocity treaties was the only positive action of the conference. Blaine's proposals for a customs union and arbitration were defeated.

Blaine resigned as secretary of state in June 1892, partly as a result of failing health, and he was dead within seven months.

JOSEPH GURNEY CANNON

(b. May 7, 1836, Guilford County, N.C., —d. Nov. 12, 1926, Danville, Ill.)

Joseph Gurney Cannon, also known as Joe Cannon, was a Republican politician who was a longtime member of the U.S. House of Representatives.

Admitted to the Indiana bar in 1858, Cannon in 1859 moved to Illinois, where he continued the practice of law and entered politics. In 1872 he was elected to the U.S. House of Representatives, where he served for 46 years (1873–91, 1893–1913, 1915–23). Cannon was a staunch conservative who, because of seniority, held important committee chairmanships and was speaker of the House for eight years (1903–11). As speaker, he exercised the power of that office in a blatantly partisan manner until March 1910, when a coalition of Democrats and insurgent Republicans passed a resolution making the speaker ineligible for membership on the committee on rules, thus divesting him of much of his power. Cannon did not originate a single major legislative measure during his 46 years in the House. He was personally liked by his colleagues, however, and was popularly known as "Uncle Joe" Cannon.

JOHN G. CARLISLE

(b. Sept. 5, 1835, Campbell County, Ky.—d. July 31, 1910, New York, N.Y.)

John Griffin Carlisle was a Democratic legislator and government official. He served as speaker of the U.S. House of Representatives (1883–89) and as secretary of the Treasury (1893–97).

Carlisle was admitted to the Kentucky bar in 1858 and practiced law in Covington before his election to a term in the state legislature (1859–61); he also served in the Kentucky state senate (1866–71) and as lieutenant governor (1871–75). Carlisle was elected to the U.S. House of

Representatives in 1876; he championed tariff reduction and rose to the post of speaker (1883). In 1890 he resigned from the House to fill an unexpired term in the Senate.

In 1893 Pres. Grover Cleveland appointed him secretary of the treasury. Carlisle's hard-money policy during the depression that followed the Panic of 1893 was extremely unpopular in the growing free-silver wing of the Democratic Party. In 1896 he abandoned the party's nominee for president, William Jennings Bryan, champion of the free-silver movement, to support John M. Palmer, candidate of the National Democratic Party (Gold Democrats). As a result of this switch of allegiance, Carlisle lost popular support in his native Kentucky; from 1897 he practiced law in New York.

John G. Carlisle. Library of Congress, Washington, D.C. (Digital File Number: cwpbh-04037)

DICK CHENEY

(b. Jan. 30, 1941, Lincoln, Neb.)

Dick Cheney is a former Republican politician who served as a representative from Wyoming in the U.S. House of Representatives (1979–91), as secretary of defense (1989–93) in the administration of Pres. George H.W. Bush, and as the 46th vice president of the United States (2001–09) in the administration of Pres. George W. Bush.

Cheney was the son of Richard Herbert Cheney, a soil-conservation agent, and Marjorie Lauraine Dickey Cheney.

Dick Cheney. The White House

Born in Nebraska, he grew up in Casper, Wyoming. He entered Yale University in 1959 but failed to graduate. Cheney earned bachelor's (1965) and master's degrees (1966) in political science from the University of Wyoming and was a doctoral candidate at the University of Wisconsin.

On Aug. 29, 1964, he married Lynne Vincent. While Cheney worked as an aid to Wisconsin governor Warren Knowles, his wife received a doctorate in British literature from the University of Wisconsin. She later served as chair of the National Endowment for the Humanities (NEH; 1986–93), where she was criticized by liberals for undermining the agency and by conservatives for opposing the closure of a controversial NEH-funded exhibit by photographer Robert Mapplethorpe in Cincinnati, Ohio. The couple have two daughters, Elizabeth and Mary.

In 1968 Cheney moved to Washington, D.C., to serve as a congressional fellow, and beginning in 1969 he worked in the administration of Pres. Richard Nixon. After leaving government service briefly in 1973, he became a deputy assistant to Pres. Gerald Ford in 1974 and his chief of staff from 1975 to 1977. In 1978 he was elected from Wyoming to the first of six terms in the U.S. House of Representatives, where he rose to become the Republican whip. In the House, Cheney took conservative positions on abortion, gun control, and environmental regulation, among other issues. In 1978 he suffered the first of several mild heart attacks, and he underwent quadruple-bypass surgery in 1988. From 1989 to 1993 he served as secretary of defense in the administration of Pres. H.W. George Bush, presiding over reductions in the military following the breakup of the Soviet Union. Cheney also oversaw the U.S. military invasion of Panama and the participation of U.S. forces in the Persian Gulf War.

After Pres. Bush lost his reelection bid in 1992, Cheney became a fellow at the American Enterprise Institute, a conservative think tank. In 1995 he became the chairman and chief executive officer of the Halliburton Company, a supplier of technology and services to the oil and gas industries.

After George W. Bush's primary victories secured his nomination for the presidency of the United States, Cheney was appointed to head Bush's vice-presidential search committee. Few expected that Cheney himself would eventually become the Republican vice-presidential candidate. Two weeks after Election Day, Cheney suffered another mild heart attack, though he quickly resumed his duties as leader of Bush's presidential-transition team.

Vice President Dick Cheney talks on the phone with Pres. George W. Bush as National Security Adviser Condoleezza Rice (seated center) and other senior staff listen at the Presidential Emergency Operations Center, Sept. 11, 2001. Eric Draper/The White House

As vice president, Cheney was active and used his influence to help shape

the administration's energy policy and foreign policy in
the Middle East. He played a central, controversial role in
promoting intelligence reports (which subsequently
proved inaccurate) that Ṣaddām Ḥussein of Iraq had
developed weapons of mass destruction in violation of
resolutions passed by the United Nations. Following the
Iraq War (2003) and the collapse of Ṣaddām's regime,
Cheney's former company, Halliburton, secured lucrative
reconstruction contracts from the U.S. government, raising suspicions of favouritism and possible wrongdoing
and damaging Cheney's reputation. Critics, who had long
charged Cheney with being a secretive public servant,
included members of Congress who brought suit against
him for not disclosing records used to form the national
energy policy. Since the end of his second vice presidential term in 2009, Cheney has publicly defended the
policies of the George W. Bush administration and vigorously criticized the new Democratic administration of
Pres. Barack Obama.

SHIRLEY CHISHOLM

(b. Nov. 30, 1924, Brooklyn, N.Y.—d. Jan. 1, 2005, Ormond Beach, Fla.)

Shirley Chisholm (née Shirley Anita St. Hill) was a
Democratic politician and the first African American
woman to be elected to the U.S. Congress.

Shirley St. Hill was the daughter of immigrants; her
father was from British Guiana (now Guyana) and her
mother from Barbados. She grew up in Barbados and in
her native Brooklyn, N.Y., and graduated from Brooklyn
College (B.A., 1946). While teaching nursery school and
serving as director of the Friends Day Nursery in
Brooklyn, she studied elementary education at Columbia
University (M.A., 1952) and married Conrad Q. Chisholm

in 1949 (divorced 1977). An education consultant for New York's day-care division, she was also active with community and political groups, including the National Association for the Advancement of Colored People (NAACP) and her district's Unity Democratic Club. In 1964–68 she represented her Brooklyn district in the New York state legislature.

In 1968 Chisholm was elected to the U.S. House of Representatives, defeating the civil rights leader James Farmer. In Congress she quickly became known as a strong liberal who opposed weapons development and the war in Vietnam and favoured full-employment proposals. As a candidate for the Democratic nomination for U.S. president in 1972, she won 152 delegates before withdrawing from the race.

Chisholm, a founder of the National Women's Political Caucus, supported the Equal Rights Amendment (ERA) and legalized abortion throughout her congressional career, which lasted from 1969 to 1983. She wrote the autobiographical works *Unbought and Unbossed* (1970) and *The Good Fight* (1973).

After her retirement from Congress, Chisholm remained active on the lecture circuit. She was Purington Professor at Mount Holyoke College (1983–87) and a visiting scholar at Spelman College (1985). In 1993 she was invited by Pres. Bill Clinton to serve as ambassador to Jamaica but declined because of poor health.

CHAMP CLARK

(b. March 7, 1850, near Lawrenceburg, Ky.—d. March 2, 1921, Washington, D.C.)

Champ Clark (byname of James Beauchamp Clark) was a Democratic politician who served as a representative

from Missouri in the U.S. House of Representatives
(1893–95, 1897–1921) and as speaker of the House (1911–
19). He narrowly lost the presidential nomination to
Woodrow Wilson at the 1912 Democratic Convention on
the 46th ballot.

Clark moved to Missouri in 1876 and settled at Bowling
Green. He was successively a country newspaper editor,
city attorney, county prosecuting attorney, and Missouri
state legislator before being elected to the U.S. House of
Representatives for the first time in 1893.

A follower of Democratic and Populist leader William
Jennings Bryan, Clark consistently supported legislation
favoured by Western and Southern agrarians. As a member
of the Rules Committee and Democratic floor leader, he
revolted against Speaker Joseph G. Cannon's dictatorial
control over the House in 1910. His reminiscences, *My
Quarter Century of American Politics*, were published in 1920.

HENRY CLAY
(b. April 12, 1777, Hanover County, Va.—d. June 29, 1852,
Washington, D.C.)

Henry Clay was an American statesman, U.S. representative (1811–14, 1815–21, 1823–25), and U.S. senator (1806–07,
1810–11, 1831–42, 1849–52). He was a major promoter of
the Missouri Compromise (1820), the compromise tariff
of 1833 (ending the Nullification crisis), and the
Compromise of 1850. For these legislative efforts to balance the rights of free and slave states, Clay became known
as the Great Compromiser. He was twice the unsuccessful
Whig candidate for president (1832, 1844).

Born of moderately well-to-do parents, young Clay
studied law under Chancellor George Wythe and was
admitted to the Virginia bar in November 1797. He then
moved to Lexington, Ky., a rising Western community and

a paradise for lawyers because of interminable lawsuits over land titles that were contested there. Endowed with great vitality, a ready but not profound intellect, and a gift for eloquent oratory, he was quick-witted and self-confident. Sociable, charming, and high-spirited, he loved to drink and gamble, qualities not distasteful to most of his contemporaries in Kentucky society. He was also hot-tempered, sensitive, and extremely ambitious.

Clay was spectacularly successful at the Kentucky bar in both civil and criminal cases, and he never lacked for clients. He acted as counsel for Aaron Burr (1806) in a Kentucky grand jury investigation of Burr's plan to establish an empire in the Southwest. Kentucky Republicans believed that Burr had been a victim of a Federalist conspiracy, and Clay's reputation did not suffer when his client's designs were later exposed.

Clay established his social position in 1799 by marrying Lucretia Hart, daughter of a wealthy Lexington businessman. By 1812 he possessed a 600-acre estate (242 hectares) known as Ashland, where he bred livestock and raised hemp, corn (maize), and rye. He and Lucretia had 11 children — 6 daughters and 5 sons.

Clay entered politics shortly after arriving in Kentucky by championing liberalization of the state's constitution. A Jeffersonian Republican, he shared that leader's distaste for slavery and was an advocate of gradual emancipation in Kentucky, but he abandoned this idea when it proved a losing cause. Like Jefferson, he learned to accept slavery, though, unlike him, he provided for the freeing of his slaves in his will. His eloquent opposition to the Alien and Sedition Acts of 1798, a series of repressive measures designed to curb the pro-French activities of the Jeffersonian Republicans, made Clay popular with Kentucky voters, and they elected him to seven terms in the state legislature (1803–09).

Clay advocated the establishment of banks, internal improvements, and manufacturing, thus foreshadowing his future national career. Twice he went to Washington to fill out unexpired terms in the U.S. Senate, and in 1811 he was elected to the U.S. House of Representatives. There, as speaker (1811–14), he was one of the leaders who pushed the country into the War of 1812. He also served as a member of the commission at Ghent that drew up the terms of peace with Britain in 1814.

During the next 10 years, Clay was Kentucky's outstanding representative in the U.S. Congress, usually serving as speaker of the House. Experience and a broadening outlook made him a neo-Jeffersonian Republican; he espoused internal improvements at national expense, a protective tariff, a national bank, and distribution of land-sale revenues to the states. Already he was developing a project of joining the industrial East and the agricultural West in a political alliance under the banner of his American System. He coveted appointment as secretary of state as a step toward the White House and was furious when Pres. James Monroe gave that post to John Quincy Adams. In 1819 he attacked Andrew Jackson for his invasion of Florida, thus earning Old Hickory's lasting enmity. In 1820 he promoted the passage of the Missouri Compromise—which maintained the balance between the slave states and free states within the Union. Then came one of the fateful crises in his career.

Clay was an unsuccessful candidate for the presidency in the election of 1824. But the decision in that election between the front-running candidates John Quincy Adams and Andrew Jackson was thrown into the House of Representatives because neither had a majority of electoral votes. As speaker of the House, Clay was in an influential position. He had decided to vote for Adams before leaving Kentucky. Conferences with Adams satisfied him that he could have any position in the government that he desired if Adams won. He threw his support to Adams, who was elected and who made Henry Clay his secretary of state. Clay never lived down the resultant cry of "bargain and sale."

His four years in the State Department were frustrating, largely because of the political machinations of the Jacksonians. Clay was thwarted in his effort to send delegates to a Pan American Congress at Panama, nor did he reach an accord with Great Britain on West Indian trade. Sneers at the "bargain" were hard to bear; a bitter attack on Clay by Sen. John Randolph led to a duel, in which neither man was wounded.

Adams was inept at political infighting, and Jackson won the election of 1828 decisively. The National Republican Party, the opposition party that had arisen in opposition to the Jacksonians, began to go to pieces and in 1834 was absorbed by the Whig Party. After Jackson's victory Clay retired for a time to Ashland, but in 1831 he returned to the Senate where he headed the opposition to the Jacksonian democracy and championed the renewal of the charter of the Second Bank of the United States, which he had helped to found in 1816. Nominated for the presidency by the National Republicans in 1832, he was defeated by Andrew Jackson, largely on the bank issue. The following year he successfully piloted through Congress the Compromise Tariff of 1833, thus ending the so-called Nullification crisis, in which South Carolina threatened to secede from the Union.

Clay remained in the Senate, leading an uphill fight against the policies of the Jacksonians and becoming a leader of the Whig Party, which gradually emerged in the middle 1830s. He refused to run for the presidency in 1836, when the Whigs put up sectional candidates, and it was with a heavy heart that he accepted reelection to the

Senate in 1837. His mood changed with the panic of 1837 and the consequent rise of Whig fortunes. He confidently expected the party's nomination in 1840, but, to his bitter disappointment, the Whig politicians turned to a military hero, Gen. William Henry Harrison, who, with John Tyler of Virginia as his running mate, was easily elected.

Clay's hopes and plans had been thwarted, and his temper had not been improved by years of political frustration. He was now bent upon dictating his party's policies from his post in the Senate. He tried to dominate Harrison, who lived only a month after his inauguration, and was determined to do the same with Tyler. The latter, a stubborn man, vetoed two bank bills that had Clay's approval, and, when other items in the Kentuckian's program of legislation were challenged from both Congress and the White House, Clay resigned from the Senate in 1842.

Confronted by a choice between Tyler and Clay as leader of the party, the Whigs rallied to Clay, nominating him for president in 1844 with a great display of enthusiasm for the "Old Prince," but once again fate proved unkind. Texas desired annexation to the Union. Clay came out against immediate annexation on the ground that it would stir up the already rising controversy over slavery and certainly involve the U.S. in war with Mexico, but the Democrats nominated James K. Polk, an ardent annexationist. Faced by a swelling tide of Manifest Destiny sentiment, Clay tried to explain his position in such a way as to satisfy pro-annexation, pro-slavery voters in the South without offending anti-slavery voters in the North. The effort was in vain, and once again his greatest ambition was unsatisfied.

Frustration continued to be Clay's lot. He opposed war with Mexico but supported its prosecution after the guns went off. He hoped for the Whig nomination in 1848, but the Whigs turned from their 71-year-old leader (even Kentucky refused to support him) and nominated a Mexican War hero, Gen. Zachary Taylor. Nevertheless, one last act of service to the nation remained for Clay.

The annexation of territory in the Southwest heightened the strife between North and South over the extension of slavery, and Clay came back to the Senate in 1849 resolved to confront the growing threat of disunion. There in a great speech (Feb. 5–6, 1850) he outlined the principal features of what became the Compromise of 1850 and put the weight of his reputation and influence behind its passage. The compromise again kept the numerical balance between slave and free states and perhaps delayed the Civil War by a decade. This was his last act of statesmanship. His health failed, and he died of tuberculosis in the National Hotel at Washington, D.C., in 1852.

Clay was a man whose charm and nationalist fervour, coupled with the appeal of his ideas to the more conservative-minded, made him a national leader loved and honoured by many thousands of Americans. Mistakes of judgment, together with the skill and good fortune of his political opponents, kept him from reaching the White House, and the passage of the years has somewhat dimmed the aura that surrounded him while he lived. During the Civil War, Pres. Abraham Lincoln and Secretary of State William H. Seward, discussing the political past, agreed that Clay's selfishness had injured the Whig Party, and historical scholarship has shown that the importance of his influence on the passage of the Compromise of 1850 was less than had been thought. But he was a staunch defender of the Union, a man who spent his life in public service and in that service helped to guide his country through some of the most difficult crises in its history.

HOWELL COBB

(b. Sept. 7, 1815, Jefferson County, Ga.—d. Oct. 9, 1868, New York, N.Y.)

Howell Cobb was a Georgia politician who championed Southern unionism during the 1850s but then advocated immediate secession following the election of Abraham Lincoln as president in 1860.

Cobb was born into the antebellum plantation elite and grew up in Athens, Ga. He graduated from the University of Georgia in 1834, studied law for two years, and in 1836 was admitted to the bar. The following year (1837) Cobb was elected solicitor general of a strongly pro-Union district in northeastern Georgia. Cobb held the office of solicitor for three years; in 1842 he was elected to the U.S. House of Representatives from essentially the same district.

Cobb served in Congress from 1842 to 1851 and again from 1855 to 1857; he supported the annexation of Texas, the war with Mexico, and the extension of slavery into the territories. But he broke with the most extreme proslavery Southerners when he advocated extending the Missouri Compromise line to the Pacific, opposed the creation of a sectional political party, and supported the Compromise of 1850.

In 1851 Cobb ran for governor of Georgia on the ticket of the newly formed Constitutional Union Party and won a solid victory over a pro-secession candidate. But in so doing, he severed all ties with pro-secessionist Democrats, became politically isolated, and was overwhelmingly defeated in 1854, when he ran for a seat in the U.S. Senate.

His pro-Union district returned Cobb to Congress in 1855, and the following year he played a major role in the nomination and election of James Buchanan as president. Buchanan made Cobb secretary of the treasury, a position

Cobb held until Lincoln was elected president in 1860.

Immediately following Lincoln's election, Cobb resigned his cabinet post, returned to Georgia, and became an ardent spokesman for secession. He served as chairman of the Montgomery, Ala., convention called to organize the Confederacy, then organized his own regiment and led it to the front. He eventually rose to the rank of major general and commanded the District of Georgia until forced to surrender at the end of the war.

Howell Cobb. Library of Congress, Washington, D.C.

A bitter opponent of Reconstruction, Cobb in his last years practiced law in Macon, Ga.

JONATHAN DAYTON

(b. Oct. 16, 1760, Elizabeth, N.J.—d. Oct. 9, 1824, Elizabeth-Town, N.J.)

Jonathan Dayton was the youngest member of the U.S. Constitutional Convention, speaker of the U.S. House of Representatives, and developer of large tracts in what later became the state of Ohio. The city of Dayton, Ohio, is named for him.

Immediately following graduation from the College of New Jersey (Princeton University) in 1776, Dayton enlisted in the New Jersey militia. He fought in the New York and New Jersey campaigns, rose to the rank of captain, was at Yorktown in 1781, and returned to civilian life two years later.

Dayton then studied law and was admitted to the bar, but his future lay more in public service than in private law practice. He served in the New Jersey Assembly 1786–87 thenat age 27 became the youngest delegate at the Constitutional Convention. Dayton was a frequent participant in the debates and opposed several aspects of the Constitution. He nonetheless signed the final document.

Elected to a seat in the first Congress, Dayton instead served in the New Jersey Council (1789) and Assembly (1790). But when elected once again to the U.S. House in 1790, he joined that body and remained there through the end of the decade. As a congressman he backed Alexander Hamilton's financial program, pressed for suppression of the Whiskey Rebellion, and supported the Jay Treaty with Great Britain (1794). During his last two terms he was speaker of the House.

Dayton was elected to the Senate, where he served for the term of 1799–1805. As a loyal Federalist he opposed Thomas Jefferson's administration by voting against the repeal of the Judiciary Act of 1801, against the Twelfth Amendment (specifying separate votes for president and vice president), and for the acquittal of Supreme Court Justice Samuel Chase. But he favoured the Louisiana Purchase of 1803.

After Dayton left the Senate in 1805, he held public office just once more in his life—a term in the New Jersey legislature (1814–15). Most of his time he devoted to developing his large landholdings (250,000 acres [101,175 hectares]) in Ohio. He apparently played some role in Aaron Burr's 1807 conspiracy to establish an empire in the Southwest, but, though indicted for high treason, he was never prosecuted.

TOM DELAY
(b. April 8, 1947, Laredo, Texas)

Tom DeLay is a Republican politician who served as a representative from Texas in the U.S. House of Representatives (1985–2006). He served as majority whip (1995–2003) and majority leader (2003–06) but resigned from the House in June 2006 in the face of corruption charges.

DeLay spent a good deal of his childhood in Venezuela because of his father's career in the oil and gas industry. He attended Baylor University in Waco, Texas, before earning a biology degree from the University of Houston (1970). He owned and operated an insect-exterminating business before winning election to the Texas State House of Representatives in 1978. He remained in office until his election to the U.S. House of Representatives in 1984.

In the House, DeLay rose swiftly through the ranks of the Republican leadership, earning the nickname "The Hammer" for his persistence and for his ability to bring fellow Republicans into line through the use of threats. In 1994 the Republican Party ousted the Democrats from power in the House of Representatives for the first time in four decades. DeLay subsequently was elected majority whip, at the same time that Rep. Newt Gingrich became speaker of the House. DeLay was a strong supporter of the Contract with America, a Republican-initiated legislative agenda that included tax cuts and a balanced budget. A vocal detractor of the Environmental Protection Agency, he was roundly criticized by Democrats for supporting a proposal to repeal air-quality regulations enacted in 1990 by amendments to the Clean Air Act. In 1998 he sharply criticized Democratic Pres. Bill Clinton for apologizing for America's role in the slave trade; DeLay said it was not right for a president to "attack" his country in such a way.

Later that year DeLay helped to lead the successful Republican effort to impeach Clinton.

Beginning in the mid-1990s, DeLay was frequently impugned by House Democrats for alleged conflicts of interest involving campaign fund-raising and his relationship with lobbyists. In 2004, while he was serving as majority leader, the House Ethics Committee issued a stern warning to DeLay to conduct his fund-raising and election dealings appropriately. His political career was dealt a sharp blow in 2005, when a Texas grand jury indicted him on charges of conspiracy to violate state election laws in a 2002 campaign fund-raising scheme. He was later indicted on charges of money laundering. Although the conspiracy charges were subsequently dropped, the money-laundering charges were not; the case was still pending in 2009. In January 2006 DeLay stepped down from his post as majority leader, and in June of that year he resigned from the House. He subsequently wrote, with Stephen Mansfield, *No Retreat, No Surrender: One American's Fight* (2007), in which he passionately denied any criminal wrongdoing.

RAHM EMANUEL

(b. Nov. 29, 1959, Chicago, Ill.)

Rahm Emanuel is a Democratic politician who served as an adviser to Pres. Bill Clinton (1993–99) before being elected to the U.S. House of Representatives (2003–09). He later became chief of staff (2009–) to Pres. Barack Obama.

His father was a doctor who immigrated to the Chicago area from Israel, and Emanuel was raised in an Orthodox Jewish household. He attended Sarah Lawrence College (B.A., 1981) before earning a master's degree (1985) in speech and communication at Northwestern University.

In the early 1980s Emanuel launched his political career. He worked for a consumer rights organization before serving on Paul Simon's successful 1984 U.S. Senate campaign. By 1989 Emanuel had established a reputation as a hard-nosed political operator. That year he was chief fund-raiser for Richard M. Daley's mayoral race in Chicago, which Daley won. In 1992 he joined Clinton's presidential campaign as finance director, and he became one of Clinton's most trusted advisers on matters of policy. Emanuel played a key role in advancing items on the Clinton agenda, most notably the North American Free Trade Agreement (NAFTA) and the 1994 ban on assault weapons. He left politics in 1999 to work for an investment bank in Chicago, and his success in that role helped to finance his successful congressional run in 2002.

Emanuel quickly reestablished himself as a major player in Democratic Party politics. After a disappointing showing nationwide in the 2004 congressional elections, the Democratic leadership turned to Emanuel, who was named head of the Democratic Congressional Campaign Committee the following year. In that role it was his job to identify vulnerable Republican candidates, recruit suitable Democratic contenders, and secure financing to make the races competitive. The 2006 midterm elections saw the Democrats pick up 30 congressional seats and secure a majority in the House of Representatives for the first time since 1995. In 2007, at the start of the new congressional session, Emanuel was elected Democratic caucus chair. After the 2008 elections, in which the Democrats won an additional 21 congressional seats, one of President-elect Obama's first appointments was to name Emanuel as his chief of staff.

Newt Gingrich
(b. June 17, 1943, Harrisburg, Pa.)

Newt Gingrich is a former Republican politician who served as speaker of the U.S. House of Representatives

(1995–98). He was the first Republican to hold the office in 40 years.

After graduating from Emory University (1965), Gingrich studied modern European history at Tulane University (M.A., 1968; Ph.D., 1971) and taught at West Georgia College (1970–78). After unsuccessful runs for the U.S. Congress in 1974 and 1976, he won a seat from a district outside Atlanta in 1978. Gingrich quickly became known for his confrontational manner and conservative policies. In 1987 he attacked the Democratic speaker of the House, Jim Wright, for questionable financial dealings; the charges forced Wright to resign in 1989. In the same year Gingrich was narrowly elected House minority whip by his Republican colleagues.

In 1994, the Republican Party gained control of Congress following that year's midterm elections. Gingrich was seen as the architect of the victory, especially noted for helping draft the Contract with America, a document outlining legislation to be enacted by the House within the first 100 days of the 104th Congress. Among the proposals were tax cuts, a permanent line-item veto, and a constitutional amendment requiring a balanced budget. In December 1994 Gingrich was chosen by the majority Republicans as House speaker, and he assumed the office the following month. With one exception, all parts of the Contract with America were passed by the House.

Shortly after becoming speaker, however, Gingrich's popularity began to wane. In late 1995 he was widely blamed for partial government shutdowns after refusing to compromise with President Clinton on the federal budget. He also faced a series of ethics investigations. In 1995 he returned a $4.5 million book advance after the House ethics committee questioned its appropriateness. The following year the committee concluded that he had violated

PRIMARY DOCUMENT: THE CONTRACT WITH AMERICA

When Democratic Pres. Bill Clinton's popularity plummeted in the summer and fall of 1994, Republican Rep. Newt Gingrich of Georgia skillfully positioned House Republicans as a viable alternative to what he described as Clinton's "failed" liberal policies. Their program for change was encapsulated in the Contract with America, reprinted below.

On the first day of the 104th Congress, the new Republican majority will immediately pass the following major reforms:

FIRST, require all laws that apply to the rest of the country also apply equally to the Congress;
SECOND, select a major, independent auditing firm to conduct a comprehensive audit of Congress for waste, fraud, or abuse;
THIRD, cut the number of House committees, and cut committee staff by one-third;
FOURTH, limit the terms of all committee chairs;
FIFTH, ban the casting of proxy votes in committee;
SIXTH, require committee meetings to be open to the public;
SEVENTH, require a three-fifths majority vote to pass a tax increase;
EIGHTH, guarantee an honest accounting of our Federal Budget by implementing zero base-line budgeting.

Thereafter, within the first 100 days of the 104th Congress, we shall bring to the House Floor the following bills.

1. THE FISCAL RESPONSIBILITY ACT: A balanced budget/ tax limitation amendment and a legislative line-item veto to restore fiscal responsibility to an out-of-control Congress.
2. THE TAKING BACK OUR STREETS ACT: An anti-crime package including stronger truth-in-sentencing, "good faith" exclusionary rule exemptions, effective death penalty provisions, and cuts in social spending to fund prison construction and additional law enforcement.
3. THE PERSONAL RESPONSIBILITY ACT: Discourage illegitimacy and teen pregnancy by prohibiting welfare to minor mothers and denying increased AFDC for additional children

while on welfare, cut spending for welfare programs, and enact a two-years-and-out provision with work requirements to promote individual responsibility.

4. THE FAMILY REINFORCEMENT ACT: Child support enforcement, tax incentives for adoption, strengthening rights of parents in their children's education, stronger child pornography laws, and an elderly dependent care tax credit to reinforce the central role of families in American society.

5. THE AMERICAN DREAM RESTORATION ACT: A $500 per child tax credit, begin repeal of the marriage tax penalty, and creation of American Dream Savings Accounts to provide middle class tax relief.

6. THE NATIONAL SECURITY RESTORATION ACT: No U.S. troops under U.N. command and restoration of the essential parts of our national security funding to strengthen our national defense and maintain our credibility around the world.

7. THE SENIOR CITIZENS FAIRNESS ACT: Raise the Social Security earnings limit which currently forces seniors out of the work force, repeal the 1993 tax hikes on Social Security benefits and provide tax incentives for private long-term care insurance to let Older Americans keep more of what they have earned over the years.

8. THE JOB CREATION AND WAGE ENHANCEMENT ACT: Small business incentives, capital gains cut and indexation, neutral cost recovery, risk assessment/cost-benefit analysis, strengthening the Regulatory Flexibility Act and unfunded mandate reform to create jobs and raise worker wages.

9. THE COMMON SENSE LEGAL REFORM ACT: "Loser pays" laws, reasonable limits on punitive damages and reform of product liability laws to stem the endless tide of litigation.

10. THE CITIZEN LEGISLATURE ACT: A first-ever vote on term limits to replace career politicians with citizen legislators.

House rules concerning a college course he taught from 1993 to 1995. It found he had wrongly used tax-exempt donations to fund the class and that he had falsely denied the involvement of GOPAC, a political action committee that he once headed, in the course's development. In

January 1997 the House of Representatives ordered Gingrich to pay a fine of $300,000. The House also reprimanded him for providing false information to the committee investigating his case. Amid the controversies, Gingrich was narrowly reelected speaker in early 1997.

In January 1998, reports surfaced alleging that President Clinton had lied before a federal grand jury concerning his involvement in an extramarital affair with a former White House intern. Gingrich backed a bid to impeach and remove the president from office. Many voters concluded that the House had overreached in its attack on Clinton, and the Republicans lost five seats to Democrats in the 1998 midterm elections. Following the election there was a backlash against Gingrich within the Republican Party, with numerous Republicans blaming him for failing to present a clear and innovative agenda to the country and instead choosing to focus party strategy upon the impeachment proceedings against a highly popular president. Faced with dwindling support, Gingrich stepped down as speaker of the House in November 1998, and in January 1999 he resigned his seat in Congress.

Gingrich has remained involved in politics, serving as a consultant and television commentator. He has written a number of books, including *Lessons Learned the Hard Way* (1998), *Winning the Future: A 21st Century Contract with America* (2005), and *Rediscovering God in America* (2006).

CARL T. HAYDEN

(b. Oct. 2, 1877, Tempe, Ariz.—d. Jan. 25, 1972, Mesa, Ariz.)

Carl Trumbull Hayden was a Democratic politician who served 56 years in both houses of the U.S. Congress (1912–69)—the longest term in the nation's history to that time.

The son of an Arizona pioneer, young Hayden entered the flour-milling business and first became active in public life in the Tempe Town Council (1902–04). After holding several county offices, he was elected to the U.S. House of Representatives in 1912 as his state's first congressman. After 14 years he won a seat in the Senate, in which he served a total of seven terms.

In Congress, Hayden concentrated on areas of special interest to his state—reclamation, irrigation, highways, and silver mining. As chairman of the Senate Appropriations Committee, he wielded great power. As president pro tempore of the Senate, he found himself in the unique position of acting vice president after the assassination of Pres. John F. Kennedy (Nov. 22, 1963). He remained second in the line of presidential succession until January 1965. In recognition of his long service, diligence, and political sagacity, he was known as dean of the Senate after 1957.

On Sept. 30, 1968, Carl Hayden Day was proclaimed at the White House in honour of the signing of the Lower Colorado River Basin Bill authorizing a $1 billion development project for central Arizona, which he had done much to promote.

HENRY HYDE

(b. April 18, 1924, Chicago, Ill.—d. Nov. 29, 2007, Chicago)

Henry Hyde was a Republican politician who served as a representative from Illinois in the U.S. House of Representatives (1975–2007).

During his freshman term he won support in 1976 for a law that prohibited federal funds for abortions (the Hyde Amendment) and was at the forefront of a group of House Republicans who in 1998 monitored the impeachment hearings of Pres. Bill Clinton. Hyde, a Roman Catholic and onetime Democrat, switched to the Republican Party and became a force in Illinois, serving in the Illinois House (1967–74) and holding the position of majority leader (1971–72).

In national politics Hyde held key positions—the ranking Republican on the House Select Committee on Intelligence (1985–91), chairman of the House Judiciary Committee (1995–2001), and chairman of the House International Relations Committee (2001–07). Shortly before his death, Hyde was awarded the Presidential Medal of Freedom.

Fiorello H. La Guardia
(b. Dec. 11, 1882, New York, N.Y.—d. Sept. 20, 1947, New York)

Fiorello Henry La Guardia was a politician and lawyer who served three terms (1933–45) as mayor of New York.

La Guardia was reared in Arizona and at the age of 16 moved to Budapest with his mother. He was employed at the U.S. consulate there, and he later served in the American consulates at Trieste and Fiume, returning to the United States in 1906. While working at Ellis Island as an interpreter for the U.S. Immigration Service, he studied law at New York University and was admitted to the bar in 1910.

La Guardia was elected to the U.S. House of Representatives as a progressive Republican in 1916, but his term was interrupted by service as a pilot in World War I. He was returned to Congress in 1918 and, after serving as president of the New York board of aldermen in 1920–21, was reelected to the House in 1922. He was reelected four more times, and in the House he opposed Prohibition and supported women's suffrage and child-labour laws. He cosponsored the Norris-LaGuardia Act (1932), which restricted the courts' power to ban or restrain strikes, boycotts, or picketing by organized labour.

In 1933 La Guardia ran successfully for mayor of New York on a "Fusion" (a Liberal and Republican party coalition) reform ticket dedicated to unseating Tammany Hall (the Democratic organization in New York) and ending its corrupt practices. As mayor, La Guardia earned a national reputation as an honest and nonpartisan reformer dedicated to civic improvement. He was an able and indefatigable administrator who obtained a new city charter, fought corrupt politicians and organized crime, improved the operations of the police and fire departments, expanded the city's social-welfare services, and began slum-clearance and low-cost-housing programs. Among his building projects were La Guardia Airport and numerous roads and bridges. A colourful figure with a flair for the dramatic, La Guardia became known as "the Little Flower" in token of his first name.

After being reelected twice, La Guardia in 1945 refused to run for a fourth term as mayor. He was appointed director of the U.S. Office of Civilian Defense (1941) and director general (1946) of the United Nations Relief and Rehabilitation Administration.

RAY LAHOOD
(b. Dec. 6, 1945, Peoria, Ill.)

Ray LaHood is a Republican politician who served as a representative from Illinois in the U.S. House of Representatives (1995–2009) before becoming U.S. secretary of transportation (2009–) in the administration of Democratic Pres. Barack Obama.

LaHood grew up in the Peoria, Ill., area, and he earned a bachelor's degree in education and sociology from Bradley University in 1971. He worked as a teacher and as an urban planner before entering politics in 1977 as an aide to U.S. Rep. Thomas Railsback. In 1982 LaHood finished the term of a retiring Illinois state representative, but he was unsuccessful in his bid to win the seat outright. The following year he joined the staff of U.S. House of Representatives Minority Leader Robert Michel, a career politician who was known for his ability to broker deals that crossed party lines. He was named Michel's chief of staff in 1990, and, upon Michel's retirement in 1994, LaHood was elected to fill his mentor's vacant congressional seat.

Although LaHood took office as a Republican when that party's congressional fortunes were on the rise, he distanced himself from party leaders such as Newt Gingrich, and he was one of a handful of Republicans who refused to sign Gingrich's Contract with America, a document outlining legislation to be enacted by the House within the first 100 days of the 104th Congress. Nonetheless, in 1998 Republican leadership selected LaHood to chair the House impeachment proceedings against Pres. Bill Clinton. Observers agreed that LaHood brought an element of impartiality and civility to the proceedings, and these traits characterized the rest of his term in Congress. He served on the House Transportation and Appropriations committees, and he secured funding for a number of infrastructure improvement projects in his district.

In 2007 he announced that he would not run for reelection. The following year he was selected by President Obama to head the Department of Transportation, and he was confirmed by the Senate in January 2009.

EDWARD LIVINGSTON

(b. May 28, 1764, Columbia County, N.Y.—d. May 23, 1836, Dutchess County, N.Y.)

Edward Livingston was a representative from New York in the U.S. House of Representatives (1795–1801, 1823–29) and a U.S. senator from New York (1829–31). He is remembered for his codifications of criminal law and procedure.

Livingston was admitted to the bar in 1785 and began to practice law in New York. In 1801, after serving six years in the House, he was appointed U.S. district attorney for New York state. In the same year he was elected mayor of New York. As district attorney, he was held responsible for public funds that had been lost through the dishonesty of one of his clerks. As a consequence, he resigned both his offices in 1803 and moved to Louisiana. He established a large law practice in New Orleans, and he prepared a provisional code of judicial procedure that was in force in Louisiana from 1805 to 1825. In 1821, a year after he became a member of the state legislature, he wrote a code of criminal law and procedure. Although not adopted by the legislature, this code gained wide influence in Europe and the United States.

In 1831, after six more years in the House and two in the Senate, Livingston was appointed secretary of state by Pres. Andrew Jackson, in which position he prepared the anti-nullification proclamation of 1832, concerning South Carolina's opposition to the protective tariff. He was minister plenipotentiary to France from 1833 to 1835.

NATHANIEL MACON

(b. Dec. 17, 1758, Edgecombe, N.C.—d. June 29, 1837, Warren County, N.C.)

Nathaniel Macon was a U.S. Congressional leader for 37 years. He is remembered chiefly for his negative views on almost every issue of the day, particularly those concerned with centralizing the government. Yet his integrity and absence of selfish motives served to strengthen his influence and to make him universally liked and respected.

Macon's long political career began in the North Carolina Senate (1781–85), shifted to the U.S. House of Representatives (1791–1815), and concluded in the U.S.

Senate (1815–28). As speaker of the House (1801–07), he was one of the most important leaders of the Jeffersonian, anti-Federalist faction, who feared that individual liberties and interests would be jeopardized by a national government. At first on close terms with Thomas Jefferson, Macon associated himself briefly (1806–09) with John Randolph and a dozen other congressmen critical of Jefferson for failing to adhere to pure Republican principles.

Returning to the party fold, he served as chairman of the House Foreign Relations Committee, which reported a bill, passed on May 1, 1810, restoring commerce with all nations but promising to revive non-intercourse against Great Britain or France if either nation were to reverse its restrictions on U.S. shipping. This bill was labelled Macon's Bill No. 2, although Macon opposed its adoption.

Macon, departing from his usual pattern of negative voting, approved the declaration of war against England in 1812 but opposed conscription and all taxes needed to wage war. His states' rights and sectional views became even more marked after the war. During his retirement years he engaged in political correspondence in which he stoutly defended slavery.

JOSEPH WILLIAM MARTIN, JR.

(b. Nov. 3, 1884, North Attleboro, Mass. — d. March 6, 1968, Fort Lauderdale, Fla.)

Joseph William Martin, Jr., was a Republican politician who was a leader of his party in Congress and speaker of the U.S. House of Representatives (1947–49, 1953–55).

The son of a blacksmith, Martin declined a scholarship to Dartmouth College (Hanover, N.H.) and instead took a job as a newspaper reporter. A few years later he joined with associates in purchasing the North Attleboro *Evening*

Chronicle. Subsequently, he bought out his partners, and he remained the paper's owner and publisher until his death.

In 1911 Martin won a seat in the Massachusetts House of Representatives; three years later he was elected to the state Senate. He was first elected to the U.S. House in 1924, launching a congressional career that would last more than 40 years. During the 1930s, Martin emerged as a leader of obstructionist forces trying to derail the New Deal. Likening the New Deal programs to those of fascism, he voted against many reform measures, including the Tennessee Valley Authority and the Securities Exchange Act.

A tireless party worker, he served on the Republican National Committee from 1936 to 1942, the last two years as chairman, and in 1940 he began a string of five consecutive Republican national convention chairmanships. From 1939 to 1959 he led the House Republicans, urging his colleagues to adhere to the conservative principles of the Grand Old Party and to block what he deemed the socialist measures of the New Deal and Fair Deal. From 1947 to 1949 and again from 1953 to 1955—periods of Republican ascendancy in the House of Representatives—Martin served as speaker of the House.

After Republicans lost heavily in the congressional elections of 1958, Martin sustained a bitter defeat at the hands of Charles Halleck for party leadership in the House. His power waned steadily, and he lost a primary contest for his seat in 1966. He retired to his home and newspaper business in North Attleboro and died while on vacation in Florida.

JOHN W. McCORMACK

(b. Dec. 21, 1891, Boston, Mass.—d. Nov. 22, 1980, Dedham, Mass.)

John William McCormack was a Democratic politician who served as speaker of the U.S. House of Representatives from 1962 to 1970.

McCormack had little formal education. He read law while working as an office boy and passed the bar examination at the age of 21. He joined the Democratic Party and won his first election to public office at age 25. He served for two years in the Massachusetts House of Representatives and for three years in the state senate. In 1928 he was elected to the U.S. House of Representatives and remained a member of Congress for the next 42 years. In 1940 he became House majority leader, and in 1962 he succeeded Sam Rayburn as speaker of the House. McCormack was known as a loyal Democrat and a skillful debater; he supported civil rights bills, antipoverty programs, and wage-and-hour laws. He opposed communism and defended U.S. military involvement in Vietnam. He retired in 1970.

THOMAS PHILIP O'NEILL, JR.

(b. Dec. 19, 1912, Cambridge, Mass.—d. Jan. 5, 1994, Boston, Mass.)

Thomas Philip O'Neill, Jr., also known as Tip O'Neill, was a Democratic politician who served as a representative from Massachusetts in the U.S. House of Representatives (1953–87) and as speaker of the House (1977–86). He was a tireless advocate for social causes, and he frequently expressed his belief that it is the responsibility of the government to contribute to the good of society by helping the poor, the underprivileged, and the unemployed.

O'Neill grew up in a working-class section of Cambridge, Mass., where his father served on the Cambridge City Council. As a teenager he joined the 1928 presidential campaign of Democratic New York Gov. Al Smith after learning that Smith, like O'Neill, was an Irish Catholic. In 1932 he campaigned for Democratic presidential candidate Gov. Franklin D. Roosevelt. He graduated from Boston College in 1936, the same year he won election to the Massachusetts state House of Representatives, where he served until 1952. In 1953 he was elected to the U.S. House of Representatives to fill the seat vacated by John F. Kennedy after Kennedy was elected to the U.S. Senate.

As a U.S. representative, O'Neill soon earned a reputation as a dyed-in-the-wool liberal Democrat who was willing to speak his mind. He was a shrewd negotiator who marshaled support in the back rooms of the Capitol rather than on the House floor. In 1967 he became one of the first members of the House to oppose Pres. Lyndon B. Johnson vocally on the Vietnam War. O'Neill served as House majority whip in 1971 and as majority leader in 1972 before being elevated to speaker in 1977. He won favour with his younger colleagues for approving legislative reforms, including a new ethics code and a limit on outside income for House members. In 1974 he publicly called on Pres. Richard M. Nixon, who had been disgraced by the Watergate scandal, to resign. O'Neill later earned the respect of many Democrats for frequently opposing the conservative administration of Pres. Ronald Reagan; he often criticized Reagan publicly.

O'Neill remained a popular figure among Democrats throughout his career. In the early 1980s, Republican-sponsored television advertisements featuring an O'Neill look-alike who was meant to symbolize a bloated free-wheeling Congress not only failed to detract from O'Neill's popularity but rather enhanced it. O'Neill himself appeared in television commercials for a credit card company and played a cameo role on the TV comedy *Cheers*.

O'Neill published his best-selling autobiography, *Man of the House*, in 1987. The publication of a book of his anecdotes and lore, *All Politics Is Local*, coincided with his death in 1994.

LEON PANETTA
(b. June 28, 1938, Monterey, Calif.)

Leon Panetta is a Democratic politician who served in the U.S. House of Representatives (1977–93) and has held office in the administrations of three presidents: as director of the Office of Civil Rights (1969–70) under Pres. Richard M. Nixon, as director of the Office of Management and Budget (1993–94) and chief of staff (1994–96) under Pres. Bill Clinton, and as director of the Central Intelligence Agency (CIA; 2009–) under Pres. Barack Obama.

Panetta's parents immigrated to the United States from Italy, and they settled in central California. Panetta grew up working in the family restaurant, and he later attended Santa Clara University, where he earned a bachelor's degree in political science in 1960 and a law degree in 1963. While at Santa Clara, he was a member of the Reserve Officers' Training Corps, and he entered the U.S. Army in 1964 as a first lieutenant. He served for two years before being honourably discharged.

Panetta's first political job came in 1966, when he moved to Washington, D.C., to serve as a legislative assistant to Republican Sen. Thomas Kuchel. In 1969 he was appointed head of the U.S. Office of Civil Rights, and he oversaw the enforcement of federal laws relating to equal opportunities in education. He recounted his experiences there in the book *Bring Us Together* (1971). Panetta returned to California in 1971, and he practiced as a private attorney until his successful run for the U.S. House of Representatives in 1976. In Congress, Panetta worked on financial and budgetary issues, as well as public health reform. President Clinton appointed him to head the Office of Management and Budget in 1993, and he was promoted to chief of staff the following year. As chief of staff, Panetta was credited with restructuring White House operations, as well as brokering deals with congressional Republicans that enabled passage of federal budgets.

Panetta left government in 1997 and, with his wife, established the nonprofit Leon & Sylvia Panetta Institute for Public Policy, at California State University's Monterey Bay campus, later that year. In 2006 he was selected to serve as a member of the bipartisan Iraq Study Group, a 10-member think tank created by Congress to assess the political, economic, and security issues in Iraq following the U.S.-led invasion. President Obama appointed him director of the CIA in 2009, a move that surprised some, as Panetta had no direct intelligence background. The Obama team emphasized Panetta's organizational strengths and extensive government experience, however, and he was confirmed by the Senate in February 2009.

CLAUDE PEPPER

(b. Sept. 8, 1900, Dudleyville, Ala.—d. May 30, 1989, Washington, D.C.)

Claude Pepper was a Democratic politician who was a representative from Florida in the U.S. House of Representatives (1963–89) and a U.S. senator from Florida (1937–51). Serving in public office for more than 60 years, he was known as a champion of the elderly.

After graduating from the University of Alabama (A.B., 1921) and Harvard University Law School (J.D., 1924), Pepper taught and practiced law before his election to the Florida legislature (1929), where he sponsored a bill allowing senior citizens to fish without a license. Elected to the U.S. Senate in 1936, he endorsed the New Deal policies of Pres. Franklin D. Roosevelt, rejected American isolationism in World War II, and supported legislation that created Social Security, minimum wages, and medical assistance for elderly people and handicapped children.

Detractors called him "Red Pepper" not for his red hair but for his liberal views, which included economic support to the Soviet Union—an unpopular sentiment in 1951, when he lost his Senate seat.

Pepper practiced law for a dozen years before returning to politics to become a member of the U.S. House of Representatives, where he became the chairman of the House Select Committee on Aging and of the Rules Committee. He was the principal architect of legislation, passed in 1986, that abolished mandatory retirement in the federal government, raised the retirement age from 65 to 70 in the private sector, and ensured continued healthcare coverage for older workers. Pepper, who was then the oldest member of Congress, was also instrumental in the passage of the Medicare Catastrophic Coverage Act (1988). He received the Medal of Freedom, the nation's highest civilian award, five days before his death.

JOHN RANDOLPH

(b. June 2, 1773, Prince George County, Va.—d. May 24, 1833, Philadelphia, Pa.)

John Randolph was a political leader who was a member of Congress for more than 30 years and an important proponent of the doctrine of states' rights in opposition to a strong centralized government.

A descendant of notable colonial families of Virginia as well as of the Indian princess Pocahontas, Randolph distinguished himself from a distant relative by assuming the title John Randolph of Roanoke, where he established his home in 1810.

In 1799 Randolph was elected to the U.S. House of Representatives, and he served in that legislative body almost continuously until 1829. His political rise was so rapid that by 1801 he was chairman of the House Ways and

Means Committee and leader of the Jeffersonian Republicans in Congress. His debating skill and biting sarcasm made him a feared opponent through the years, and he anticipated the states' rights theories of John C. Calhoun by passionately defending state sovereignty on every occasion. He thus opposed a national bank, protective tariffs, federally financed internal improvements (such as roads and canals), and federal interference with the institution of slavery—though he freed his own bondsmen in his will.

After his failure as manager of the impeachment trial of Supreme Court Justice Samuel Chase in 1804–05, in addition to his opposition to Pres. Thomas Jefferson's efforts to acquire Florida, Randolph drifted away from the Jeffersonian Republican Party. He returned to national prominence in 1820 when he represented Southern planters in resisting the Missouri Compromise, which outlawed slavery in new western territory north of the 36°30' parallel. During those years, when party feelings ran high, Randolph's denunciation of Rep. Henry Clay's support of John Quincy Adams for the presidency in the disputed election of 1824–25 led him into a duel with Clay from which both emerged unscathed.

He served briefly in the Senate (1825–26) and three years later was a prominent member of the convention that drafted a new Virginia constitution. In 1830 Pres. Andrew Jackson sent him on a special mission to Russia, but ill health forced him to return to the United States after only a few weeks at his post.

Sam Rayburn

(b. Jan. 6, 1882, Roane County, Tenn.—d. Nov. 16, 1961, Bonham, Texas)

Sam Rayburn was a Democratic politician who served as speaker of the U.S. House of Representatives for nearly 17 years. In 1912 he was elected to the U.S. House of Representatives and served there continuously for 48 years and 8 months, which, at the time of his death, was a record tenure. He was elected to Congress 25 consecutive times.

Rayburn's family, of predominantly Scottish origin, moved from Tennessee to Texas in 1887, and there Rayburn grew up on a 40-acre farm. He worked his way through East Texas Normal College (now Texas A&M University, Commerce), taught school, and became a lawyer. He served in the Texas House of Representatives for six years (1907–13) and in 1911 was elected speaker. The following year he was elected to the U.S. House of Representatives, where he remained for almost a half century.

Energetic, studious, ambitious, and affable, Rayburn quickly became influential behind the scenes in government and in party politics. As chairman (1931–37) of the powerful House Committee on Interstate and Foreign Commerce, he was a major architect of the New Deal. As a member of the House of Representatives, he was coauthor of six important laws—the Emergency Railroad Transportation Act, the "Truth-in-Securities" Act, the Stock Exchange Act, the Federal Communications Act, the Rural Electrification Act, and one of the most bitterly contested of all New Deal laws, the Public Utility Holding Company Act.

Rayburn was elected Democratic leader of the House of Representatives in 1937 and became speaker of the House on Sept. 16, 1940. He held the latter office for almost 17 years, exceeding by a wide margin the previous record set by Kentucky statesman Rep. Henry Clay in the first quarter of the 19th century. Noted for his tart common sense, his honesty, and his unflagging patriotism, Rayburn was a trusted adviser to presidents Franklin D. Roosevelt, Harry Truman, Dwight D. Eisenhower, and John F. Kennedy. A dedicated party man who described himself as a Democrat "without prefix, without suffix, and without apology," Rayburn was often called "Mr. Democrat." He was permanent chairman of the Democratic National Conventions in 1948, 1952, and 1956. After he won the battle in 1961 to enlarge the House Committee on Rules—the hardest internal House struggle in 50 years—Rayburn's health failed quickly. Before Congress adjourned that year, he went home to Bonham, Texas, where he died.

At the time of his death, Rayburn was regarded as an extraordinarily able legislator who had gone on to become the most effective speaker since Rep. Joe Cannon was divested of his power in 1910. That assessment of Rayburn did not change in the decades following his death. His pivotal role in the House as a broker between the Northern and Southern wings of the Democratic Party, however, was later better understood and appreciated. During Rayburn's tenure, power in the House was lodged in the hands of committee chairs who gained their positions through seniority. Because the American South still was overwhelmingly Democratic and the Republican Party was not competitive there, Southern Democrats in the House—with their seniority and their control over chairs of committees—tended to have great power. Northern Democrats tended to be more liberal than their Southern counterparts, but their lack of seniority and committee chairs diminished their influence in the House. Rayburn brokered the interests of both wings of the Democratic Party.

Although the office of speaker at that time lacked great formal powers, Rayburn used the limited influence of the office to maximum advantage. He also relied heavily on his personal prestige, his skill at persuasion, and personal friendships built up over decades in the House to bridge the regional differences within the Democratic Party and to forge a working majority in the House. His leadership style usually resulted in congenial relations not only between the Northern and Southern wings of the Democratic Party but also between Rayburn and the Republican leadership of the House—a considerable accomplishment, especially when viewed in the light of the divisive House of Representatives in the early 21st century.

THOMAS B. REED

(b. Oct. 18, 1839, Portland, Maine—d. Dec. 7, 1902, Washington, D.C.)

Thomas Brackett Reed was a vigorous U.S. Republican Party leader who, as speaker of the U.S. House of Representatives (1889–91, 1895–99), introduced significant procedural changes (the Reed Rules) that helped ensure legislative control by the majority party in Congress.

After he was admitted to the bar in 1865, Reed began his law practice in Portland and was elected to the Maine House of Representatives in 1868 and to the state senate two years later. He was elected to Congress on the Republican ticket in 1877 and served continuously until the end of the century. In 1882 he was appointed to the House Committee on Rules, and when the Republicans regained control of the House in 1889, Reed was elected speaker. As a strong speaker, he arranged for the control of the Rules Committee by the majority party in Congress.

The Reed Rules, adopted in February 1890, provided that every member present in the House must vote unless financially interested in a measure; that members present and not voting be counted for a quorum; and that no dilatory motions be entertained by the chair. Reed claimed these innovations enhanced legislative efficiency and helped ensure Democratic (majority) control of the House; many thought they made a major contribution to the U.S. political system by establishing the principle of party responsibility. His dictatorial methods were bitterly attacked by the opposition, however, who called him Czar Reed. Nevertheless, the Reed Rules and methods were adopted by the Democratic leadership in 1891–95, and the power of the Rules Committee was increased.

Though denied the 1896 presidential nomination he had sought, Reed nonetheless supported the domestic programs of Pres. William McKinley and exercised a powerful influence in guiding bills through Congress. In 1899, however, he broke with the Republican administration over what he considered its expansionist policy toward Cuba and Hawaii. He resigned from the House in protest and retired to New York to practice law and to write.

BILL RICHARDSON

(b. Nov. 15, 1947, Pasadena, Calif.)

Bill Richardson is a Democratic politician who has served as a member of the U.S. House of Representatives (1983–97), as a member of Pres. Bill Clinton's cabinet (1997–2001), and as governor of New Mexico (2003–). In 2008 he unsuccessfully sought the Democratic nomination for president.

Richardson's father, an American and a bank executive, met his mother while working in Mexico City, and she traveled to Pasadena, Calif., to give birth so there would be no questions regarding her son's citizenship status. Richardson lived in Mexico City until age 13, when he was sent to the elite Middlesex School in Concord, Mass. He later attended Tufts University (near Boston), earning bachelor's degrees in political science and French in 1970 and a master's degree from the Fletcher School of Law and Diplomacy the following year.

After graduation, Richardson moved to Washington, D.C., and spent much of the next decade in various staff positions within the U.S. government. In 1978 he moved with his family to New Mexico. Richardson rose quickly within the state's Democratic Party ranks, and he made an unsuccessful bid for a seat in the U.S. House of Representatives in 1980. Fortunes changed two years later when he was elected to the first of seven consecutive terms. His eighth term was cut short in 1997 when he accepted an appointment by Pres. Bill Clinton to serve as the U.S. ambassador to the United Nations (UN). He served in Clinton's cabinet as secretary of energy from 1998 to 2001 and worked as a private consultant before returning to New Mexico in 2002.

Richardson was elected governor of New Mexico in 2002 and retained his position with a landslide victory in 2006. His 2008 presidential campaign focused on many of the same issues that he had faced throughout his political career—the economy, energy and the environment, foreign policy, education, and immigration reform. However, Richardson failed to place higher than fourth in both the Iowa caucus and the New Hampshire primary, and he withdrew from the race in January 2008. Later that year President-elect Barack Obama selected Richardson to serve as secretary of commerce, a post that requires Senate confirmation. In January 2009 Richardson asked to be withdrawn from consideration for the cabinet position because

Bill Richardson. Governor Bill Richardson

of an investigation into whether his administration had awarded state contracts to one of his political donors. Richardson has chronicled his life and views in *Between Worlds: The Making of an American Life* (2005).

PETER RODINO

(b. June 7, 1909, Newark, N.J.—d. May 7, 2005, West Orange, N.J.)

Peter Rodino was a Democratic politician who served for 40 years as a representative from New Jersey in the U.S. House of Representatives (1949–89). As chairman of the House Judiciary Committee, he steered the 1974 impeachment hearings of Pres. Richard M. Nixon during the Watergate scandal. He was known for his advocacy of civil rights and immigration reform and for having introduced the bill that made Columbus Day a national holiday.

The son of Italian immigrants, Rodino grew up in a tenement in the Little Italy section of Newark, N.J. He graduated from the University of Newark and then took night courses at the New Jersey Law School, earning his law degree in 1937; both schools are now part of Rutgers University. Rodino was admitted to the bar in 1938 and worked as a lawyer in Newark until joining the United States Army (1941–46) to serve in Italy and North Africa during World War II. In 1948 he was elected to the U.S. House of Representatives. Until the 1970s he was little known outside his New Jersey district.

In 1973 Rodino was elected chairman of the House Judiciary Committee. After Nixon was implicated in illegal activities related to the burglary and wiretapping of the Democratic National Committee headquarters in the Watergate office complex, the Judiciary Committee initiated impeachment hearings against the president. In preparation for the hearings, Rodino read about the impeachment of Pres. Andrew Johnson in 1868 and studied the Watergate evidential record intensively. Although many legislators, including some Democrats, questioned whether Rodino was fully qualified to lead the hearings, he impressed his colleagues throughout the proceedings with his patience and fairness. The House Judiciary Committee voted to recommend three articles of impeachment: for obstruction of justice, abuse of power, and failure to comply with congressional subpoenas. On Aug. 5, 1974, in compliance with a Supreme Court ruling, Nixon submitted to the Judiciary Committee transcripts of a taped conversation in which he discussed plans to halt an investigation into the Watergate break-in by the Federal Bureau of Investigation (FBI); he resigned the presidency three days later. The hearings earned Rodino widespread popularity among the American people, who believed he had handled the situation with sympathy and honesty.

Rodino was later appointed a manager by the House of Representatives in the impeachment trials of district Court Judge Harry E. Claiborne (1986) and district Court Judge Alcee Lamar Hastings (1988). He also served as chairman of the Committee on the Judiciary (1973–88). After retiring from political office in 1989, he was a professor of law at Seton Hall University until his death.

JAMES C. WRIGHT, JR.
(b. Dec. 22, 1922, Fort Worth, Texas)

James Claude Wright, Jr., is a Democratic politician and legislator who became speaker of the U.S. House of Representatives in 1986 but had to resign from office in 1989 owing to charges of financial improprieties.

Wright was educated at Weatherford College and the University of Texas before serving in the Army Air Force during World War II. After the war he entered politics as a Democrat and was elected to the Texas House of Representatives in 1946. He was defeated for reelection after serving one term and subsequently served as mayor of Weatherford, Texas, from 1950 to 1954. He then successfully sought election to the U.S. House of Representatives in 1954 and was reelected consecutively 16 times. He made an unsuccessful run for the Senate in 1961.

In 1976 Wright was elected majority leader by his fellow Democrats in the House of Representatives, and in 1986 he was elected speaker to succeed Rep. Thomas P. O'Neill. Wright was an assertive leader of the House, but in June 1988 the House ethics committee began to investigate allegations of financial improprieties on his part. In April 1989 the committee unanimously accused Wright of five counts comprising 69 separate violations of the House's ethics rules. Wright was accused of having received unusually high fees that in essence violated the House's limits on outside earned income and with having received discounted housing and other gifts that he had failed to list on his financial disclosure statements. Wright announced on May 31, 1989, that he would resign the speakership and his seat in Congress, and he did so a week later, when Thomas Foley was elected to succeed him as speaker. Wright was the first speaker of the House to resign his post in the middle of his term because of scandal.

ANDREW YOUNG
(b. March 12, 1932, New Orleans, La.)

Andrew Young is a Democratic politician, a civil rights leader, and a clergyman.

Young was reared in a middle-class black family, attended segregated Southern schools, and later entered Howard University (Washington, D.C.) as a premed student. But he turned to the ministry and graduated in 1955 from the Hartford Theological Seminary (Hartford, Conn.) with a divinity degree.

A pastor at several black churches in the South, Young became active in the civil rights movement—especially in voter registration drives. His work brought him in contact with Dr. Martin Luther King, Jr., and Young joined with King in leading the Southern Christian Leadership Conference (SCLC). Following King's assassination in 1968, Young worked with Ralph Abernathy until he resigned from the SCLC in 1970.

Defeated that year in his first bid for a seat in the U.S. House of Representatives, Young ran again in 1972 and won. He was reelected in 1974 and 1976. In the House he opposed cuts in funds for social programs while trying to block additional funding for the war in Vietnam. He was an early supporter of Jimmy Carter, and, after Carter's victory in the 1976 presidential elections, Young became the U.S.' ambassador to the United Nations. His apparent sympathy with countries of the developing world made him controversial in the United States, and he was finally forced to resign in 1979 after it became known that he had met with a representative of the Palestine Liberation Organization. In 1981 Young was elected mayor of Atlanta, and he was reelected to that post in 1985, serving through 1989.

For a list of all Speakers of the House of Representatives, see table on page 343.

Chapter 3 The Senate

The Senate, along with the House of Representatives, was established in 1789 under the Constitution of the United States. The Senate shares with the House responsibility for all lawmaking within the United States; for an act of Congress to be valid, both houses must approve an identical document. In addition, the Senate possesses certain important and exclusive powers, such as ratifying treaties and approving appointments to high federal offices.

HISTORY AND FUNCTIONS

The role of the Senate was conceived by the Founding Fathers as a check on the popularly elected House of Representatives. Thus each state, regardless of size or population, is equally represented. Further, until the Seventeenth Amendment of the Constitution (1913), election to the Senate was indirect, by the state legislatures. They are now elected directly by voters of each state.

IN FOCUS: THE SEVENTEENTH AMENDMENT

The Seventeenth Amendment (1913) to the Constitution of the United States provided for the direct election of U.S. senators by the voters of the states. It altered the electoral mechanism established in Article I, Section 3 of the Constitution, which had provided for the appointment of senators by the state legislatures. Adopted in the Progressive era of democratic political reform, the amendment reflected popular dissatisfaction with the corruption and inefficiency that had come to characterize the legislative election of U.S. senators in many states.

The amendment changed the wording of Article I, Section 3, Paragraph 1 to state that "two senators from each state" should be "elected by the people thereof" rather than "chosen by the legislature thereof." It also revised Paragraph 2 of Section 3 to allow the state executive to fill vacancies in the Senate by making temporary appointments to serve until new elections could be held. The full text of the amendment is:

The Senate of the United States shall be composed of two senators from each state, elected by the people thereof, for six years; and each senator shall have one vote. The electors in each state shall have the qualifications requisite for electors of the most numerous branch of the state legislatures.

When vacancies happen in the representation of any state in the Senate, the executive authority of such state shall issue writs of election to fill such vacancies: Provided, that the legislature of any state may empower the executive thereof to make temporary appointments until the people fill the vacancies by election as the legislature may direct.

This amendment shall not be so construed as to affect the election or term of any Senator chosen before it becomes valid as part of the Constitution.

By the time of the amendment's adoption, many states had already established mechanisms that effectively allowed voters to choose the senators of their state (e.g., by having the legislature appoint the winners of party primaries). Nevertheless, the amendment was widely seen as necessary to reduce the influence of big business and other special interests on the selection of senators and to prevent vacancies or frequent turnover in the Senate caused by party wrangling or changes of party leadership at the state level. In the late 20th century some conservative political scholars called for the repeal of the Seventeenth Amendment on the grounds that it undermined the proper balance of power between the federal government and the states.

Each state elects two senators for six-year terms, the terms of about one-third of the Senate membership expiring every two years. The constitutional provisions regarding qualifications for membership of the Senate specify a minimum age of 30, citizenship of the United

States for nine years, and residence in the state from which elected.

The Senate is given important powers under the "advice and consent" provisions (Article II, section 2) of the Constitution...

[The President] shall have Power, by and with the Advice and Consent of the Senate, to make Treaties, provided two-thirds of the Senators present concur; and he shall nominate, and by and with the Advice and Consent of the Senate, shall appoint Ambassadors, other public Ministers and Consuls, Judges of the supreme Court, and all other Officers of the United States, whose Appointments are not herein otherwise provided for, and which shall be established by Law: but the Congress may by Law vest the Appointment of such inferior Officers, as they think proper, in the President alone, in the Courts of Law, or in the Heads of Departments.

Ratification of treaties requires a two-thirds majority of all senators present and a simple majority for approval of important public appointments, such as those of cabinet members, ambassadors, and judges of the Supreme Court. The Senate also adjudicates impeachment proceedings initiated in the House of Representatives, a two-thirds majority being necessary for conviction.

As in the House of Representatives, political parties and the committee system dominate procedure and organization. Each party elects a leader, generally a senator of considerable influence in his own right, to coordinate Senate activities. The Senate leaders also play an important role in appointing members of their party to the Senate committees, which consider and process legislation and exercise general control over government agencies and departments. Sixteen standing committees are grouped mainly around major policy areas, each having staffs, budgets, and various subcommittees. Among important standing committees are those on appropriations, finance, government operations, and foreign relations. At "mark-up" sessions, which may be open or closed, the final language for a law is considered. Select and special committees are also created to make studies or to conduct investigations and report to the Senate—for example, the Select Committee on Ethics and the Special Committee on Aging.

The smaller membership of the Senate permits more extended debate than is common in the House of Representatives. Indeed, unlike the House of Representatives, in which speaking time is limited by rule, the Senate allows unlimited debate on a bill. Occasionally a minority of senators (sometimes even a single senator), using a parliamentary tactic known as a filibuster, will attempt to delay or prevent action on a bill by talking so long that the majority either grants concessions or withdraws the bill. In 1957 Sen. Strom Thurmond of South Carolina talked for more than 24 hours, the longest individual filibuster on record, as part of an unsuccessful attempt by Southern senators to obstruct civil rights legislation. To check a filibuster, three-fifths of the Senate membership must vote for cloture (or closure); if the bill under debate would change the Senate's standing rules, cloture may be invoked only on a vote of two-thirds of those present. The cloture motion itself is not debatable. Debate on the bill is then limited to an additional 30 hours.

There is a less-elaborate structure of party control in the Senate than there is in the House. The position taken by influential senators may be more significant than the position (if any) taken by the party.

NOTABLE MEMBERS OF THE SENATE

For a number of reasons, the Senate enjoys a special prestige that is not possessed by the House. The Constitution reserves to the Senate certain very important powers, such as ratifying treaties and confirming presidential nominations; senators are elected to longer terms than members of the House; senators represent the interests of entire states—and indeed the state level of government—rather than circumscribed districts; and the number of senators is limited to two per state, making the relative powers of individual senators greater than those of individual representatives. Because of its power and prestige, the Senate has frequently been regarded as a springboard to the presidency, and in fact many presidents have been drawn from its ranks. Many cabinet heads and Supreme Court justices also were senators before their appointments. Some of the more prominent members of the Senate are discussed in the remainder of this chapter.

SELECT CURRENT MEMBERS

SAM BROWNBACK
(b. Sept. 12, 1956, Garnett, Kan.)

Sam Brownback is a Republican politician who has served as a representative from Kansas in the U.S. House of Representatives (1995–96) and as a U.S. senator from Kansas (1996–). He unsuccessfully pursued the 2008 Republican presidential nomination.

Brownback was raised on his family's farm near Parker, Kan., and was the state president of the Future Farmers of America in high school, where his passion for politics began. He graduated from Kansas State University (where he was student body president) in 1978 and received a law degree from the University of Kansas in 1982. After graduating from law school, Brownback worked as an attorney in Manhattan, Kan., for four years before turning to public service. He was appointed secretary of the state board of agriculture in 1986, a position he held until 1993, and he was a White House fellow in 1990. In 1994 Brownback was elected to the U.S. House of Representatives as part of the landslide that gave the Republicans a majority. After Kansas Sen. Bob Dole resigned his position to campaign for the presidency in 1996, Brownback won a special election to fill the vacant Senate seat by running on a strongly conservative plat-

Sam Brownback. U.S. Senator Sam Brownback

form. He was easily reelected in 1998 and 2004, in the latter election garnering the highest number of votes for any office in Kansas history.

During his tenure as senator, Brownback has focused primarily on domestic social issues and international relations. He has been a member of the Senate's appropriations and judiciary committees and has served on the Joint Economic Committee and on the Commission on Security and Cooperation in Europe (the Helsinki Commission). His political philosophy is outlined in his *From Power to Purpose: A Remarkable Journey of Faith and Compassion* (2007). In his presidential campaign, Brownback supported tax reform and opposed abortion rights, but his initial support for a stalled immigration-reform bill cost him the support of some social conservatives. In October

2007 he withdrew from the race because of campaign fund-raising shortfalls.

ROLAND BURRIS

(b. Aug. 3, 1937, Centralia, Ill.)

Roland Burris is a Democratic politician who represents Illinois in the U.S. Senate (2009–). He was the first African American elected to statewide office in Illinois, and his appointment as U.S. senator to fill the seat vacated by Pres. Barack Obama made him only the fourth African American to serve in the Senate since Reconstruction.

Burris grew up in downstate Illinois, and he earned a bachelor's degree in political science from Southern Illinois University in 1959. He received a law degree from Howard University in 1963, and, after moving to Chicago, became a bank examiner for the U.S. Department of the Treasury. He left the job a year later to work in the tax division of Continental Illinois, then one of the 10 largest banks in the United States. While there, he made his first foray into politics, with a failed bid for the Illinois House of Representatives in 1968. Having risen to the rank of vice president, Burris left the bank in 1973 to join the cabinet of Illinois Gov. Dan Walker. After an unsuccessful campaign for state comptroller in 1976, he worked as director of Jesse Jackson's Operation PUSH in 1977. In 1978 Burris ran again for state comptroller, this time winning and becoming the first African American to be elected to statewide office in Illinois.

Burris easily won reelection in 1982 and 1986, and in 1990 he campaigned for the office of Illinois attorney general. That November he narrowly defeated the Republican candidate, Jim Ryan. While in office (1991–95), Burris established himself as a quietly effective administrator. His electoral fortunes waned in succeeding years, though, with three unsuccessful bids for governor (1994, 1998, 2002) and a crushing defeat in the 1995 race for mayor of Chicago—in which Burris ran as an independent—that pitted him against popular incumbent Richard M. Daley.

The election of Barack Obama as president in November 2008 left open one of Illinois's seats in the U.S. Senate, and the power to appoint Obama's successor fell to Illinois Gov. Rod Blagojevich. Before the appointment could be made, U.S. Attorney Patrick Fitzgerald filed criminal charges against Blagojevich, alleging, among other things, that he had solicited donations from potential candidates in a "pay for play" scheme. Nevertheless, on Dec. 30, 2008, Blagojevich appointed Burris to serve as Illinois's newest senator. Burris's appointment met with controversy at both the state and federal level. Illinois Secretary of State Jesse White refused to sign the paperwork that would endorse Burris, and Senate Majority Leader Harry Reid stated that anyone appointed by Blagojevich would not be seated.

On Jan. 6, 2009, Burris arrived at the Capitol for the opening of the 111th Congress. He was refused entry on the grounds that his credentials had not been properly authorized by state officials (specifically, they lacked the signature of the secretary of state). Burris evoked sympathy in a rain-soaked press conference outside the Capitol, and public opinion shifted to his support. Over the following days, Senate leaders met with Burris and his legal team, and Burris was officially sworn in on Jan. 15, 2009. In February, however, he faced more controversy after revealing that, prior to his appointment as senator, he had been in contact with several of Blagojevich's associates and had tried unsuccessfully to raise money for the governor (Blagojevich was impeached in January). Burris had failed to mention these dealings during his testimony before the state's House Special Investigative Committee in early January.

ROBERT C. BYRD

(b. Nov. 20, 1917, North Wilkesboro, N.C.)

Robert Carlyle Byrd is a Democratic politician who has served as a representative from West Virginia in the U.S. House of Representatives (1953–59) and as a U.S. senator from West Virginia (1959–). In his decades-long Senate career, Byrd has held various leadership positions, including Democratic whip (1971–77), majority leader (1977–80, 1987–88), minority leader (1981–86), and president pro tempore (1989–95, 2001–03, 2007–). In 2006 he became the longest-serving U.S. senator in history.

The son of working-class parents, Byrd was raised in southern West Virginia. After graduating from high school in a class of fewer than 30 students, he was a part-time student at Beckley College, Concord College, Morris Harvey College, and Marshall College (now Marshall University), all in West Virginia. Although he did not complete his bachelor's degree from Marshall University until 1994, he earned a law degree (1963) from American University in Washington, D.C., while serving in the Senate. In the early 1940s Byrd organized a local Ku Klux Klan chapter, although years later he had a change of heart and became a strong supporter of civil rights. He worked as a butcher, a coal miner, and a grocery store proprietor before launching his political career by getting elected to the West Virginia House of Delegates in 1946. He served in the state senate (1951–52) before winning election to the U.S. House of Representatives in 1952 and to the U.S. Senate in 1958.

As a senator, Byrd soon earned a reputation as a strong advocate for the working class as he sought to ensure accessibility to health care and greater educational and employment opportunities for his constituents. As minority and later majority leader during the 1980s, he often found himself at odds with Pres. Ronald Reagan (1981–89); he implored the president to withdraw U.S. marines from Lebanon in 1984 and criticized him sharply during the Iran-Contra Affair in 1986. After Pres. George H. W. Bush (1989–93) signed into law the Clean Air Act (1990), which threatened the livelihood of coal miners in his home state, Byrd worked to bring industry and federal jobs to West Virginia through his position as chairman of the Senate Appropriations Committee (1988–2008). He also provided needed guidance on procedural matters during Senate hearings on the impeachment of Pres. Bill Clinton (1993–2001) in 1998. Byrd opposed the reorganization of federal security agencies undertaken by Pres. George W. Bush (2001–09)—including the creation of the Department of Homeland Security—in the wake of the September 11 attacks in 2001, and he has been a vocal critic of the Iraq War (2003).

Byrd is a distinguished expert on the Senate's vast historical record, and he has frequently given impromptu speeches in which he recounts long-forgotten episodes of Senate history. His celebrated four-volume series *The Senate, 1789–1989* (1989–94) was followed by *The Senate of the Roman Republic* (1994), *Losing America: Confronting a Reckless and Arrogant Presidency* (2004), and *Letter to a New President* (2008). His memoir—*Child of the Appalachian Coalfields* (2005)—examines not only his political career but also the embarrassment he still feels over his early ties to the KKK.

Chris Dodd
(b. May 27, 1944, Willimantic, Conn.)

Chris Dodd is a Democratic politician who served as a representative from Connecticut in the U.S. House of Representatives (1975–81) and now serves in the U.S. Senate (1981–).

Dodd grew up around politics—his father was a four-term U.S. representative (1953–57) and senator (1959–71)—and began his own public service at an early age. He joined the Peace Corps after graduating from Providence College in Rhode Island in 1966 and spent two years working in the Dominican Republic. He served in the U.S. Army, first in the National Guard and later in the reserves, from 1969 to 1975. In 1972 Dodd received a law degree from the University of Louisville in Kentucky. The following year he was admitted to the Connecticut bar and opened a private practice in New London. Dodd was elected to the first of three terms as a U.S. representative in 1974, the midterm election bringing a large influx of Democrats to Congress during ongoing investigation into the Watergate scandal. Following his father's career path, Dodd ran for and was elected to the Senate in 1980. He was reelected in 1986, 1992, 1998, and 2004—the first Connecticut senator to be elected to five consecutive terms.

Chris Dodd. Congressional Pictorial Directory of the 110th Congress

Dodd's time in Congress has been marked by an interest in child welfare, fiscal reform, and education. He has served on the Senate's committees on banking, housing, and urban affairs (chair from 2007); foreign relations; health, education, labour, and pensions; and rules and administration (chair 2001–03). In 1995–97 he served as general chair of the Democratic National Committee. In

January 2007 Dodd announced that he planned to pursue the 2008 Democratic presidential nomination. His bid for the presidency never garnered widespread public support, and he withdrew from the race after finishing sixth in the Iowa Democratic caucus in January 2008.

RICHARD J. DURBIN
(b. Nov. 21, 1944, East St. Louis, Ill.)

Richard Joseph Durbin, also known as Dick Durbin, is a Democratic politician who has represented Illinois in the U.S. House of Representatives (1983–97) and in the U.S. Senate (1997–), where he has been majority whip since 2005.

Durbin attended Georgetown University in Washington, D.C., where he earned a B.A. (1966) and a law degree (1969). Thereafter he practiced law in Springfield, Ill., where he also worked as legal counsel to the state's lieutenant governor, Paul Simon (1969–72), and as an associate professor of law at Southern Illinois University School of Medicine (1978–83).

In 1982 he won election to the U.S. House of Representatives. Representing a rural district in central Illinois, Durbin sought to become a friend of farmers. He won a seat on the House Agriculture Committee and later on the Appropriations Committee, where he was a member of the Subcommittee on Agriculture. He was a strong supporter of the use of ethanol, an industrial chemical derived from sugar crops; ethanol manufacturing provided a valuable market for corn farmers in Illinois. He distinguished himself as a critic of big tobacco companies when he sponsored a successful ban (1988) on smoking on commercial airline flights. After Simon, his former employer, announced his retirement from the U.S. Senate in 1996, Durbin ran successfully for his seat.

As a senator, Durbin has continued his advocacy for farmers; in 2000 he secured funding for an ethanol research pilot plant to be built near Edwardsville, Ill. He also sponsored legislation (2001) designed to improve the quality of the country's food supply by consolidating a dozen federal food-safety agencies into a single agency. Durbin was also an outspoken opponent of Republican Pres. George W. Bush. An advocate for global AIDS research and treatment, in 2002 he criticized Bush for failing to propose adequate funding for these efforts. Durbin spoke out against the Iraq War (2003) and several domestic initiatives of the Bush administration, including the No Child Left Behind Act (2001). The year after he became majority whip (2005), Durbin pressed the Bush administration to be more forthcoming about the treatment of detainees held by the U.S. military at the Guantánamo Bay detention camp in Cuba. Durbin was a strong supporter of the successful presidential campaign in 2008 of fellow senator from Illinois Barack Obama.

DIANNE GOLDMAN FEINSTEIN

(b. June 22, 1933, San Francisco, Calif.)

Dianne Goldman Feinstein (née Dianne Emiel Goldman) is a Democratic politician who was the first woman mayor of San Francisco (1978–88). She is the first woman to represent California in the U.S. Senate, where she has served since 1992.

Feinstein grew up in San Francisco's upscale Presidio Terrace district. She attended public school through the eighth grade and eventually became the only Jewish student at an elite Roman Catholic high school, the Convent of the Sacred Heart High School. In 1951 she entered Stanford University, first as a premed student and then as a political science and history major. After graduating in 1955 with a B.S. degree, she interned at the Coro Foundation in San Francisco, an organization whose goal was to provide young people with political experience.

From 1960 to 1966 she worked on the California Women's Board of Terms and Parole. She chaired San Francisco's Advisory Committee for Adult Detention from 1966 to 1968, and in 1969 she won a seat on the San Francisco Board of Supervisors. She served in this role for nine years and was the board's first female president (1970–71, 1974–75, 1978).

In 1971 and again in 1975, she ran unsuccessfully for mayor of San Francisco. In 1978, when Mayor George Moscone and City Supervisor Harvey Milk were assassinated, Feinstein, as president of the Board of Supervisors, succeeded to the mayoral position. Just a few days before the assassinations, the followers of Jim Jones—most of whom were former Bay Area residents—had committed mass suicide at their compound in Guyana. Feinstein's leadership during this difficult time in the city's history earned her much respect and public support. She was elected mayor in her own right in 1979 and served until 1988. While in office, she received high marks for improving city services such as garbage collection and transportation and for furthering gay rights. In 1982, however, she opposed a measure that would have granted registered domestic partners the right to some benefits, such as insurance; this position cost her the support of much of her constituency.

After serving the maximum of two terms as mayor, Feinstein ran as the Democratic candidate for governor of California in 1990, losing to Republican Sen. Pete Wilson. When Wilson won the election and vacated his Senate position, she was elected to his seat. She was sworn into office in November 1992 for a special two-year term and was reelected to a full six-year term in 1994. She was reelected again in 2000 and 2006.

In office Feinstein wrote legislation that included a ban on the manufacture, sale, and possession of semiautomatic military combat weapons and drafted the California Desert Protection Act, which called for the protection of more than 3 million acres (1.2 million hectares) of desert, national parks, and nature reserves. During her career she has continued to focus on criminal justice and environmental concerns. She has served on several committees, including the Senate Judiciary Committee, the Foreign Relations Committee, the Appropriations Committee, the Rules and Administration Committee, and the Select Committee on Intelligence. In 2007, when the Democrats regained control of the U.S. Senate, Feinstein became the first woman to serve as chair of the Senate Rules and Administration Committee.

AL FRANKEN
(b. May 21, 1951, New York, N.Y.)

Al Franken is a comedian, political commentator, and Democratic U.S. senator from Minnesota (2009–).

When Franken was four years old, his family moved from New York to Minnesota, where his father ran a factory. Franken earned a bachelor's degree (1973) in political science at Harvard University. After graduation he returned to Minnesota to perform in Minneapolis's Brave New Workshop comedy troupe, which in 1975 led to a job with NBC television's *Saturday Night Live* (*SNL*). On the show Franken was best known for playing the character of self-help guru Stuart Smalley. Franken worked for *SNL* as a writer and performer until 1980, again during 1985–95, and briefly in 2008. He shared four Emmy Awards for writing on the show and received an additional nine nominations. He also did some acting, wrote and starred in a 1995 film featuring his Stuart Smalley character, and penned the screenplay for the dramatic film *When a Man Loves a Woman* (1994).

After leaving *SNL* in 1995, Franken became an outspoken political satirist for the left, publishing a number of books, including *Rush Limbaugh Is a Big Fat Idiot and Other Observations* (1999), *Lies and the Lying Liars Who Tell Them: A Fair and Balanced Look at the Right* (2004), and *The Truth (with Jokes)* (2005). He was also, from 2004 to 2007, the host of the Air America radio program *The Al Franken Show* (originally called *The O'Franken Factor*, which was a play on Bill O'Reilly's conservative show, *The O'Reilly Factor*). Conceived by Franken as a weapon in the fight to get Republican Pres. George W. Bush "unelected," the program used interviews and commentary to advance Franken's progressive political views. The show's final episode, on Feb. 14, 2007, ended with a bang when Franken announced his candidacy for the Minnesota Senate seat. Franken gained respect—if grudging from some quarters—for his tireless campaigning. Running on the Democratic-Farmer-Labor Party ticket, he emerged as a real threat to the incumbent Republican senator, Norm Coleman.

Although in the initial count Coleman outpolled Franken by a narrow margin in the November 2008 election, a mandatory recount of 2.9 million undisputed ballots (along with thousands of other disputed and absentee ballots) left Franken ahead by 225 votes. Coleman contested the result, but on April 13, 2009, Franken was again declared the winner. Coleman then took his fight to the courts. After a statewide recount ended with Franken ahead by 312 votes, Coleman again appealed the result, but on June 30 the Minnesota Supreme Court dismissed the challenge and ruled that Franken was entitled to be certified the winner. Because Coleman's term had expired on January 3, Minnesota's Senate seat had been left vacant for six months while the matter played out in the courts. When Franken took office on July 7, the Senate Democrats (supported by two independents) acquired a filibuster-proof 60–40 majority.

Orrin G. Hatch

(b. March 22, 1934, Homestead Park, Pa.)

Orrin Grant Hatch is a Republican politician who serves as a U.S. senator from Utah (1977–). The state's longest-serving senator, he chaired the Senate Judiciary Committee from 1995 to 2001 and again from 2003 to 2005.

Hatch, who was raised a Mormon, earned a bachelor's degree from Brigham Young University (1959) and a law degree from the University of Pittsburgh (1962). He worked as a lawyer in Pittsburgh from 1963 to 1969, when he relocated his practice to Salt Lake City, Utah. In 1977 he was elected to the Senate, where he was consistently recognized as a crusader for conservative values. In the wake of *Roe* v. *Wade* (1973), the U.S. Supreme Court decision that legalized abortion in the United States, he proposed in 1977 an amendment to the U.S. Constitution that would have made abortion illegal. In 1978 he helped to defeat the proposed Labor Law Reform Act, which would have expanded the power of labour unions. Five years later he voted against the Equal Rights Amendment (ERA), a proposed amendment to the Constitution that would have invalidated state and federal laws that discriminate on the basis of sex. Hatch co-sponsored the Missing Children Act (1982), which established the National Center for Missing and Exploited Children, as well as the Comprehensive Smoking Education Act

(1984), which required that cigarette packaging carry warnings from the surgeon general about the dangers of smoking.

Throughout the 1990s and into the 21st century, Hatch has continued to serve as a powerful voice for conservatives. He voted in favour of the Religious Freedom Restoration Act (1993), which would have prohibited the federal government from placing a substantial "burden [on] a person's exercise of religion" in all but a few exceptional circumstances. The law was struck down in 1997, however, when the Supreme Court ruled that Congress did not have the power to grant such expansive religious rights. Hatch announced in 1999 that he would run for the Republican nomination for the presidency, but he dropped out of the race after several disappointing primary finishes behind front-runner George W. Bush. After the September 11 attacks in 2001, Hatch helped to draft the controversial USA PATRIOT Act, which gave the federal government broader search-and-surveillance powers for use in preventing acts of terrorism. In 2006, as in previous years, he worked for passage by the Senate of a proposed Constitutional amendment that would make it illegal to burn the American flag, but it failed by one vote.

Despite his ardent conservatism, Hatch occasionally votes in favour of legislation sponsored or supported by Democrats. In 1988, for example, he was the only Republican to support federal funding of AIDS education. Two years later he voted for the Ryan White Comprehensive AIDS Resources Emergency Act (1990), which allocated more than $4 billion to address the crisis on a national level. In 2001 he became one of the few Republican advocates of stem cell research; he favoured harvesting the cells from umbilical cords rather than from human embryos. He has been frequently criticized within

his party for the close relationship he maintained with
Democratic Sen. Edward M. Kennedy.

Hatch is the author of *Square Peg: Confessions of a Citizen
Senator* (2002).

JOHN KERRY

(b. Dec. 11, 1943, Denver, Colo.)

John Kerry is a Democratic politician who has represented Massachusetts in the U.S. Senate since 1985. He
was the Democratic Party's nominee for the U.S. presidency in 2004.

Kerry was born in a Denver military hospital, the son
of Richard Kerry, a World War II pilot and diplomat, and
Rosemary Forbes Kerry, a member of the wealthy Forbes
family and a descendant of John Winthrop, first governor
of Massachusetts Bay Colony. John Kerry, educated in

John Kerry, 2004. Sharon
Farmer

New England and Switzerland,
was a successful student and
athlete who nurtured a longtime interest in politics. After
graduating from Yale
University in 1966, he enlisted
in the U.S. Navy and served in
the Vietnam War as an officer
of a gunboat in the Mekong
delta. By the time he returned
from Vietnam in 1969, he had
achieved the rank of lieutenant
and had been honoured with a
Silver Star, a Bronze Star, and
three Purple Hearts.

Concluding his military
service in 1970, he questioned
the purpose and execution of

the war and was a cofounder of the Vietnam Veterans of America and a spokesperson for the Vietnam Veterans Against the War. In this role he gained national attention in 1971 when he testified before the Senate Foreign Relations Committee. The following year he ran unsuccessfully for the U.S. House of Representatives and enlisted in the Naval Reserve. In 1976 he graduated from Boston College Law School and became assistant district attorney in Middlesex county, Massachusetts, winning notice for his tough stance on organized crime. From 1979 he practiced law privately for a few years before resuming his political career. In 1982 he was elected lieutenant governor of Massachusetts, and in 1984 he won election to the U.S. Senate. He was reelected three times (1990, 1996, 2002).

As senator, Kerry has fought for campaign finance reform, investment in public education, and deficit reduction. In his freshman term he began an unofficial investigation that persuaded a bipartisan congressional committee to open hearings on the Iran-Contra Affair. He also pursued scandals in banking. Along with Republican Sen. John McCain of Arizona, he helped to normalize U.S. relations with Vietnam by clearing up the status of American veterans declared POW/MIA (prisoner of war or missing in action). Kerry has chaired several committees, most notably the Foreign Relations Committee (2009–).

Kerry's first marriage, to Julia Thorne (1970), ended in divorce in 1988. In 1995 he married Teresa Heinz, widow of John Heinz (a Republican senator from Pennsylvania) and heiress to the Heinz Company fortune.

After securing the Democratic nomination, Kerry chose as his running mate John Edwards, a U.S. senator from North Carolina who had contended ably for the primary nomination. Campaigning in the general election against incumbent Pres. George W. Bush, Kerry touted plans to reduce joblessness and the national deficit, increase access to health care, and roll back Bush's tax cuts for the wealthiest. Kerry also called for greater diplomacy in foreign affairs and pointed to the administration's failure to capture terrorist Osama bin Laden and to achieve peace in Iraq. In an election with a huge voter turnout, Kerry suffered a narrow defeat.

Kerry is the author of *The New War: The Web of Crime That Threatens America's Security* (1997) and *A Call to Service* (2003).

Jon Kyl
(b. April 25, 1942, Oakland, Neb.)

Jon Kyl is a Republican politician who served as a representative from Arizona in the U.S. House of Representatives (1987–95) and now serves in the U.S. Senate (1995–).

Kyl earned bachelor's (1964) and law (1966) degrees from the University of Arizona, where he served as president of the *Arizona Law Review*. After being admitted to the state bar in 1966, he practiced at a Phoenix law firm for the next 20 years before running for a seat in the U.S. House of Representatives in 1986. In 1994 he successfully campaigned for a seat in the U.S. Senate.

Early in his career as a senator, Kyl pushed for a constitutional amendment that would require a two-thirds majority in both the House and the Senate before federal taxes could be raised. He also supported the rights of Medicare recipients to negotiate private contracts with their doctors. In 1998 Kyl and Democratic Sen. Dianne Feinstein proposed a constitutional amendment in the form of a crime victims' bill of rights, which Pres. Bill

Clinton first supported and later opposed. When Vice Pres. Al Gore championed a very similar amendment during his 2000 presidential campaign, Kyl harshly criticized him for ensuring the earlier amendment's failure.

Since the late 1990s Kyl has been a vocal opponent of research using stem cells taken from human embryos. In 2006 he voted in favour of a bill to authorize the construction of a 700-mile (1,130-km) fence along the U.S.-Mexico border in order to limit illegal immigration. A year later, however, he angered many of his constituents by compromising with Democratic senators, including Edward M. Kennedy, to support a bill that would provide a path to citizenship and temporary guest-worker status for illegal immigrants in the country. The bill failed in the Senate in a June 2007 vote. In 2009 Kyl joined Sen. Blanche Lincoln to sponsor a measure that would reduce or eliminate the estate taxes paid by some wealthy taxpayers.

JOSEPH LIEBERMAN
(b. Feb. 24, 1942, Stamford, Conn.)

Joseph Lieberman is a politician who has represented Connecticut in the U.S. Senate since 1989. Elected originally as a Democrat, he won reelection in 2006 as an independent after losing the Democratic Party primary. In 2000 he was the Democratic vice presidential nominee—the first Jewish candidate on a major party's presidential ticket.

Lieberman studied at Yale University, where he earned both a B.A. (1964) and LL.B. (1967). During the 1960s he was active in the civil rights movement and briefly practiced law. In 1970 (in a campaign in which future U.S. President Bill Clinton, then a student at Yale, served as a volunteer) Lieberman was elected to the Connecticut Senate, and he was majority leader from 1975 to 1981. In 1980 he was defeated in a bid for a seat in the U.S. House of Representatives, but two years later he was elected Connecticut attorney general. In 1988 he won election to the U.S. Senate, becoming the first Orthodox Jew to sit in that body, and he was reelected in 1994. Lieberman, who served as the chairman of the Democratic Leadership Council, took a generally centrist stance. Although he supported Democratic positions on issues such as campaign finance reform, abortion rights, and gun control, he broke ranks with his party by advocating school vouchers, cuts in capital gains taxes, and limits on liability awards.

In 2000 Lieberman was chosen by Al Gore, the Democratic presidential candidate, to be his running mate. The decision was seen as a bold one, but it was met with widespread approval. Lieberman's religious beliefs had a pervasive influence on his life and work. He had been the first Democratic senator to publicly criticize Pres. Bill Clinton for his behaviour in the Monica Lewinsky affair—in which Clinton first denied and then admitted having had a sexual relationship with a White House intern—although he later voted against removing Clinton from office. It was thought that one of the benefits of Lieberman's candidacy would be to help distance the Democratic ticket from the scandals of the Clinton administration. Although Gore and Lieberman won more popular votes than their Republican opponents (George W. Bush and Dick Cheney), they were narrowly defeated (271–266) in the electoral college. Lieberman, however, had also appeared on the Connecticut ballot for reelection to the Senate, a contest he won easily.

In January 2003 Lieberman announced his intention to run for the Democratic nomination for the 2004 presidential election. He failed to garner the endorsement of Gore, and many Democrats questioned his support of the Iraq War. After losing the New Hampshire primary in February 2004, he withdrew from the race.

Lieberman's position on the war proved particularly problematic during his 2006 Senate reelection, at a time when many Democrats were becoming increasingly frustrated by the Bush administration's handling of the war. Running against him in the Democratic primary was the relatively unknown antiwar candidate Ned Lamont, who narrowly defeated the incumbent. In response, Lieberman announced that he would continue in the race as an independent (or, as he phrased it, an "independent Democrat") and defeated Lamont in the election by a comfortable margin. Though elected as an independent, Lieberman opted to caucus with the Democrats—thus helping them secure a tenuous majority—and became chairman of the Senate Committee on Homeland Security and Governmental Affairs. However, Lieberman continued to roil Democrats, endorsing Republican John McCain for president in 2008 and criticizing the Democratic nominee, Barack Obama. In November 2008, shortly after Obama won the presidential election, the Democratic caucus approved a resolution that condemned campaign comments made by Lieberman and removed him as chairman of an environmental and public works subcommittee. However, he was allowed to continue as head of the powerful Senate Committee on Homeland Security and Governmental Affairs.

Lieberman is the author of numerous books, including the memoir *In Praise of Public Life* (2000; with Michael D'Orso) and, with his wife, Hadassah, *An Amazing Adventure: Joe and Hadassah's Personal Notes on the 2000 Campaign* (2003; with Sarah Crichton).

JOHN MCCAIN

(b. Aug. 29, 1936, Panama Canal Zone)

John McCain is a Republican politician who served as a representative from Arizona in the U.S. House of Representatives (1983–87) and now serves in the U.S. Senate (1987–). In 2008 he was his party's nominee for the U.S. presidency. A self-described conservative "foot soldier in the Reagan revolution," McCain has clashed with his party's right wing on a wide range of issues. McCain has long been a favourite of reporters, who admire what they see as his directness. Their attention has helped him gain a reputation as a political maverick

McCain has strong Southern roots—his great-great-grandfather, William A. McCain, owned a Mississippi plantation with more than 50 slaves and died fighting for the Confederacy in 1863—but he believes that his heritage lies almost entirely inside the country's military. The son and grandson of U.S. Navy admirals, he graduated from the United States Naval Academy near the bottom of his class in 1958, his low class rank attributed to indifference both to disciplinary rules and to academic subjects he did not enjoy. He then served in the Navy as a ground-attack pilot. In 1967, during the Vietnam War, McCain was nearly killed in a severe accidental fire aboard the aircraft carrier USS *Forrestal*, then on active duty in the Gulf of Tonkin.

Later that year McCain's plane was shot down over Hanoi, and, badly injured, he was captured by the North Vietnamese. In captivity he endured torture and years of solitary confinement. When his father was named commander of all U.S. forces in the Pacific in 1968, the North Vietnamese, as a propaganda ploy, offered early release to the younger McCain, but he refused unless every American captured before him was also freed. Finally released in 1973, he received a hero's welcome home as well as numerous service awards, including the Silver Star and the Legion of Merit.

McCain retired from the Navy in 1981, after his life had changed course. In 1977 he became the Navy's liaison to the U.S. Senate, which he later called his "real entry into the world of politics and the beginning of my second career as a public servant." Three years later his first marriage ended in divorce, which he confessed was due to his own infidelities; soon after, he married Cindy Lou Hensley of Phoenix, a teacher who was

John McCain. Office of U.S. Senator John McCain

also the only child of Marguerite Smith and Jim Hensley, founder of the third largest Anheuser-Busch beer distributorship in the country. Having acquired the personal connections and financial resources required to realize his political ambitions, McCain relocated to Arizona and was elected to the House of Representatives in 1982. After serving two terms, he successfully ran for a seat in the U.S. Senate in 1986; he was reelected in 1992, 1998, and 2004.

The war-hero senator gained national visibility by delivering a well-received address to the 1988 Republican National Convention. But McCain also became embroiled in the most spectacular case to arise out of the savings and loan scandals of the 1980s, as a result of his connections with Charles Keating, Jr., the head of the Lincoln Savings and Loan Association of Irvine, Calif., who had engaged in fraud. Although cleared by the Senate in 1991 of illegalities in his dealings on Keating's behalf, McCain was mildly rebuked for exercising "poor judgment." Duly embarrassed, McCain became a champion of campaign finance reform; he collaborated with the liberal Democratic senator Russ Feingold of Wisconsin, and, after a seven-year battle, the pair saw the McCain-Feingold Bipartisan Campaign Reform Act signed into law in 2002. The legislation, which restricted the political parties' use of funds not subject to federal limits, is McCain's signal achievement on Capitol Hill.

On most issues—including military spending, labour legislation, abortion, and gun regulation—McCain's record in the Senate has been basically conservative. Yet quite apart from campaign reform, McCain has taken stands on specific issues that distance him from the conservative Republican mainstream in Washington. Despite his years in captivity in Vietnam, McCain strongly advocated restoring diplomatic relations with that country, finally achieved in 1995. He led unsuccessful efforts to enact a new federal tax on tobacco products that would fund antismoking campaigns and help the states pay for smoking-related health costs. On immigration reform, health care, restriction of so-called greenhouse gas emissions (a primary cause of global warming), reduction of pork-barrel government spending, regressive tax cuts, and the political power of religious conservatives, McCain has stood out. His critics claim that his contrarian stance is calculated and mostly for show and that the favourable impression it makes inside the news media far outweigh the political risks.

In 2000, promising the country "straight talk" and extensive government reform, McCain ran for the Republican presidential nomination, competing against Texas Gov. George W. Bush. Bush prevailed after a strenuous fight, including an especially brutal effort by the Bush campaign in the South Carolina primary. McCain eventually recovered from his devastating defeat, campaigned hard for Bush's reelection in 2004, gave unswerving support to the Iraq War (2003), and, after initially opposing Bush's tax cuts, voted against their repeal.

In 2007 McCain announced that he would once again seek the Republican presidential nomination. Despite his rapprochement with the Bush family, his campaign seemed to be in serious trouble as the election year approached, lacking money and a clear political base. But after a decisive victory in New Hampshire and a strong showing on Super Tuesday, McCain took a commanding lead, and he secured the nomination with his victories on March 4, 2008. In late August he chose Sarah Palin, the governor of Alaska, as his vice presidential running mate.

McCain faced a challenging political climate in the general election. After 40 years of conservative dominance, the public seemed eager to start anew. By aligning himself with Pres. Bush, McCain gained powerful political resources, but it remained to be seen how much Bush's hard-core supporters, especially among religious conservatives, would rally to McCain's cause, despite his efforts to court them. By sidling up to Bush, McCain also contradicted his reputation for independence, made himself look inconsistent on key issues (including taxes), and identified himself with a president who in his second term earned the longest sustained period of public disapproval ever. McCain remained far more popular with the public than his party did, but, as he took on Democrat Barack Obama, he faced the humbling irony that, having been defeated by George W. Bush in 2000, he might find himself defeated by the legacy of Bush's presidency in 2008.

Indeed, in the event, McCain lost to Obama. Trailing in the initial opinion polls, McCain appeared to rebound following the Republican national convention in early September. His choice of Palin, a social conservative, as his running mate—the first female ever nominated to a

Republican national ticket—initially stirred great excitement, particularly within the party's social conservative base. But Palin soon received harsh criticism from many commentators, including conservatives, who claimed her lack of experience raised doubts about McCain's judgment. The outcome became almost inevitable when, later in September, the failure of some major investment houses and banks signaled the start of what became widely described as the worst financial crisis since the Great Depression. McCain strangely suspended his campaign, just prior to the first scheduled presidential debate, in order to work on a congressional bailout of the financial industry. He then just as suddenly decided to participate in the debate, which made him look erratic—and when House Republicans rejected the proposed bailout bill, he looked ineffectual as well. Obama wound up winning nearly 53 percent of the popular vote—a decisive margin, but no landslide—yet also captured not only all of those states that had gone for John Kerry in 2004 but also a number of historically Republican states won by Bush in the 2000 and 2004 elections, including Colorado, Florida, Nevada, North Carolina, Ohio, Indiana, and Virginia.

McCain has coauthored several books on his experiences and values. They include *Faith of My Fathers* (1999), *Worth the Fighting For: A Memoir* (2002), *Why Courage Matters: The Way to a Braver Life* (2004), and *Hard Call: Great Decisions and the Extraordinary People Who Made Them* (2007).

MITCH McCONNELL

(b. Feb. 20, 1942, Tuscumbia, Ala.)

Mitch McConnell is a Republican politician who serves as a U.S. senator from Kentucky (1985–). He is the state's longest-serving senator. In the Senate he has served as majority whip (2003–07) and minority whip (2007–).

During his early childhood, McConnell was afflicted with, but eventually overcame, polio. His family moved from Alabama to Louisville, Ky., when he was 13. He graduated from the University of Louisville in 1964 and from the University of Kentucky Law School in 1967. From 1968 to 1970 McConnell was a legislative assistant to U.S. Sen. Marlow Cook. He later served as deputy assistant U.S. attorney general in the administration of Pres. Gerald R. Ford (1974–75) and as judge/executive (chief judge) of Jefferson County, Ky. (1978–85). In 1993 he married Elaine Chao, who later served as secretary of labour under Pres. George W. Bush.

McConnell was elected to the U.S. Senate in 1984, becoming the first Republican since 1968 to win a statewide election in Kentucky. As chairman of the Senate Ethics Committee in 1995, he garnered national attention for resisting Democratic attempts to investigate sexual assault accusations against Republican Sen. Bob Packwood of Oregon. In a speech on the Senate floor, McConnell threatened to launch investigations into Democratic politicians who had faced similar charges in the past, among them Sen. Edward M. Kennedy. His Democratic colleagues prevailed, however, and McConnell publicly changed his mind about Packwood, who resigned later that year under the weight of evidence against him.

McConnell earned a reputation as a tough opponent of campaign finance reform and campaign spending limits. From the 1990s he consistently voted against a series of such measures, including some sponsored by fellow Republicans. When a popular bipartisan measure sponsored by Republican Sen. John McCain and Democratic Sen. Russell D. Feingold was signed into law by Pres. Bush in 2002, McConnell promptly sued the Federal Election Commission, calling the law a violation of free speech. In a December 2003 decision, the U.S. Supreme Court upheld the constitutionality of the law.

In subsequent years McConnell has shown greater willingness to compromise. In 2005 he served on a bipartisan Senate committee that made recommendations for broad changes to the Department of Homeland Security, the government agency charged with protecting the country against terrorist attacks in the wake of the September 11 attacks of 2001. The following year he introduced a compromise bill that brought the Republican and Democratic parties closer to agreement about which interrogation techniques could be used by U.S. authorities on detainees held as suspected terrorists or terrorist sympathizers. In 2007 he opposed Democratic calls to set in place a timetable for the withdrawal of U.S. troops from Iraq, arguing that it was not within the power of Congress to make such a judgment.

HARRY REID

(b. Dec. 2, 1939, Searchlight, Nev.)

Harry Reid is a Democratic politician who served as a representative from Nevada in the U.S. House of Representatives (1983–87) and now serves as a U.S. senator from Nevada (1987–). He has been the Senate's Democratic party whip (1999–2005), minority leader (2005–07), and majority leader (2007–).

Reid was raised in a Mormon family in a small mining town outside Las Vegas. To attend high school, he hitchhiked to nearby Henderson, Nev., every Monday and lived with relatives during the week before returning home for the weekend. He earned degrees from Utah State University (1961) and George Washington School of Law

(1964). Reid served as city attorney for Henderson (1964–66), as Nevada's lieutenant governor (1970–74), and as chairman of the Nevada Gaming Commission (1977–81). In the latter role he found himself the target of attempted violence by organized crime after he instituted measures to reduce mob influence in the state's casinos.

In 1982 Reid was elected to the first of two terms in the U.S. House of Representatives, where he served as one of only two representatives from Nevada. Because he could not join a Democratic congressional delegation from his own state (he was the only Nevada Democrat in Congress), he joined the California Democratic Congressional Delegation instead, becoming its secretary-treasurer in 1985. He won election to the Senate in 1986.

Reid has gained a reputation for being more conservative than many of his Democratic colleagues. He supported a Republican-sponsored constitutional amendment to ban the burning of the American flag and a bill to prohibit an abortion technique known as intact dilation and evacuation ("partial-birth" abortion). He has also sided with the mining industry against environmentalists by opposing environmental legislation that would impose restrictions on mining in Nevada.

Despite his election as Senate minority leader in November 2004, some of his colleagues questioned his devotion to the party and to traditional Democratic causes. As Pres. George W. Bush's leadership of the Iraq War was increasingly questioned by members of both parties, Reid's occasional support for Bush's policies met with renewed criticism among Democrats. Nevertheless, Reid quickly proved his allegiance to the Democrats in January 2005, when he demanded that Bush address concerns about the Iraq War in his State of the Union address, and again in September of that year, when he opposed Republican efforts to limit federal aid to victims of Hurricane Katrina. After the Democrats swept the midterm elections in 2006, Reid became Senate majority leader. In that position he challenged the president in 2007 after Bush announced plans to increase troop levels in Iraq. In 2009 Reid continued as majority leader during the administration of Democratic Pres. Barack Obama.

Select Past Members

John Ashcroft
(b. May 9, 1942, Chicago, Ill.)

John Ashcroft is a former Republican politician who served as attorney general of the United States (2001–05) and as a U.S. senator (1995–2001) from Missouri. He is known for his conservative policies and his support of the USA PATRIOT Act.

After graduating from Yale University (B.A., 1964) and the University of Chicago (J.D., 1967), Ashcroft taught business law at Southwest Missouri State University. In 1972 he unsuccessfully ran for the U.S. House of Representatives as a Republican. After serving as state auditor (1973–75), Ashcroft in 1976 was elected to the first of two terms as state attorney general, a post in which he earned much attention for his enforcement of a state law that restricted abortions.

In 1984 Ashcroft was elected governor of Missouri, and he was reelected in 1988. During his tenure as governor, he promoted fiscally and socially conservative policies. In 1994 he was elected to the U.S. Senate but was defeated in 2000, when he lost to Mel Carnahan, who had died shortly before the election and whose name remained on the ballot (Carnahan's position in the Senate was taken by his wife). Subsequently, he was nominated by Pres. George W. Bush as U.S. attorney general. Ashcroft faced intense questioning in the Senate, particularly on his attitudes toward African Americans and homosexuals and on his ability as a fundamentalist Christian to uphold U.S. law, but he was confirmed by a vote of 58 to 42.

As attorney general, Ashcroft was at the centre of policy changes adopted by the Department of Justice (DOJ) during 2002. Following the September 11 terrorist attacks in 2001, he pressed for the passage of the USA PATRIOT

John Ashcroft. U.S. Department of Justice

Act, which expanded the government's power to detain noncitizens, conduct surveillance and search, and investigate persons suspected of involvement in criminal activity. Ashcroft approved giving agents of the Federal Bureau of Investigation permission to monitor people in public areas—in libraries and on the Internet, for example— without evidence that a crime had been committed. Perhaps no actions were more controversial, however, than his department's handling of some 1,200 people jailed after the attacks. These included immigration violators whose cases were heard in secret and two U.S. nationals classified as "enemy combatants" and thus denied the legal rights of citizens. Ashcroft and the DOJ vigorously resisted challenges to its actions from the courts and from members of the U.S. Congress and the press.

On Nov. 9, 2004, Ashcroft announced his resignation as attorney general and was succeeded in February
2005 by Alberto Gonzales. Ashcroft subsequently
founded a strategic consulting firm and became a professor at Regent University in Virginia. He has written a
number of books, including *Lessons from a Father to His
Son* (1998) and *Never Again: Securing America and Restoring
Justice* (2006).

WILLIAM BENTON

(b. April 1, 1900, Minneapolis, Minn.—d. March 18, 1973, New York, N.Y.)

William Benton was the American publisher of *Encyclopædia
Britannica* (1943–73), an advertising executive, and a U.S.
senator (1949–53) from Connecticut government official.

The descendant of missionaries and educators, Benton
was greatly influenced by his indomitable mother, a professor's widow, pioneer woman school superintendent,
and Montana homesteader who instilled in him the drive
to excel. As a schoolboy he spent summers helping his
mother "prove up" her homestead claim. After a year at
Carleton College (Northfield, Minn.), he transferred to
Yale University, where he demonstrated an ability to write,
became chairman of the *Yale Record*, and graduated in 1921.
He also made one of the most influential friendships of his
life with his classmate Robert M. Hutchins.

Benton was attracted to the advertising business, and,
after eight years of increasing success in New York and
Chicago, he took on as partner Chester Bowles and
founded the New York agency of Benton and Bowles in
1929. The agency flourished through the Great Depression,
due in part to its innovations in radio entertainment programs sponsored by advertisers. By 1935 it was the
sixth-largest advertising firm in the world, but Benton had

grown restive in the profession and sold out to his partners for approximately $1 million.

Hutchins, who had become president of the University of Chicago, urged Benton to come to the university as a vice president. In 1937 Benton agreed. His restless energy was well-suited to the educational ferment Hutchins was developing there, and his advertising and radio background enabled him to develop the distinguished "University of Chicago Round Table" of the air into an extremely popular national radio forum. While at the university, he played a significant role in helping one of its trustees, Paul G. Hoffman, organize the Committee for Economic Development. He was also, prior to U.S. involvement in World War II, active with Hutchins in the America First movement. There he came to know Robert E. Wood, chairman of Sears, Roebuck and Company.

Surprised to learn that the mail-order company reluctantly owned *Encyclopædia Britannica*, Benton suggested that Sears give the encyclopaedia to the university, and Wood shortly thereafter agreed. But the trustees were hesitant to take on responsibility for operating capital and general management, and Benton offered to put up his own money. The university accepted the gift, committing management and common stock to Benton and retaining preferred stock and a royalty contract. Later, Benton acquired all the stock, and the royalty arrangements were modified; by the year after his death, the accumulated royalties to the university amounted to $47.8 million.

In 1945 Benton resigned from the university to become U.S. assistant secretary of state. He converted for peacetime use the U.S. Information Service, the cultural exchange programs, and the Voice of America, and he organized U.S. participation in the establishment of UNESCO, in which he later (1963–69) served as U.S. representative.

He also lobbied the Fulbright Scholarship Act and the Foreign Service Act of 1946 through Congress.

Appointed to a vacant U.S. Senate seat from Connecticut in 1949, Benton won reelection in 1950 to the remaining two years of that term. In the Senate he was among the first to decry the tactics for which Sen. Joseph R. McCarthy of Wisconsin was eventually censured. He was defeated for a full term in the Republican electoral landslide of 1952.

Thereafter, for the first time since 1945, he devoted sustained attention to Encyclopædia Britannica, Inc., which he led on an unprecedented course of acquisition and expansion. He acquired an educational filmmaker, ERPI, from Western Electric and renamed it Encyclopædia Britannica Films (1943; later given to his four children); he published the 54-volume *Great Books of the Western World* (1952) and *Enciclopedia Barsa* (Spanish, 1957; Portuguese, 1964); and he set in motion joint ventures leading to the publication of major foreign encyclopaedias (*Encyclopædia Universalis,* French, 1968–75; *Britannica International Encyclopædia,* Japanese, 1972–75). He acquired *Compton's Pictured Encyclopedia* (1961), G. & C. Merriam Company (1964; Webster's dictionaries), and Frederick A. Praeger, Inc. (1964–76). Shortly thereafter he authorized a massive effort to create the 15th edition of the *Britannica,* the costs of which were ultimately $32 million. He died a year before publication. In accordance with his wishes, the ownership of the *Britannica* went to the William Benton Foundation, a support foundation for the University of Chicago; the foundation held the *Britannica* until 1996. His own writings include two books: *This Is the Challenge* (1958) and *The Voice of Latin America* (1961). In 1968 Benton was honoured by the University of Chicago with the first William Benton Distinguished Service Medal.

LLOYD BENTSEN

(b. Feb. 11, 1921, Mission, Texas—d. May 23, 2006, Houston, Texas)

Lloyd Bentsen was a Democratic politician who was a longtime U.S. Democratic senator from Texas (1971–93). In 1988 he achieved national prominence as the vice-presidential running mate of presidential candidate Michael Dukakis in their unsuccessful bid for election. Bentsen, who distinguished himself as an able fund-raiser and public speaker, was famously remembered during the vice-presidential debate for his riposte to Sen. Dan Quayle, who had likened himself to Pres. John F. Kennedy. Bentsen declared, "Senator, you're no Jack Kennedy."

After earning a law degree from the University of Texas (1942), Bentsen was a combat pilot in the U.S. Army Air Forces. He served as a judge in Hidalgo County, Texas(1946–48), and was a member of the U.S. House of Representatives (1949–55). He left government, complaining that he could not support his family on the $12,500 salary he earned. With help from relatives, he founded Consolidated American Life Insurance Co.—later called Lincoln Consolidated, Inc., in Houston, and he reportedly became a millionaire as president of the firm. He reentered politics in 1970, beating George Bush in the Senate race, and served as chairman of the powerful U.S. Senate Finance Committee. After leaving the Senate, he served as Treasury Secretary (1993–94) in the cabinet of Pres. Bill Clinton.

WILLIAM E. BORAH

(b. June 29, 1865, Fairfield, Ill.—d. Jan. 19, 1940, Washington, D.C.)

William Edgar Borah was a Republican politician who served as a U.S. senator from Idaho for 33 years. He was

best known for his major role at the end of World War I
(1918) in preventing the United States from joining the
League of Nations.

Borah practiced law in Boise, Idaho, and in 1892
became chairman of the Republican State Central
Committee. He first won election to the U.S. Senate in
1906 and was returned to office five times by large majorities, making his tenure one of the longest in U.S. history.
Borah's distrust of government centralization limited his
commitment to social reform, but he did sponsor bills
establishing the Department of Labor as well as the federal Children's Bureau. He also strongly supported the
federal income tax and fought the trusts.

Isolationism dominated Borah's attitudes toward foreign policy. He did, however, sponsor a congressional
resolution (1921) calling for an international naval disarmament conference in Washington, D.C., resulting in the
Naval Armament Limitation Treaty concluded Feb. 6,
1922. Assuming the chairmanship of the Senate Committee
on Foreign Relations in 1924, he wielded enormous power
in this area for the next 16 years.

Borah did not object to international compacts so long
as the enforcement mechanism was limited to moral sanctions; thus he lent his support to the Kellogg-Briand Pact
(Paris, 1928) — an ineffective multilateral agreement theo-
retically outlawing war as an instrument of national policy.
He consistently upheld diplomatic recognition of the
Soviet Union and also helped establish the Good Neighbor
policy toward Latin America by advocating a fair deal for
Mexico during the controversy over foreign-held oil prop-
erties (1926–28).

During the Great Depression of the 1930s, Borah supported many New Deal measures designed to relieve
internal economic conditions. As European tensions

mounted, however, he held fast to his isolationist stance by resisting all attempts to involve the U.S. on the side of the Allies.

BILL BRADLEY

(b. July 28, 1943, Crystal City, Mo.)

Bill Bradley is a former collegiate and professional basketball player who served as a Democratic U.S. senator from New Jersey (1979–97).

Bradley began to play basketball at age nine and became one of the best players in Missouri high school basketball history. At Princeton University Bradley, a forward, was a playmaker and high scorer, averaging 30.1 points a game during three seasons. He led the team to three straight Ivy League titles, earning All-American recognition each time. He was the first basketball player to win the Amateur Athletic Union's Sullivan Award for the amateur athlete of the year (1965). He played on the U.S. team that won the gold medal at the 1964 Olympic Games in Tokyo. After graduation he deferred a contract offer from the New York Knicks of the National Basketball Association (NBA) in order to study at Oxford University (M.A., 1968) as a Rhodes scholar. He joined the Knicks during the 1967–68 season and played with them until his retirement in 1977. During Bradley's career the Knicks won two NBA championships (1970, 1973), with disciplined, aggressive defense. He was elected to the Naismith Memorial Basketball Hall of Fame in 1983. Bradley wrote two books about his NBA experiences: *Life on the Run* (1977) covers professional basketball players during two weeks of the 1973–74 season, and *Values of the Game* (1998) contains essays in which Bradley reflects on the qualities necessary to succeed at both basketball and life.

After his retirement from professional basketball, Bradley immediately turned to politics. Without having held a lesser office he was elected to the U.S. Senate from New Jersey in 1978 and served three six-year terms. A liberal Democrat, he announced his candidacy for the U.S. presidency on Jan. 12, 1999, but lost the Democratic nomination to Al Gore.

Edward Brooke
(b. Oct. 26, 1919, Washington, D.C.)

Edward Brooke is a former Republican politician who became the first African American popularly elected to the U.S. Senate, where he served two terms (1967–79).

Brooke earned his undergraduate degree at Howard University (Washington, D.C.) in 1941 and served as an infantry officer during World War II, achieving the rank of captain. After being discharged, he earned two law degrees at Boston University and was editor of the *Boston University Law Review*.

Brooke began practicing law in 1948 and became a successful Boston attorney. Entering politics, he was defeated in attempts to win a seat in the Massachusetts legislature in 1950 and 1952. He also failed in his 1960 bid to become the Massachusetts secretary of state. From 1961 to 1962 he served as chairman of the Boston Finance Commission, seeking evidence of corruption in city politics.

In 1962 Brooke, a Republican in an overwhelmingly Democratic state, was elected attorney general of Massachusetts. A vigorous prosecutor of official corruption, he was reelected in 1964 by a large margin, despite the success of Democrats that year (Democratic Pres. Lyndon Johnson captured more than 75 percent of the vote in Massachusetts against Republican Barry Goldwater).

In 1966 Brooke ran for a seat in the U.S. Senate and won by nearly half a million votes. That year he also published *The Challenge of Change: Crisis in Our Two-Party System*, which focused on self-help as a way to address the social issues facing the United States during the 1960s. He established a reputation as a soft-spoken moderate on civil rights and a leader of the progressive wing of his party. In 1972 he was overwhelmingly reelected. In 1978, however, beset by personal problems including accusations of financial misdeeds and a divorce, Brooke lost his bid for a third term. In 2008 journalist Barbara Walters revealed that she and Brooke had engaged in an affair for several years prior to his divorce.

After leaving the Senate in 1979, Brooke became chairman of the National Low-Income Housing Coalition and resumed the practice of law. In 2004 he was awarded the Presidential Medal of Freedom. His memoir, *Bridging the Divide* (2007), explores issues of race and class as viewed from his experiences as an African American Republican politician from a largely Democratic state.

BLANCHE K. BRUCE

(b. March 1, 1841, Prince Edward County, Va. — d. March 17, 1898, Washington, D.C.)

Blanche Kelso Bruce was an African American U.S. senator from Mississippi during the Reconstruction era.

The son of a slave mother and white planter father, Bruce was well educated as a youth. After the American Civil War, he moved to Mississippi, where in 1869 he became a supervisor of elections. By 1870 he was an emerging figure in state politics. After serving as sergeant at arms in the state senate, he held the posts of county assessor, sheriff, and member of the Board of Levee

Blanche K. Bruce. Library of
Congress, Washington, D.C.

Commissioners of the Mississippi River. Through these positions he amassed enough wealth to purchase a plantation in Floreyville, Miss.

In 1874 Mississippi's Republican-dominated state legislature elected Bruce, a Republican, to a seat in the U.S. Senate. He served from 1875 to 1881, advocating just treatment for both African Americans and Indians and opposing the policy excluding Chinese immigrants. He sought improvement of navigation on the Mississippi and advocated better relations between the races. Much of his time and energy he devoted to fighting fraud and corruption in federal elections.

Bruce lost his political base in Mississippi with the end of Reconstruction governments in the South. He remained in Washington when, at the conclusion of his Senate term, he was appointed register of the Treasury. He served in that post from 1881 to 1885 and again from 1895 to 1898. He was also recorder of deeds in the District of Columbia (1889–95) and a trustee of Howard University.

JAMES F. BYRNES

(b. May 2, 1879, Charleston, S.C. — d. April 9, 1972, Columbia, S.C.)

James Francis Byrnes was a Democratic Party politician and administrator who, during World War II, was popularly known as "assistant president for domestic affairs" in his capacity as U.S. director of war mobilization (1943–45). He also served effectively as secretary of state (1945–47) in the challenging postwar period.

A self-taught lawyer, Byrnes entered public life in 1908 as public prosecutor in South Carolina. He served in the U.S. House of Representatives (1911–25) and in the Senate (1931–41), where he soon emerged as the actual majority leader. A member of Pres. Franklin D. Roosevelt's "Brain Trust," he helped pilot numerous New Deal measures through Congress. He later rejected many administration concepts as too radical, but was a key figure in launching important defense preparedness legislation on the eve of World War II.

After serving briefly on the U.S. Supreme Court (1941–42), Byrnes was appointed director of economic stabilization and later head of the Office of War Mobilization. He was thus vested with authority over production, procurement, and distribution of all civilian and military goods, manpower allocation, and economic stabilization.

After attending the Yalta (Big Three) Conference with Roosevelt in February 1945, Byrnes resigned but was recalled to active service by Pres. Harry S. Truman as secretary of state and accompanied Truman to the Potsdam Conference in the same year. His experiences in dealing with the Soviet Union, particularly over the issue of German reunification, soon converted him from an advocate of friendly cooperation to a hard-line fighter in the Cold War. Byrnes called for the United States to maintain a military establishment in western Europe to prevent Soviet expansion there. He resigned from the cabinet in 1947 in a disagreement with Truman.

Byrnes served as governor of his state from 1951 to 1955. In later years he defended racial segregation in the schools.

HATTIE OPHELIA CARAWAY

(b. Feb. 1, 1878, near Bakerville, Tenn. — d. Dec. 21, 1950, Falls
Church, Va.)

Hattie Ophelia Caraway (née Hattie Ophelia Wyatt) was
a politician who became the first woman elected to the
U.S. Senate.

Hattie Wyatt grew up in her native Bakerville, Tenn.,
and in nearby Hustburg. She graduated (1896) from
Dickson Normal School and for a time thereafter taught
school. In 1902 she married Thaddeus H. Caraway, who
subsequently became a congressman and then a U.S. senator for Arkansas.

When Thaddeus died in November 1931 Hattie
Caraway was appointed by the governor to fill her husband's seat until a special election could be held; she
thereby became the second
woman (after Rebecca Felton,
1922) to be seated in the U.S.
Senate. She won a special election (January 1932) to fill the
few remaining months of her
late husband's term. She won
reelection in her own right to
the seat later in 1932 with the
help of Louisiana governor
Huey Long, who campaigned
for her. Caraway was reelected
again in 1938 but failed in her
bid for a third term in 1944. In
her 13 years in the Senate, she
was the first woman to preside
over a session of that body and
the first to serve as a committee chairman.

Hattie Ophelia Caraway. Library of Congress, Washington,
D.C.; neg. no. LC USZ 62 12692

In her voting Caraway generally supported the New Deal and other legislation of the Franklin D. Roosevelt administration. She opposed isolationism, supported veterans and organized labour, and in 1943 became the first woman in Congress to cosponsor the Equal Rights Amendment. Her reelection in 1938 after a primary victory over Rep. John L. McClellan firmly established her as a senator in her own right, and her dry humour and homely sayings made her a favourite national figure. In the 1944 Democratic primary in Arkansas she was defeated by Rep. J. William Fulbright, and she left the Senate in 1945.

DeWitt Clinton

(b. March 2, 1769, Little Britain, N.Y.—d. Feb. 11, 1828, Albany, N.Y.)

DeWitt Clinton was a political leader who promulgated the idea of the Erie Canal, which connects the Hudson River to the Great Lakes. He served as New York state senator (1798–1802, 1806–11), U.S. senator (1802–03), mayor of New York (1803–15 except for two annual terms), lieutenant governor (1811–13), and governor (1817–23, 1825–28). As mayor of New York, he advocated free and widespread public education, promoted legislation that removed voting restrictions against Roman Catholics, and established various public-welfare institutions in the city. He was an unsuccessful presidential candidate in 1812, being defeated by James Madison.

In 1811 Clinton introduced a bill into the New York Senate to appoint a commission to explore suggested routes for a canal across New York state to link the Northeast coastal trade with the Great Lakes via Lake Erie. He and Gouverneur Morris, chairman of the commission, were sent to Washington, D.C., to seek federal aid for the project but were unsuccessful. After the War of 1812 ended (1814), the canal idea was revived, and Clinton went to the state capital at Albany, urging acceptance of a detailed canal plan. After much persuasion, the legislature agreed to finance the canal as a state project (April 1816) and appointed Clinton to the commission.

Elected governor at this opportune time and serving almost continuously until his death, he was in an advantageous position to oversee the entire project. As bitter opposition to his administration developed under Martin Van Buren and Tammany Hall, Clinton refused to run for a third term in 1822. But his dismissal as canal commissioner in 1824 caused such indignation statewide that he was swept into the governorship the next year and served until his death. With the opening of the Erie Canal on Oct. 25, 1825, Clinton assured the 19th-century development of New York as the major port of trade with the Midwest.

Clinton was also profoundly interested in the arts and the natural sciences, and he published an excellent summary of the state of scientific knowledge in the United States in a work entitled *An Introductory Discourse* (1814).

HILLARY RODHAM CLINTON
(b. Oct. 26, 1947, Chicago, Ill.)

Hillary Rodham Clinton (née Hillary Diane Rodham) is a Democratic politician who served as a U.S. senator from New York (2001–09) and as secretary of state (2009–) in the administration of Pres. Barack Obama. She was also the first lady (1993–2001) during the administration of her husband, Bill Clinton, the 42nd president of the United States.

The first president's wife born after World War II, Hillary Rodham was the eldest child of Hugh and Dorothy Rodham. She grew up in Park Ridge, Illinois, a Chicago suburb, where her father's textile business provided the family with a comfortable income. Her parents' emphasis on hard work and academic excellence set high standards.

A student leader in public schools, she was active in youth programs at the First United Methodist Church. Although she later became associated with liberal causes, during this time she adhered to the Republican Party of her parents. She campaigned for Republican presidential candidate Barry Goldwater in 1964 and chaired the local chapter of the Young Republicans. A year later, after she enrolled at Wellesley College, her political views began to change. Influenced

Hillary Rodham Clinton, 2009.
U.S. Department of State

by the assassinations of Malcolm X, Robert F. Kennedy, and Martin Luther King, Jr., she joined the Democratic Party and volunteered in the presidential campaign of antiwar candidate Eugene McCarthy.

After her graduation from Wellesley in 1969, Hillary entered Yale Law School, where she came under the influence of Yale alumna Marian Wright Edelman, a lawyer and children's rights advocate. Through her work with Edelman, she developed a strong interest in family law and issues affecting children.

Although Hillary met Bill Clinton at Yale, they took separate paths after graduation in 1973. He returned to his native Arkansas, and she worked with Edelman in Massachusetts for the Children's Defense Fund. In 1974 Hillary participated in the Watergate inquiry into the possible impeachment of Pres. Richard M. Nixon. When her

assignment ended with Nixon's resignation in August
1974, she made what some people consider the crucial
decision of her life—she moved to Arkansas. She taught at
the University of Arkansas School of Law, and, following
her marriage to Bill Clinton on Oct. 11, 1975, she joined the
prominent Rose Law Firm in Little Rock, Ark., where she
later became a partner.

After Bill was elected governor of Arkansas in 1978,
she continued to pursue her career and retained her
maiden name (until 1982), bringing considerable criticism
from voters who felt that her failure to change her name
indicated a lack of commitment to her husband. Their
only child, Chelsea Victoria, was born in 1980.

Throughout Bill's tenure as governor (1979–81, 1983–
92), Hillary worked on programs that aided children and
the disadvantaged; she also maintained a successful law
practice. She served on the boards of several high-profile
corporations and was twice named one of the nation's 100
most influential lawyers (1988, 1991) by the *National Law
Journal*. She also served as chair of the Arkansas Education
Standards Committee and founded the Arkansas
Advocates for Children and Families. She was named
Arkansas Woman of the Year in 1983 and Arkansas Young
Mother of the Year in 1984.

In Bill's 1992 presidential campaign, Hillary played a
crucial role by greeting voters, giving speeches, and serving as one of her husband's chief advisers. Her appearance
with him on the television news program *60 Minutes* in
January 1992 made her name a household word.
Responding to questions about Bill's alleged 12-year sexual relationship with an Arkansas woman, Gennifer
Flowers, Bill and Hillary discussed their marital problems, and Hillary told voters to judge her husband by his
record—adding that, if they did not like what they saw,
then, "heck, don't vote for him."

With a professional career unequaled by any previous presidential candidate's wife, Hillary was heavily scrutinized. Conservatives complained that she had her own agenda, because she had worked for some liberal causes. During one campaign stop, she defended herself from such criticism by asserting that she could have "stayed home and baked cookies." This impromptu remark was picked up by the press and used by her critics as evidence of her lack of respect for women who are full-time homemakers.

Some of Hillary's financial dealings raised suspicions of impropriety and led to major investigations after she became first lady. Her investment in Whitewater, a real estate development in Arkansas, and her commodities trading in 1978–79 — through which she reportedly turned a $1,000 investment into $100,000 in a few months — came under close scrutiny.

During the 1992 campaign, Bill Clinton sometimes spoke of a "twofer" ("two for the price of one") presidency, implying that Hillary would play an important role in his administration. Early indications from the Clinton White House supported this interpretation. She appointed an experienced staff and set up her own office in the West Wing, an unprecedented move. Her husband appointed her to head the Task Force on National Health Care, a centrepiece of his legislative agenda. She encountered sharp criticism when she closed the sessions of the task force to the public, and doctors and other health care professionals objected that she was not a "government official" and had no right to bar them from the proceedings. An appeals court later supported her stand, ruling that presidents' wives have "a longstanding tradition of public service...act[ing]...as advisers and personal representatives of their husbands." To promote the findings of the task force, she appeared before five congressional committees and received considerable and mostly favourable press coverage for her expertise on the subject. But Congress ultimately rejected the task force's recommendations, and her role in the health care debate galvanized conservatives and helped Republicans recapture Congress in the 1994 elections.

Hillary was criticized on other matters as well, including her role in the firing of seven staff members from the White House travel office ("Travelgate") and her involvement in legal maneuvering by the White House during the Whitewater investigation. As the 1996 election approached, she was less visible and played a more traditional role as first lady. Her first book, *It Takes a Village: And Other Lessons Children Teach Us* (1996), described her views on child rearing and prompted accolades from supporters and stark criticism from her opponents.

Revelations about Pres. Clinton's affair with White House intern Monica Lewinsky brought the first lady back into the spotlight in a complex way. She stood faithfully by her husband during the scandal—in which her husband first denied and then admitted to having had a sexual relationship with Lewinsky—and throughout his ensuing impeachment and trial in the Senate.

In 1999 Hillary Rodham Clinton made history of a different sort when she launched her candidacy for the U.S. Senate seat from New York

Hillary Rodham Clinton (left) being sworn in as secretary of state by Joe Biden (right) as Bill Clinton, Chelsea Clinton, and Dorothy Rodham look on, Feb. 2, 2009. Michael Gross/U.S. Department of State

being vacated by Daniel Patrick Moynihan. To meet the state's residency requirement, she moved out of Washington, D.C., on Jan. 5, 2000, to a house that she and the president purchased in Chappaqua, New York. After a bitter campaign, she defeated Republican Rick Lazio by a substantial margin to become the first first lady to win elective office. Although often a subject of controversy, Hillary showed that the ceremonial parts of the first lady's job could be merged with a strong role in public policy and that the clout of the first lady could be converted into a personal political power base.

Sworn into office on Jan. 3, 2001, Hillary continued to push for health care reform, and she remained an advocate for children. She served on several senatorial committees, including the Committee for Armed Services. Following the September 11 terrorist attacks in 2001, she supported the U.S.-led invasion of Afghanistan but grew highly critical of Pres. George W. Bush's handling of the Iraq War. In 2003 Hillary's much-anticipated memoir of her White House years, *Living History*, was published and set sales records; she had received an advance of about $8 million for the book. In 2006 she was easily reelected to the Senate.

The following year Hillary announced that she would seek the Democratic Party's presidential nomination for 2008. She began the primary season as the front-runner for the nomination but placed a disappointing third in the first contest, the Iowa caucus, on Jan. 3, 2008. Her campaign quickly rebounded, and she won the New Hampshire primary five days later. On Super Tuesday, February 5, Clinton won important states such as California, Massachusetts, and New York, but she failed to gain a significant lead over Barack Obama in the number of pledged convention delegates. Obama won 11 consecutive states following Super Tuesday to take over the delegate lead and become the new favourite for the nomination, but Clinton rebounded in early March with key victories in Ohio and Texas, and in April she added to her momentum by winning the Pennsylvania primary. However, Clinton's narrow victory in Indiana and substantial loss in North Carolina in early May severely limited the possibility of her garnering enough delegates to overtake Obama before the final primaries in June. On June 3, following the final primaries in Montana and South Dakota, Obama passed the delegate threshold and became the presumptive Democratic nominee. He officially secured the party's nomination on August 27 at the Democratic National Convention in Denver and went on to win the general election on November 4. In December 2008 Obama selected Clinton to serve as secretary of state, and she was easily confirmed by the Senate in January 2009. Since becoming secretary of state she has addressed a wide range of foreign-policy problems, including the growing influence of the Taliban in Pakistan and the menace to international security posed by North Korea.

ROSCOE CONKLING
(b. Oct. 30, 1829, Albany, N.Y.—d. April 18, 1888, New York, N.Y.)

Roscoe Conkling was a prominent U.S. Republican leader in the post—Civil War period. He served as a representative from New York in the U.S. House of Representatives (1859–65) and as a U.S. senator from New York (1867–81). He was known for his support of severe Reconstruction measures toward the South and his insistence on the control of political patronage in his home state.

Admitted to the bar in 1850, Conkling soon established a reputation as a lawyer, orator, and Whig Party leader. In 1858 he ran as a Republican and was elected to the U.S. House of Representatives. In the House,

Conkling consistently sup- ported the administration of Pres. Abraham Lincoln in his conduct of the Civil War (1861–65). He became a leader of the Radical Republicans, who advocated firm military supervision of the defeated Confederate states and broader rights for freedmen. In addition, he was an avid supporter of the Fourteenth (due process) Amendment to the Constitution (1868). As a U.S. senator Conkling influenced the administration of Pres. Ulysses S. Grant (1869–77) in its overall policy toward the South.

Roscoe Conkling. Library of Congress, Washington, D.C.

To maintain a tight grip on the reins of political power in his home state, Conkling insisted on the need for senators to have personal control over all federal appointments within state boundaries. He thus vigorously resisted the efforts of the Republican president Rutherford B. Hayes (served 1877–81) to introduce civil-service reform legislation.

At the party convention of 1880 Conkling headed the so-called Stalwart faction supporting a third term for former president Grant. As a result of this movement, the convention was split and a compromise candidate, James A. Garfield, was nominated and elected. Conkling resigned from office (May 1881) in a dispute with the new president over the patronage issue. He declined a nomination to the U.S. Supreme Court in 1882 and practiced law in New York until his death.

JOHN J. CRITTENDEN

(b. Sept. 10, 1787, near Versailles, Ky.—d. July 26, 1863, Frankfort, Ky.)

John Jordan Crittenden was a statesman best known for the so-called Crittenden Compromise, his attempt to resolve sectional differences on the eve of the American Civil War. He served intermittently in the U.S. Senate, from 1817 through 1861.

Two years after his graduation (1807) in law from the College of William and Mary, Crittenden became territorial attorney general in Illinois. During the War of 1812, having returned to Kentucky, he was elected to the legislature of that state.

Crittenden left the U.S. Senate in 1840 to become U.S. attorney general in William Henry Harrison's Whig administration but resigned, along with others, after John Tyler, having acceded to the presidency on Harrison's death (April 4, 1841), had vetoed a national banking act favoured by the Whigs.

Crittenden returned to the Senate in 1842 and left again to serve as governor of Kentucky (1848–50). During his last years in the Senate (1855–61), the controversial Kansas-Nebraska Act of 1854, enunciating the doctrine of local option in the territories concerning slavery, led to the breakup of the Whig Party, whereupon Crittenden first joined the American, or Know-Nothing, Party (1856) and then switched to the Constitutional Union Party (1859), which sought to unite the sections by ignoring the slavery issue.

After Abraham Lincoln's election as president, Crittenden introduced his resolutions (December 1860) proposing a collection of compromises on the slavery issue, but they were defeated, and he went home to try to save Kentucky for the Union. In May 1861 he was chairman of the Frankfort convention of border-state leaders that asked the South to reconsider its position on secession from the Union. He then returned to Congress as a representative. One of his sons, Thomas, was a major general in the Union Army; another son was a major general in the Confederate Army.

TOM DASCHLE
(b. Dec. 9, 1947, Aberdeen, S.D.)

Tom Daschle is a former Democratic politician who served as a U.S. senator from South Dakota (1987–2005) and as Senate majority leader (2001–03).

Daschle was the first member of his family to attend college, and in 1969 he graduated from South Dakota State University with a B.A. in political science. From 1969 to 1972 he served in intelligence in the Air Force Strategic Air Command. For five years, from 1972 to 1977, he was a congressional aid to U.S. Sen. James Abourezk, and in 1978 he was elected to the first of four terms in the House of Representatives.

In 1986 Daschle, a Democrat, defeated incumbent James Abdnor to win election to the Senate, and he was reelected overwhelmingly in 1992 and 1998. He became a member of the powerful Finance Committee while still a freshman senator and in 1988 was appointed cochair of the Democratic Policy Committee. Other legislative interests of Daschle included veterans' and Indian affairs and agriculture. He compiled a record that was generally liberal on economic matters and moderate on social issues. Daschle gained a reputation for looking out for the interests of his constituents, and every year he drove himself throughout South Dakota to visit each of its 66 counties and talk to voters. In 1994 Daschle won the position of Democratic leader by one vote, and he became minority leader in the Senate at the beginning of the 1995 session. A soft-spoken man, he had a reputation for being fair and inclusive, but he was a skillful tactician and could be tough when needed.

On June 6, 2001, Daschle became the new majority leader when the Senate passed from Republican to Democratic control. The shift occurred when Sen. James Jeffords of Vermont left the Republican Party to become an independent, which gave the Democrats a 50–49 majority. The Democrats under Daschle found themselves with greater power to determine the legislative agenda and to pass judgment on the appointments and judicial nominees of Pres. George W. Bush. Daschle opposed Bush's tax-cut bill on the grounds that it was fiscally irresponsible and that it unduly benefited the wealthy. He also declared that parts of the Bush legislative program, including drilling for oil in the Arctic National Wildlife Refuge and quick deployment of a missile defense system, would not pass the Senate. In the first three weeks under Daschle's leadership, a patients' bill of rights, guaranteeing certain protections to those who were covered under managed-care health insurance, cleared the Senate despite the president's threat to veto it; the House of Representatives later passed a weaker version of the bill, and both proposals ultimately stalled in Congress. Later in the year Daschle took the lead in blaming the Bush tax cut for the disappearance of the budget surplus.

Daschle remained the majority leader until 2003, when Republicans regained control of the Senate. In 2004 he was defeated in his reelection bid by Republican challenger John Thune. Daschle subsequently returned to the private sector. In November 2008 President-elect Barack Obama selected Daschle to serve as secretary of health and human services, a post requiring Senate confirmation. The following February, however, Daschle asked to be withdrawn from consideration for the cabinet position after problems surfaced concerning back taxes.

JEFFERSON DAVIS

(b. June 3, 1808, Christian County, Ky.—d. Dec. 6, 1889, New Orleans, La.)

Jefferson Davis was a political and military leader who served as a representative from Mississippi in the U.S. House of Representatives (1845–46) and as a U.S. senator from Mississippi (1847–53, 1857–61). He was president of the Confederate States of America throughout its existence during the American Civil War (1861–65). After the war he was imprisoned for two years and indicted for treason but never tried.

Jefferson Davis was the 10th and last child of Samuel Emory Davis, a Georgia-born planter of Welsh ancestry. When he was three his family settled on a plantation called Rosemont at Woodville, Miss. At seven he was sent for three years to a Dominican boys' school in Kentucky, and at 13 he entered Transylvania College, Lexington, Ky. He later spent four years at the United States Military Academy at West Point, graduating in 1828.

Davis served as a lieutenant in the Wisconsin Territory and afterward in the Black Hawk War under the future president, Col. Zachary Taylor, whose daughter Sarah Knox he married in 1835. In 1835 Davis resigned his commission and became a planter near Vicksburg, Miss. Within three months his bride died of malarial fever. Grief-stricken, Davis stayed in virtual seclusion for seven years, creating a plantation out of a wilderness and reading prodigiously in constitutional law and world literature.

In 1845 Davis was elected to the U.S. House of Representatives and, in the same year, married Varina Howell, a Natchez aristocrat who was 18 years his junior. In 1846 he resigned his seat in Congress to serve in the war with Mexico as colonel in command of the First Mississippi volunteers, and he became a national hero for winning the Battle of Buena Vista (1847). After returning, severely wounded, he entered the U.S. Senate and soon became chairman of the Military Affairs Committee. Pres. Franklin Pierce made him secretary of war in 1853.

During the period of mounting intersectional strife, Davis spoke widely in both the North and South, urging harmony between the sections. When South Carolina withdrew from the Union in December 1860, Davis still opposed secession, though he believed that the Constitution gave a state the right to withdraw from the original compact of states. He was among those who believed that the newly elected president, Abraham Lincoln, would coerce the South and that the result would be disastrous.

On Jan. 21, 1861, twelve days after Mississippi seceded, Davis made a moving farewell speech in the Senate and pleaded eloquently for peace. Before he reached his Brierfield plantation, he was commissioned major general to head Mississippi's armed forces and prepare its defense. But within two weeks the Confederate Convention in Montgomery, Ala., chose him as provisional president of the Confederacy. He was inaugurated on Feb. 18, 1861.

During the ensuing Civil War, Davis had innumerable troubles, including a squabbling Congress, a dissident vice president, and the constant opposition of extreme states'-rights advocates, who objected vigorously to the conscription law he had enacted over much opposition in 1862. But despite a gradually worsening military situation, unrelieved internal political tensions, continuing lack of manpower and armament, and skyrocketing inflation, he remained resolute in his determination to carry on the war, and Gen. Robert E. Lee, commander of the Army of Northern Virginia and later of all Southern armies, remained both his most valuable field commander and his most loyal personal supporter.

After Lee surrendered to the North at Appomattox Courthouse (1865) without Davis's approval, Davis was captured by Union forces near Irwinville, Ga. He remained a prisoner under guard for two more years. Finally, in May 1867, he was released on bail and went to Canada to regain his shattered health. Davis died in 1889 in New Orleans of a complicated bronchial ailment.

EVERETT McKINLEY DIRKSEN
(b. Jan. 4, 1896, Pekin, Ill.—d. Sept. 7, 1969, Washington, D.C.)

Everett McKinley Dirksen was a Republican politician who was leader of the Senate Republicans during the administrations of presidents John F. Kennedy and Lyndon B. Johnson.

Dirksen attended the University of Minnesota, left before graduating to serve in World War I, and, after his discharge, returned to Pekin, where he pursued a number of business interests. In 1926, with his election to the office of city finance commissioner in Pekin, Dirksen began what was to become a lifelong career in public service. Defeated in 1930 in his bid for a congressional seat, he ran again in 1932 and won. A conservative Republican, Dirksen voted against most New Deal measures—except Social Security. He also opposed Pres. Franklin D. Roosevelt's foreign policy, adhering to an isolationist stance. In a foreshadowing of his later moderation and flexibility, however, Dirksen switched to bipartisan support of presidential foreign policy with U.S. entry into World War II.

A severe eye ailment forced Dirksen to resign his House seat in 1948. He returned to Pekin to practice law, having gained admittance to the bar by examination while serving in Congress. By 1950 his health was fully restored, and he ran successfully for a seat in the Senate. Throughout the 1950s, Dirksen belonged to the so called old-guard conservative wing of the Republican Party. He backed Sen. Robert A. Taft for the 1952 presidential nomination, and he supported the anti communist crusade of Joseph R. McCarthy until the Wisconsin senator was discredited in the middle of the decade.

Elected minority leader of the Senate in 1959, Dirksen continued to voice support for several conservative policies, including the permitting of prayer in public schools. He played a crucial role in securing passage of major pieces of legislation in the 1960s: the Nuclear Test Ban Treaty, the Civil Rights Act of 1964, and the Voting Rights Act of 1965.

In his constituency, in the Senate, and through the medium of television, Dirksen became something of a folk hero for his rich bass voice and imposing oratorical style, attributes for which his critics dubbed him "the wizard of ooze." He won his last election in 1968 and served in the Senate until his death the following year.

Bob Dole
(b. July 22, 1923, Russell, Kan.)

Bob Dole is a former Republican politician who served as a representative from Kansas in the U.S. House of Representatives (1961–69) and as a U.S. senator from Kansas (1969–96). He was his party's candidate for the U.S. presidency in 1996.

Dole was born into a working-class family and left the University of Kansas to serve in the army during World War II. He became a second lieutenant and was seriously wounded during fighting in Italy. His recuperation from almost total paralysis took nearly four years, and, despite three major operations, he was left without the use of his right arm and hand. He returned to school and graduated with a law degree from Washburn Municipal University in Topeka, Kansas.

From 1951 to 1953 Dole was a Republican member of the Kansas state legislature, and he thereafter served four terms as the Russell County prosecuting attorney before being elected to the U.S. House of Representatives in 1960. He was first elected to the U.S. Senate in 1968 and was reelected repeatedly thereafter. He also served as chairman of the Republican National Committee (1971–73) under Pres. Richard M. Nixon.

In 1984 Dole became leader of his party in the Senate, and he twice served as majority leader (1984–86, 1994–96). He was selected by Pres. Gerald R. Ford as the vice presidential candidate in the 1976 election, and after their defeat he unsuccessfully sought the Republican presidential nomination in 1980 and 1988. After finally clinching his party's nomination for president in March 1996, he retired from the Senate in June to devote himself wholly to the campaign, naming former congressman Jack Kemp as his running mate. Dole was defeated in November when Pres. Bill Clinton won election to a second term.

Dole's political career was characterized by pragmatic conservatism. His second wife, Elizabeth Hanford Dole, whom he married in 1975, also held a number of influential U.S. governmental posts.

STEPHEN A. DOUGLAS
(b. April 23, 1813, Brandon, Vt. — d. June 3, 1861, Chicago, Ill.)

Stephen Arnold Douglas was a Democratic politician and orator who espoused the cause of popular sovereignty in relation to the issue of slavery in the territories before the American Civil War (1861–65). He served as a representative from Illinois in the U.S. House of Representatives (1843–1847) and as a U.S. senator from Illinois from 1847 until his death. During his 1858 Senate campaign he engaged in a series of eloquent debates with the Republican candidate, Abraham Lincoln, who defeated him in the presidential race two years later.

Douglas left New England at the age of 20 to settle in Jacksonville, Ill., where he quickly rose to a position of leadership in the Illinois Democratic Party. In 1843 he was elected to the U.S. House of Representatives; one of its youngest members, Douglas gained early prominence as a dedicated worker and gifted speaker. Heavyset and only five feet four inches (1.6 metres) tall, he was dubbed the "Little Giant" by his contemporaries.

Douglas embraced a lifelong enthusiasm for national expansion, giving consistent support to the annexation of Texas (1845) and the Mexican War (1846–48), taking a vigorous stance toward Great Britain in the Oregon boundary dispute (1846), and advocating both government land grants to promote transcontinental railroad construction and a free homestead policy for settlers.

Douglas was elected in 1846 to the U.S. Senate, where he became deeply involved in the nation's search for a solution to the slavery problem. As chairman of the Committee on Territories, he was particularly prominent in the bitter debates between the North and South on the extension of slavery westward. Trying to remove the onus from Congress, he developed the theory of popular sovereignty (originally called squatter sovereignty), under which the people in a territory would themselves decide whether to permit slavery within their region's boundaries. Douglas himself was not a slaveholder, though his wife was. He was influential in the passage of the Compromise of 1850 (which tried to maintain a congressional balance between free and slave states), and the organization of the Utah and New Mexico territories under popular sovereignty was a victory for his doctrine.

The climax of Douglas's theory was reached in the Kansas-Nebraska Act (1854), which substituted local options toward slavery in the Kansas and Nebraska territories for that of congressional mandate, thus repealing the Missouri Compromise of 1820. The act's passage was a triumph for Douglas, although he was bitterly condemned and vilified by antislavery forces. A strong contender for the Democratic presidential nomination in both 1852 and 1856, he was too outspoken to be chosen by a party that was still trying to bridge the sectional gap.

The Supreme Court struck indirectly at popular sovereignty in the Dred Scott Decision (1857), which held that neither the Congress nor territorial legislatures could prohibit slavery in a territory. The following year Douglas engaged in a number of widely publicized debates with Lincoln in a close contest for the Senate seat in Illinois, and although Lincoln won the popular vote, Douglas was elected 54 to 46 by the legislature. In the debates, Douglas enunciated his famous "Freeport Doctrine," which stated that the territories could still determine the existence of slavery through unfriendly legislation and the use of police power, in spite of the Supreme Court decision. As a result, Southern opposition to Douglas intensified, and he was denied reappointment to the committee chairmanship he had previously held in the Senate.

When the "regular" (Northern) Democrats nominated him for president in 1860, the Southern wing broke away and supported a separate ticket headed by John C. Breckinridge of Kentucky. Although Douglas received only 12 electoral votes, he was second to Lincoln in the number of popular votes polled. Douglas then urged the South to acquiesce in the results of the election. At the outbreak of the Civil War, he denounced secession as criminal and was one of the strongest advocates of maintaining the integrity of the Union at all costs. At Pres. Lincoln's request, he undertook a mission to the Border States and to the Northwest to rouse Unionist sentiments among their citizenry. Douglas's early and unexpected death was partly the result of these last exertions on behalf of the Union.

JOHN EDWARDS

(b. June 10, 1953, Seneca, S.C.)

John Edwards is a Democratic politician who served as a U.S. senator from North Carolina (1999–2005) and in 2004 was the running mate of John Kerry, the Democratic Party's nominee for the U.S. presidency.

He is the son of Wallace Edwards, a textile-mill worker, and Catherine ("Bobbie") Wade Edwards, a textile worker and later postal worker. He grew up in the mill town of Robbins, N.C. The first in his family to attend college, Edwards received a bachelor's degree in textile management from North Carolina State University in 1974 and a law degree from the University of North Carolina at Chapel Hill in 1977. That year he also married a fellow law student, Elizabeth Anania. Edwards became a successful attorney, first in Nashville, Tenn., and then in Raleigh, N.C., winning multimillion-dollar verdicts in personal-injury lawsuits. The death of his 16-year-old son, Wade, in an automobile accident in 1996 helped to impel Edwards into public service and philanthropy, and in 1998 he was elected to the U.S. Senate from North Carolina.

As a senator, Edwards cosponsored a patients' bill of rights and supported education reform. As a member of the Senate Select Committee on Intelligence, he proposed legislation to strengthen homeland security. Seeking the Democratic presidential nomination in 2004, Edwards struck a populist tone, with charismatic stump speeches that evoked his modest upbringing in Robbins. Though Edwards's presidential bid was unsuccessful, John Kerry, the party's eventual nominee, chose him as his running mate. The pair was narrowly defeated in the November elections by incumbent Pres. George W. Bush and Vice Pres. Dick Cheney.

Edwards subsequently devoted much of his time to antipoverty efforts, becoming director of the newly created Center on Poverty, Work, and Opportunity at the University of North Carolina in 2005. The following year he announced that he would seek the Democratic Party's presidential nomination in 2008. Edwards's bid for the presidency got off to an inauspicious start, as he finished second in the Iowa caucus, third in the New Hampshire primary, and third in the South Carolina primary (his native state) in January 2008. Later that month he withdrew from the race. In August 2008 Edwards publicly admitted to having had an extramarital affair in 2006, and in 2009 he faced a federal investigation into allegedly improper campaign spending by his political action committee in 2006–07.

John Edwards. John Edwards for President

SAMUEL J. ERVIN, JR.
(b. Sept. 27, 1896, Morganton, N.C.—d. April 23, 1985, Winston-Salem, N.C.)

Samuel James Ervin, Jr., was a Democratic politician who served as a U.S. senator from North Carolina (1955–74). He was best known as chairman of the Select Committee on Presidential Campaign Activities, which investigated the Watergate Scandal during the administration of Republican Pres. Richard M. Nixon.

The son of a lawyer, Ervin graduated from the University of North Carolina in 1917 and earned a law degree from Harvard University in 1922. He returned to North Carolina to practice law and later held several state judicial posts, including justice of the North Carolina Supreme Court. In 1954 Ervin won election to the U.S. Senate and quickly established a reputation as an expert on—and defender of—the Constitution. He sat on the Senate committee that censured Sen. Joseph McCarthy, and he helped investigate labour racketeering in the late 1950s. During the 1960s he led Southern filibusters against civil rights laws, while simultaneously acting as one of the leading champions of civil liberties.

Ervin supported Pres. Nixon on the war in Vietnam but disagreed vehemently with Nixon's refusal to spend funds authorized by Congress for social programs. Chosen to head the seven-member committee investigating the Watergate scandal, he became something of a folk hero for his unceasing pursuit of evidence against White House claims of executive privilege. His earthy humour, distinctive accent, and unfailing charm made him a popular figure throughout the televised hearings.

After 20 years in the Senate, Ervin declined to run for reelection in 1974 and returned to his hometown of Morganton, N.C., the next year to resume private legal practice. He wrote two books: *The Whole Truth: The Watergate Conspiracy* (1980), his version of the eventual triumph of the U.S. Constitution in the Watergate ordeal, and *Humor of a Country Lawyer* (1983).

REBECCA ANN FELTON

(b. June 10, 1835, near Decatur,
Ga.—d. Jan. 24, 1930, Atlanta, Ga.)

Rebecca Ann Felton (née Rebecca Ann Latimer) was a political activist, writer, and lecturer and the first woman seated in the U.S. Senate.

Rebecca Latimer graduated first in her class from the Madison Female College, Madison, Ga., in 1852 and the following year married William H. Felton, a local physician active in liberal Democratic politics. She assisted her husband in his political career (as a U.S. congressman and later in

Rebecca Ann Felton. Library of Congress, Washington, D.C.; neg. no. LC USZ 62 20175

the state legislature), writing speeches, planning campaign strategy, and later helping to draft legislation. Together the Feltons promoted penal reform, temperance, and women's rights. Rebecca Felton was equally outspoken in her prejudice against African Americans and Jews and her advocacy of child labour and lynching, views for which her column in the *Atlanta Journal* was a popular forum. She served on the board of lady managers of the Chicago Exposition (1893), as head of the women's executive board of the Cotton States and International Exposition (1894–95) in Atlanta, Georgia, and on the agricultural board at the Louisiana Purchase Exposition (1904) in St. Louis, Mo.

In 1922 Gov. Thomas W. Hardwick of Georgia, in a symbolic gesture, appointed Felton to fill the U.S. Senate seat left vacant by the death of Sen. Thomas E. Watson, whose antagonism to former Pres. Woodrow Wilson and all of his policies she heartily shared. She served only two days, Nov. 21–22, 1922, before being succeeded by Walter F. George, the duly elected senator. Her writings include *My Memoirs of Georgia Politics* (1911), *Country Life in Georgia in the Days of My Youth* (1919), and *The Romantic Story of Georgia Women* (1930).

HAMILTON FISH

(b. Aug. 3, 1808, New York, N.Y.—d. Sept. 6, 1893, New York, N.Y.)

Hamilton Fish was a politician and government official who served as a U.S. senator (1851–57) from New York and as U.S. secretary of state (1869–77). In his diplomatic role he skillfully promoted the peaceful arbitration of explosive situations with Great Britain and Latin America.

A lawyer involved in New York Whig politics, Fish transferred his allegiance to the newly formed Republican Party while serving in the U.S. Senate. During the American Civil War (1861–65) he became chairman of the Union Defense Committee to expedite the supply of arms and troops and later served as a War Department commissioner to investigate and alleviate the poor conditions of Federal prisoners in the South.

In March 1869 Pres. Ulysses S. Grant appointed Fish head of the State Department, in which position he served for eight years. His entry into office coincided with a crisis between the United States and Great Britain over the *Alabama* claims, which arose from the Civil War depredations of the British-built Confederate cruiser *Alabama*. By tactful management of Congress on the one side and of the British government on the other, Fish calmed the quarrel. Cooperating with British diplomats, he brought about the conference that drafted the Treaty of Washington

(May 1871), providing for the first major international arbitration of modern history.

At the same time, Fish conducted a contest with American interventionists who wished to land troops in Cuba in order to help rebels attempting an overthrow of Spanish rule. Their pressure became almost irresistible when in 1873 Spanish authorities seized on the high seas the ship *Virginius,* belonging to the Cuban revolutionary committee in New York, and shot 53 Americans and Britons. Fish managed to maintain peace, however, and Spain restored the *Virginius* with apologies and indemnities.

As the most experienced and most respected member of Grant's cabinet, Fish helped to counteract the period's low political standards by leading the element of Grant's inner circle who laboured to keep the president vigilant against trickery and graft, to save him from improper appointment of old friends, and to prevent gross violations of the civil liberties of blacks. Returning to private life in New York in 1877, Fish devoted his last years to public-spirited activities, especially to the development of Columbia University.

FREDERICK THEODORE FRELINGHUYSEN

(b. Aug. 4, 1817, Millstone, N.J. — d. May 20, 1885, Newark, N.J.)

Frederick Theodore Frelinghuysen was a politician and government official who served as a U.S. senator from New Jersey (1866–69, 1871–77) and as a U.S. secretary of state. He is remembered for obtaining Pearl Harbor in Hawaii as a U.S. naval base.

Frelinghuysen was born into a family that had long been prominent in politics. Left an orphan at the age of three, he was adopted by his uncle, Theodore

Frelinghuysen. He graduated from Rutgers College in 1836, studied law in his uncle's law office, and succeeded to the latter's large practice in 1839. Frelinghuysen was one of the founders of the Republican Party in New Jersey and served as the state's attorney general from 1861 to 1866.

In 1866 he was appointed to the U.S. Senate to fill a vacancy and was elected the following year to fill the unexpired term. Defeated for the Senate in 1869, he was elected for a full six-year term beginning in 1871. He was one of the Senate's ablest debaters and did important work as chairman of the Committee on Foreign Affairs during the negotiations over the *Alabama* claims. Pres. Chester A. Arthur appointed Frelinghuysen secretary of state in 1881 to succeed James G. Blaine. Patient and firm in his handling of diplomatic affairs, he favoured closer commercial relations with Latin America and negotiated a change in the treaty with Hawaii to secure a U.S. naval base at Pearl Harbor. He also opened treaty relations with Korea (1882) and mediated several international disputes.

BILL FRIST
(b. Feb. 22, 1952, Nashville, Tenn.)

Bill Frist is a physician and former American Republican politician who served as a U.S. senator (1995– 2007) from Tennessee and as Senate majority leader from (2003–2007).

Frist graduated from Princeton University in 1974 with a degree in health care policy. He then attended Harvard Medical School, graduating with honours in 1978. He received surgical training at various hospitals and was hired in 1985 by the Vanderbilt University Medical Center in Nashville, where he founded and directed the school's renowned transplant centre. A board-certified heart surgeon, Frist performed numerous heart transplants and the first successful heart-lung transplant in the southeastern United States.

Frist was elected to the U.S. Senate in November 1994, defeating three-term Democratic incumbent James Sasser after mounting an aggressive campaign; he became the first physician to be elected to the Senate since 1928. Even after entering politics, Frist had numerous opportunities to put his medical skills to work. In July 1998, after a gunman in the U.S. Capitol killed two police officers and injured a tourist, Frist provided aid to the victims and even resuscitated the gunman and escorted him to the hospital.

In 2000 Frist won reelection overwhelmingly. In the Senate he specialized in health care policy and issues in bioethics, specifically the treatment of HIV/AIDS. An opponent of cloning, in 2001 Frist announced his support for strictly regulated embryonic stem-cell research. After the September 11 attacks on the United States in 2001 and the discovery of anthrax spores in mail sent to two U.S. senators and various media companies, Frist was increasingly consulted as a leading Senate expert on bioterrorism (terrorism committed with biological agents or biological weapons). He also expanded his areas of expertise, sitting on committees dealing with such areas as foreign relations, the federal budget, banking, commerce, finance, and education.

Praised for his bipartisanship and hard work, Frist quickly ascended the Republican Senate hierarchy. In 2000 he was elected to head the National Republican Senatorial Committee, helping the party win majority control of the chamber in the 2002 midterm elections. In January 2003 Frist became Senate majority leader after Sen. Trent Lott was forced to resign the post amid criticism of his controversial remarks at a 100th-birthday party for Sen. Strom Thurmond.

During 2003 Frist was successful in shepherding much of Pres. George W. Bush's legislative agenda through the Senate, particularly his reform of Medicare. Nevertheless, Frist drew fire from Republican colleagues for agreeing to cap Bush's $726 billion tax-cut package at $350 billion. Frist supported a constitutional amendment prohibiting same-sex marriage—a position that won him praise from conservative allies and criticism from liberals. In 2005 he was at the centre of the controversy surrounding Terry Schiavo, a brain-damaged Florida woman whose family was locked in a fierce legal battle over whether to remove her from life support. After viewing video footage of Schiavo, Frist challenged the opinion of doctors who had examined her in person, stating that because she responded to visual stimuli he doubted they were correct about the extent of her brain damage. When autopsy reports later confirmed her doctors had been correct, he defended his remarks by saying that they had never been intended to constitute a diagnosis. Frist remained Senate majority leader until 2007, when he resigned his Senate seat. In May 2009 Frist joined the board of directors of the drug-testing laboratory Aegis Sciences Corporation; he has also advised the company on health care matters.

Frist is the author of *When Every Moment Counts: What You Need to Know About Bioterrorism from the Senate's Only Doctor* (2002) and *A Heart to Serve: The Passion to Bring Health, Hope, and Healing* (2008).

J. WILLIAM FULBRIGHT

(b. April 9, 1905, Sumner, Mo.—d. Feb. 9, 1995, Washington, D.C.)

James William Fulbright was a Democratic politician who served as a representative from Missouri in the U.S. House of Representatives (1943–45) and as a U.S. senator from

Missouri (1945–74). He initiated the international exchange program for scholars known as the Fulbright scholarship. He was also known for his vocal and articulate criticism of U.S. military involvement in South Vietnam during his tenure as chairman of the Senate Foreign Relations Committee.

Fulbright graduated from the University of Arkansas, then went to Oxford—where he earned two degrees—as a Rhodes scholar. Back in the United States, he received his law degree from George Washington University (Washington, D.C.) and taught law at the University of Arkansas, serving as president of the latter from 1939 to 1941.

In 1942 Fulbright won a seat as a Democrat in the U.S. House of Representatives, thus beginning a political career that was to last more than three decades. His most notable achievement in the House was the 1943 Fulbright Resolution, putting the House on record as favouring U.S. participation in a postwar international organization. This organization at its founding in 1945 was named the United Nations.

In 1944 Fulbright ran successfully for the Senate. The following year he initiated the Fulbright Act, establishing an educational exchange program for scholars between the United States and foreign countries.

Fulbright voted against funding for Sen. Joseph R. McCarthy's anticommunist investigations, an action that made him popular among liberals. He consistently opposed efforts to integrate schools and promote the civil rights of blacks, however, making it possible for him to be reelected from Arkansas in 1950, 1956, 1962, and 1968.

As chairman of the Senate Foreign Relations Committee (1959–74), Fulbright advised Pres. Kennedy not to invade Cuba, and he vigorously opposed Pres. Johnson's 1965 intervention in the Dominican Republic.

The American public came to know Fulbright best for his probing, articulate opposition to the Vietnam War, despite the fact that he initially supported U.S. involvement. Indeed, as an old friend and former Senate colleague of Pres. Johnson, Fulbright had shepherded the Gulf of Tonkin Resolution through the Senate. In 1966, however, his committee held televised hearings on U.S. military involvement in Southeast Asia, from which he emerged as a leading proponent for an end to the U.S. bombing of North Vietnam and for peace talks to settle the Vietnamese conflict.

Fulbright was defeated in the Arkansas Democratic primary contest for the Senate in 1974, and he retired later that year. He presented his views of U.S. foreign policy in a number of books, including *Old Myths and New Realities* (1964), *The Arrogance of Power* (1966), and *The Crippled Giant* (1972).

JOHN NANCE GARNER

(b. Nov. 22, 1868, Red River County, Texas—d. Nov. 7, 1967, Uvalde, Texas)

John Nance Garner was a Democratic politician who served as a representative from Texas in the U.S. House of Representatives (1903–33) and as the 32nd vice president of the United States (1933–41) in the Democratic administration of Pres. Franklin D. Roosevelt. He maintained his conservatism despite his prominent position in Roosevelt's New Deal administration.

Garner was the son of farmers John Nance Garner III and Sarah Guest. After playing semiprofessional baseball and dropping out of Vanderbilt University, he studied law and was admitted to the Texas bar in 1890. He served two terms in the state legislature (1898–1902) before being elected to the U.S. House of Representatives in 1902. As a congressman, Garner was especially expert at backstage maneuvering to expedite legislation. He supported the graduated income tax and the Federal Reserve System and came to be regarded by 1917 as one of the most influential politicians in Congress. Although he considered retirement after the Republican Party won control of Congress in 1918, he ran for reelection in part to stress his opposition to the Ku Klux Klan. After serving successively as Democratic whip and floor leader, he was elected speaker of the House (1931).

At the 1932 Democratic National Convention, Garner was a candidate for the presidency, but after the third ballot he released his delegates from Texas and California to ensure Roosevelt's nomination. His selection as Roosevelt's vice presidential running mate particularly assuaged conservatives within the Democratic Party. As vice president Garner never felt comfortable with the New Deal, which he deemed "too liberal." Although reelected in 1936, he broke with the administration in 1937 over its efforts to "pack" (enlarge) the Supreme Court and worked to defeat some of the administration's legislative proposals. Opposed to Roosevelt's effort to win an unprecedented third term, Garner challenged him for the Democratic presidential nomination in 1940 but lost. At the end of his second term he retired to his Texas ranch.

CARTER GLASS

(b. Jan. 4, 1858, Lynchburg, Va. — d. May 28, 1946, Washington, D.C.)

Carter Glass was a Democratic politician who became a principal foe in the Senate of Pres. Franklin D. Roosevelt's New Deal in the 1930s.

In the main self-educated, having left school at the age of 13, Glass followed his father's path into journalism, finally becoming proprietor of the *Lynchburg Daily News* and the *Daily Advance*. A lifelong Democrat, he served in the U.S. House of Representatives (1902–18), where his most notable contribution was the framing and sponsoring of the Federal Reserve Act (1913). Pres. Woodrow Wilson appointed him secretary of the Treasury in 1918, and he supported Wilson's fight for U.S. adherence to the League of Nations.

In 1920 Glass accepted an interim appointment as senator from Virginia and thereafter won election and reelection until his death. As senator his main role was one of opposition. He was a leader of the conservative Southern Democratic bloc in the Senate. He supported Roosevelt for president in 1932 but soon became one of his sharpest critics. His bitterest assault on Roosevelt came during the controversy over "packing" the U.S. Supreme Court (1937). One of the greatest experts on monetary matters ever to serve in Congress, Glass was the principal author of the Glass-Steagall Act (1933), which established the Federal Deposit Insurance Corporation and helped curb bank speculation.

John H. Glenn, Jr. NASA

JOHN H. GLENN, JR.
(b. July 18, 1921, Cambridge, Ohio)

John Herschel Glenn, Jr., is a former Democratic politician who was one of the first U.S. astronauts and later served as a U.S. senator from Ohio (1975–99). In 1962 he became the first American to orbit the Earth, completing three orbits in 1962. (Soviet cosmonaut Yury Gagarin, the first person in space, made a single orbit of the Earth in 1961.)

Glenn joined the U.S. Marine Corps in 1943 and flew 59 missions during World War II and 90 missions during the Korean War. He was a test pilot from 1954 and was promoted to lieutenant colonel in 1959. Of the seven U.S. military pilots selected in that year for Project Mercury astronaut training, he was the oldest. Glenn served as a backup pilot for Alan B. Shepard, Jr., and Virgil I. Grissom, who made the first two U.S. suborbital flights into space. Glenn was selected for the first orbital flight, and on Feb. 20, 1962, his space capsule, *Friendship 7*, was launched from Cape Canaveral, Florida. Its orbit ranged from approximately 99 to 162 miles (159 to 261 km) in altitude, and Glenn made three orbits, landing in the Atlantic Ocean near the Bahamas.

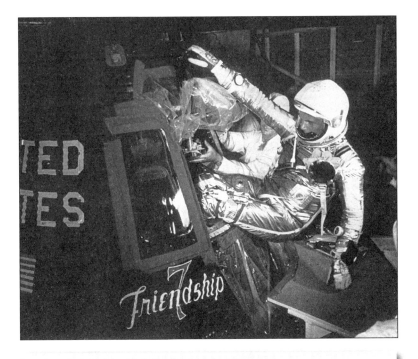

Astronaut John H. Glenn, Jr., entering Friendship 7 *to begin the first American manned mission to orbit Earth, February 1962.* NASA

Glenn retired from the space program and the Marine
Corps in 1964 to enter private business and to pursue his
interest in politics. In 1970 he sought the Democratic
nomination for a U.S. Senate seat in Ohio but lost narrowly in the primary. He was elected U.S. senator from
that state in 1974 and was reelected three times thereafter.
Glenn was unsuccessful, however, in his bid to become the
1984 Democratic presidential candidate.

On Oct. 29, 1998, Glenn returned to space as a payload
specialist on a nine-day mission aboard the space shuttle
Discovery. The oldest person ever to travel in space, Glenn
at age 77 participated in experiments that studied similari-
ties between the aging process and the body's response to
weightlessness.

BARRY GOLDWATER

(b. Jan. 1, 1909, Phoenix, Ariz.—d. May 29, 1998, Paradise Valley, Ariz.)

Barry Goldwater was a Republican politician who served
as a U.S. senator from Arizona (1953–64; 1969–87) and was
his party's presidential candidate in 1964.

Goldwater dropped out of college and began working
in his family's Phoenix department store, Goldwater's, of
which he was president from 1937 to 1953. He was elected
to the Phoenix city council in 1949, and in 1952 he narrowly won election to the U.S. Senate. He was reelected in
1958 by a large majority. A conservative Republican, he
called for a harsher diplomatic stance toward the Soviet
Union, opposed arms-control negotiations with that
country, and charged the Democrats with creating a quasi-
socialist state at home.

After winning several key victories in the 1964 primary
elections, Goldwater won the Republican presidential
nomination on the first ballot. He fought a determined
campaign against the incumbent president, Lyndon B.

Johnson, but national prosperity worked in Johnson's favour, and Goldwater was handicapped by the charge that he was an extreme anticommunist who might carry the country into war with the Soviet Union. Goldwater and his vice presidential running mate, William E. Miller, were decisively defeated in the election; they carried only Arizona and five states in the Deep South.

In 1968 Goldwater was reelected to the Senate and was reelected thereafter until he retired in 1987. He led the delegation of senior Republican politicians who on Aug. 7, 1974, persuaded Pres. Richard M. Nixon to resign from office. Goldwater moderated many of his views in later years and became a symbol of high-minded conservative Republicanism. His published works included *The Conscience of a Conservative* (1960), *The Coming Breakpoint* (1976), and *With No Apologies* (1979).

JOHN BROWN GORDON

(b. Feb. 6, 1832, Upson County, Ga.—d. Jan. 9, 1904, Miami, Fla.)

John Brown Gordon was a Confederate military leader and post American Civil War politician who symbolized the shift from agrarian to commercial ideals in the Reconstruction South. He served as a U.S. senator from Georgia from 1873 to 1880.

Gordon accomplished little of note during his first 29 years. He attended but did not graduate from the University of Georgia. He became a lawyer but abandoned his practice to develop coal mines in Georgia's northwestern tip. Then came the Civil War. Although lacking any military education or experience, Gordon was elected captain of a company of mountaineers and displayed remarkable capabilities. He quickly climbed from captain to brigadier general (1862) to major general (1864) to lieutenant general (1865). He was at many major Civil War battles—Seven Pines, Malvern Hills, Chancellorsville, Gettysburg, Spotsylvania, and Petersburg—and he commanded one wing of Gen. Robert E. Lee's army just prior to Appomattox.

A hero to Georgians at the age of just 33, Gordon returned to his home state and began to practice law once again. He vigorously opposed federal Reconstruction policies, but, when he ran for governorship as a Democrat in 1868, he was defeated by his Republican opponent. Unquestionably a symbol of the age of white supremacy to his Georgian constituents, Gordon was rumoured to be a Grand Dragon in the Ku Klux Klan.

Gordon was elected to the U.S. Senate in 1873. Though he was reelected, he resigned in 1880 to take an important position with a railroad company, thereby leading the shift of the New South to commercialism and industrialism. He returned to politics in 1886 for one term as governor and, at the conclusion of that term in 1890, was sent back to the U.S. Senate, where he served until 1897.

When the United Confederate Veterans organization was formed in 1890, Gordon was made commander in chief, a position he occupied until his death. He published memoirs of his military exploits in *Reminiscences of the Civil War* (1903).

MIKE GRAVEL

(b. May 30, 1930, Springfield, Mass.)

Mike Gravel is a Democratic politician who served as a U.S. senator from Alaska (1969–81) and who unsuccessfully sought the 2008 Democratic and Libertarian presidential nominations.

After serving in the U.S. Army from 1951 to 1954, Gravel attended Columbia University in New York and received a bachelor's degree in 1956. He held a variety of jobs—including railroad brakeman and cab driver—before serving in the Alaska House of Representatives from 1963 to 1966. After losing a bid for election to the U.S. House of Representatives in 1966, Gravel was elected to the U.S. Senate in 1968 and became one of the most outspoken senatorial critics of the Vietnam War. In 1971 he made headlines when he undertook a five-month-long one-man filibuster that succeeded in killing legislation to extend the draft. In

Mike Gravel. Mike Gravel for President 2008

the same year he introduced the Pentagon Papers into the public record by reading portions of them aloud in a subcommittee meeting. Gravel lost his reelection bid in 1980 and spent much of the following 25 years promoting increased citizen participation in government, in part through the Democracy Foundation, a nonprofit organization he established in 2001. Gravel later campaigned for the 2008 Democratic presidential nomination but eventually left the party to compete for the presidential nomination of the Libertarian Party, which he failed to win.

WADE HAMPTON

(b. March 28, 1818, Charleston, S.C.—d. April 11, 1902, Columbia, S.C.)

Wade Hampton was a Confederate war hero during the American Civil War who restored Southern white rule to

South Carolina following Radical Reconstruction. He represented South Carolina in the U.S. Senate from 1879 to 1891.

Born into an aristocratic plantation family, Hampton graduated from South Carolina College in 1836 and studied law. He never practiced, however, instead devoting himself to the management of his family's landholdings in Mississippi and South Carolina.

From 1852 to 1861 Hampton served in the South Carolina legislature. He consistently upheld a conservative position on slavery and secession. When the South seceded, Hampton gave unstintingly of himself and his fortune to the Confederacy. Though lacking military experience, he organized and commanded "Hampton's Legion" of South Carolina troops. He rose from colonel to lieutenant general and saw combat in many key battles. He served as second in command to Gen. J.E.B. Stuart and, after Stuart's death, led the cavalry corps. Wounded three times, he survived to become a military hero to the defeated South and a symbol of the nobility and gallantry of the "Lost Cause."

Hampton backed Pres. Andrew Johnson's plans for Reconstruction and sought reconciliation between North and South. But with the imposition of Radical policies, Hampton took the lead in South Carolina in the fight to restore white supremacy. With the Republicans firmly in control from 1868 to 1876, however, he devoted himself primarily to restoring his greatly depleted fortune. In 1876 he campaigned vigorously as the Democratic candidate for governor. His triumph was largely attributable to systematic efforts by his backers to prevent blacks from voting.

Reelected in 1878, Hampton resigned the following year after being elected to the U.S. Senate. He was defeated for reelection by Ben Tillman. The transition from Hampton to Tillman represented the end of rule by genteel antebellum aristocrats in the South. Hampton served as a commissioner of Pacific Railways from 1893 to 1897 before retiring to Columbia.

MARK HANNA

(b. Sept. 24, 1837, New Lisbon, Ohio—d. Feb. 15, 1904, Washington, D.C.)

Mark Hanna was an industrialist who served as a Republican U.S. senator from Ohio (1897–1904). The prototype of the political kingmaker, he successfully promoted the presidential candidacy of William McKinley in the election of 1896 and personified the growing influence of big business in American politics.

The prosperous owner of a Cleveland coal and iron enterprise, Hanna soon expanded his interests to include banking, transportation, and publishing. Convinced that the welfare of business (and consequently the prosperity of the nation) was dependent upon the success of the Republican Party, he began as early as 1880 to work among industrialists to ensure the financial support of likely candidates for office. He was especially impressed by Ohio congressman William McKinley's successful sponsorship in 1890 of a high protective tariff, and thenceforth he devoted all his energies to McKinley's political advancement, first as governor (1892–96) and then as president (1897–1901). In preparation for the 1896 contest with the Democrat-Populist candidate, William Jennings Bryan, Hanna was reputed to have poured more than $100,000 of his own money into preconvention expenses alone. Raising an unprecedented fund from wealthy individuals and corporations, the dynamic Hanna skillfully directed the $3.5 million campaign—the costliest and best organized the nation had ever witnessed. At a rate of spending exceeding his opponents by 20 to 1, his 1,400 paid workers inundated the country with millions of pamphlets promising continuing prosperity with McKinley. Hanna succeeded in stunting Bryan's grass-roots appeal with a continual barrage of posters and propaganda that preceded and followed Bryan at every whistle-stop of his campaign train.

Once in office, McKinley helped to fulfill Hanna's life-long ambition by appointing Sen. John Sherman secretary of state, thus creating a vacancy in the U.S. Senate. Hanna was elected to fill the vacancy (March 1897) and remained in the Senate until his death.

GARY HART
(b. Nov. 28, 1936, Ottawa, Kan.)

Gary Hart is a former Democratic politician who served as a U.S. senator from Colorado (1975–87). He ran for the Democratic presidential nomination in 1984 and again in 1988 but suspended the latter campaign soon after the *Miami Herald* newspaper reported that he was having an extramarital affair.

Hart earned degrees at Bethany (Okla.) Nazarene College and Yale Divinity School with the intention of going into the ministry. Sen. John F. Kennedy's 1960 presidential campaign, however, inspired him to change his goals from preaching and teaching to law and politics; four years later he graduated from Yale Law School. Hart first made a name for himself as the campaign manager for Sen. George McGovern's run for the presidency in 1972. His organizational and fund-raising strategies enabled the liberal McGovern to capture the Democratic nomination. Two years after his candidate lost the general election to Richard Nixon, Hart was elected by Colorado voters to the U.S. Senate. By the time he won reelection in 1980, he was considerably more conservative than the long-haired Hart of the McGovern days.

In 1984 Hart ran a close race against Sen. Walter Mondale for the Democratic presidential nomination. Although Hart won 26 states to Mondale's 19, Mondale's superior organization netted him enough delegates for victory. Hart had gained momentum in the campaign until Mondale ridiculed his "new ideas" with the barb, "Where's the beef?" which came from a TV commercial criticizing hamburgers that were more bun than beef.

Hart made a bid for the 1988 Democratic presidential nomination. In 1987, exasperated by rumours of infidelity, Hart invited *New York Times* reporters to follow him and see for themselves that he was not unfaithful to his wife. In May of that year, with his wife, Lee, away in Colorado, *Miami Herald* reporters staked out Hart's home in Washington, D.C., and spotted him leaving it with fashion model Donna Rice, who, they alleged, had stayed there overnight. The front-page story was published at a time when Hart already faced public doubts about his character. For a week he continued campaigning, but when the *Washington Post* threatened to release details about an affair with yet another woman, Hart quit the race. In December, however, he once again made headlines by dramatically announcing that he was back in the running for president, but after a disappointing finish in the New Hampshire primary, he withdrew from the race for the second and final time.

After his retirement from the Senate and abrupt departure from national politics in 1988, Hart turned his attention to teaching and to national security issues. He has served as cochair of the U.S. Commission on National Security/21st Century and as a visiting lecturer at such universities as Oxford, Yale, and the University of Colorado at Denver. He has also worked as senior counsel for the international law firm Coudert Brothers. He is the author of several books, including *Right from the Start: A Chronicle of the McGovern Campaign* (1973), *Russia Shakes the World: The Second Russian Revolution* (1991), *Restoration of the Republic: The Jeffersonian Ideal in 21st Century America* (2002), and *Under the Eagle's Wing: A National Security Strategy for the United States* (2009).

S.I. Hayakawa

(b. July 18, 1906, Vancouver, B.C., Can. — d. Feb. 27, 1992, Greenbrae, Calif.)

Samuel Ichiyé Hayakawa was a scholar, university president, and U.S. senator from California (1977–83). He was best known for his popular writings on semantics and for his career as president of San Francisco State College (now San Francisco State University).

Hayakawa was educated at the University of Manitoba, McGill University, and the University of Wisconsin. He taught English and language arts at the University of Wisconsin, the Illinois Institute of Technology, the University of Chicago, and San Francisco State College. His first book, *Language in Action* (1941), was a popular treatment of the semantic theories of Alfred Korzybski and was followed by years of teaching, writing, and lecturing in that field.

In 1968, after a period of student rioting at San Francisco State College, Hayakawa was appointed acting president and immediately took a firm stand against what he regarded as the excesses of student protesters. He acquired a national reputation as a foe of student leftism and a symbol of the conservative in action. In 1969 he was given permanent status as president. He retired in 1973, saying that he had accomplished his mission of restoring order. Three years later he was elected, as a Republican, to the U.S. Senate, where he served for one term.

JESSE HELMS
(b. Oct. 18, 1921, Monroe, N.C.—d. July 4, 2008, Raleigh, N.C.)

Jesse Helms was a Republican politician who served as a U.S. senator from North Carolina (1973–2003) and was a longtime leader of the right wing of his party. Nicknamed "Senator No," he was perhaps best known for his vehement opposition to civil rights and gay rights.

Helms, the son of the chief of police in Monroe, N.C., attended Wingate Junior College and Wake Forest College (now Wake Forest University, in Winston-Salem) but abandoned his schooling in 1941. He served as a recruiter for the U.S. Navy (1942–45) before becoming city editor for *The Raleigh Times*, and from 1948 to 1951 he was program director for the radio station WRAL in Raleigh. He then served as an aide to North Carolina senators Willis Smith (1951–53) and Alton Lennon (1953). In 1953 he became the executive director of the North Carolina Bankers Association, a position he held until 1960. That year he began working as a political commentator for WRAL, WRAL-TV, and the Tobacco Radio Network.

Originally a Democrat, Helms left the party in 1970. His political transformation was in large part due to his opposition to the Civil Rights Act (1964) that was passed under Pres. Lyndon B. Johnson. In 1972 Helms was elected to the U.S. Senate as a Republican. As senator, he maintained a staunchly conservative stance on social issues, leading crusades against abortion and homosexuality, supporting prayer in public schools, and opposing the busing of students for racial integration. A polarizing political figure, Helms was reelected four times (1978, 1984, 1990, 1996) but never garnered more than 55 percent of the vote. His campaigns were often criticized for their adversarial tone, as when in 1990, while running against Harvey Gantt, an African American candidate, Helms employed what many considered a blatantly racist television ad that attacked affirmative action.

Helms served as the Senate Agriculture Committee chair (1981–87) and as chair of the Senate Foreign Relations Committee (1995–2000). In the latter position, he supported military governments in Latin America, actively opposed arms control, and fought against nearly all foreign aid programs, claiming that such efforts were analogous to "pouring money down foreign rat holes." Portrayed by his critics as a demagogue, an extremist, and a bigot—he famously opposed the creation of a national holiday in honour of Martin Luther King, Jr.—Helms nevertheless displayed formidable skills as a politician, utilizing the power of his chairmanship to influence debate on foreign policy issues and to stall the confirmation of Pres. Bill Clinton's nominees.

Toward the end of his career, Helms was influenced by the activism of rock musician Bono, who encouraged him to reconsider his position on AIDS. Though Helms had in the past opposed federal spending on AIDS in the U.S.—claiming that the disease was a result of homosexual behaviour—in his final year in the Senate he sponsored a bill that provided relief to AIDS victims in Africa, where transmission of the disease occurs largely through heterosexual contact. While his "Old South" opinions on social issues were sometimes problematic even for those in his own party, Helms stood as an influential icon of Republican conservatism.

Helms published *Here's Where I Stand: A Memoir* in 2005.

GEORGE FRISBIE HOAR

(b. Aug. 29, 1826, Concord, Mass.—d. Sept. 30, 1904, Worcester, Mass.)

George Frisbie Hoar was a Republican politician who served as a representative from Massachusetts in the U.S. House of Representatives (1869–77) and as a U.S. senator from Massachusetts (1877–1904). He was one of the leading organizers of the modern Republican Party and a lifelong crusader for good government.

George Frisbie Hoar. Library of Congress, Washington, D.C. (Digital File Number: cwpbh-03673)

Hoar graduated from Harvard College (1846) and Harvard Law School (1849) and then went into private law practice in Worcester. His political life, which spanned more than half a century, began with his support of the Free Soil Party. During the 1850s he was busily organizing the Republican Party in Massachusetts while serving terms in both houses of the state legislature. He did not enter national politics until elected to the U.S. House of Representatives in 1869, but he was afterward in the House and the Senate continuously for the rest of his life.

Hoar served on several important committees in both houses of Congress, and he was a member of the electoral commission selected to determine the winner of the Hayes-Tilden presidential contest in 1876. For many years he was chairman of the Senate Judiciary Committee, and he drafted the Presidential Succession Act of 1886.

Hoar fought for civil-service reform, and he was an outspoken opponent of the American Protective Association—an anti-Catholic, anti-immigrant organization. He broke with his own party in protesting imperialistic U.S. policies toward the Philippines after the Spanish-American War, but he was so greatly admired for his honesty that he was decisively re-elected.

Always interested in education and scholarship, Hoar served as an overseer of Harvard, trustee of the Worcester Polytechnic Institute and Clark University, regent of the Smithsonian Institution, and president of the American Antiquarian Society and the American Historical Association.

SAM HOUSTON

(b. March 2, 1793, Rockbridge County, Va.—d. July 26, 1863, Huntsville, Texas)

Sam Houston was a politician and a leader of the struggle by U.S. emigrants in Mexican territory to win control of Texas (1834–36) and make it part of the United States. He served as a representative from Tennessee in the U.S. House of Representatives (1823–27) and as one of the first two U.S. senators from Texas (1847–59).

In his youth Houston moved with his family to a farm in rural Tennessee after the death of his father in 1807. He ran away in his mid-teens and lived for nearly three years with the Cherokee Indians in eastern Tennessee, where he took the name Black Raven and learned the native language, skills, and customs. Houston thus developed a rapport with the Indians that was unique for his day. As a consequence, after service in the War of 1812 and an interlude of study and teaching, in 1817 Houston became a U.S. subagent assigned to manage the removal of the Cherokee from Tennessee to a reservation in the Arkansas Territory. He returned to Nashville to practice law before being elected in 1823 to the U.S. House of Representatives, where he served as a U.S. congressman until 1827. In 1827 he was elected governor of Tennessee. After a brief, unsuccessful marriage to Eliza Allen in 1829, he resigned his office; he again sought refuge among the Cherokee and was formally adopted into the tribe. He twice went to Washington, D.C., to expose frauds practiced upon the Indians by government agents and in 1832 was sent by Pres. Andrew Jackson to Texas, then a Mexican province, to negotiate Indian treaties for the protection of U.S. border traders.

Houston's arrival in Texas coincided with the heated contest between U.S. settlers and Mexicans for control of the area. He established a home there by 1833, and he quickly emerged as one of the settlers' main leaders. When they rose in rebellion against Mexico in November 1835, he was chosen commander in chief of their army. The revolt suffered reverses during the winter, but on April 21, 1836, Houston and a force of roughly 800 Texans surprised and defeated 1,500 Mexicans under Gen. Antonio López de Santa Anna at San Jacinto. This triumph secured Texan independence and was followed by Houston's election as president (1836–38, 1841–44)

Sam Houston, photograph by Mathew Brady. Library of Congress, Washington, D.C.

of the Republic of Texas. He was influential in gaining the admission of Texas to the United States in 1845. Houston was elected one of the new state's first two senators in 1846, serving as a Union Democrat from 1846 to 1859. His views on the preservation of the union were unpopular with the Texas legislature, however, and on the eve of the Civil War he was not reelected—although he was chosen governor once more in 1859. In this position he tried unsuccessfully to prevent the secession of his state in 1861, and upon his refusal to swear allegiance to the Confederacy, he was declared deposed from office in March.

He spent his last two years quietly at home in Huntsville with Margaret Lea, his wife from 1840 and mother of his eight children. The city of Houston, Texas, was named in his honour.

CORDELL HULL

(b. Oct. 2, 1871, Overton County, Tenn.—d. July 23, 1955, Bethesda, Md.)

Cordell Hull was a Democratic politician and government official who served as a representative from Tennessee in the U.S. House of Representatives (1907–21, 1923–31), as a U.S. senator from Tennessee (1931–33), and as U.S. secretary of state (1933–44) in the administration of Democratic Pres. Franklin D. Roosevelt (1933–45). His initiation of the reciprocal trade program to lower tariffs set in motion the mechanism for expanded world trade in the second half of the 20th century. In 1945 he received the Nobel Prize for Peace for his part in organizing the United Nations.

As a young Tennessee attorney, Hull early identified with the Democratic Party. He served in the U.S. House of Representatives for 22 years and in the Senate for two years. Appointed secretary of state by Pres. Franklin D. Roosevelt at the beginning of the New Deal, he called for a reversal of high tariff barriers that had increasingly stultified U.S. foreign trade since the 19th century. He first won presidential support and public acclaim for such proposals at the inter-American Montevideo Conference (December 1933). He next succeeded in getting Congress to pass the Reciprocal Trade Agreements Act (March 1934), which set the pattern for tariff reduction on a most-favoured-nation basis and was a forerunner to the international General Agreement on Tariffs and Trade (GATT), begun in 1948.

Throughout the 1930s Hull did much to improve the United States' relations with Latin America by implementing what came to be known as the Good Neighbor Policy. At the Montevideo Pan-American Conference (1933) his self-effacing behaviour and acceptance of the principle of nonintervention in the internal affairs of other nations began to counteract the distrust built up through decades of Yankee imperialism in Latin America. He also attended the Pan-American Conference at Buenos Aires (1936) and a special foreign ministers' conference at Havana (1940). Because of the favourable climate of opinion that he had largely created, Hull successfully sponsored a united front of American republics against Axis aggression during World War II.

In East Asia, he rejected a proposed Japanese Monroe Doctrine that would have given that country a free hand in China (1934). When Japan served notice later that year that it would not renew the naval-limitation treaties (due to expire in 1936), Hull announced a policy of maintenance of U.S. interests in the Pacific, continuing friendship with China, and military preparedness.

With the outbreak of World War II, Hull and Roosevelt felt that efforts to maintain American neutrality would only encourage aggression by the Axis powers; they therefore decided to aid the Allies. In the crucial negotiations with Japan in the autumn of 1941, Hull stood firm for the rights of China, urging Japan to abandon its military conquests on the mainland.

When the United States entered the war, Hull and his State Department colleagues began planning an international postwar peacekeeping body. At the Moscow Conference of Foreign Ministers (1943)—despite his frail health and advancing age—he obtained a four-nation pledge to continue wartime cooperation in a postwar world organization aimed at maintaining peace and security. For this work, Roosevelt described Hull as the "father of the United Nations," and universal recognition of his key role came with the Nobel Prize. He resigned after the 1944 presidential election and wrote his *Memoirs of Cordell Hull* (1950).

NANCY LANDON KASSEBAUM

(b. July 29, 1932, Topeka, Kan.)

Nancy Landon Kassebaum (née Nancy Landon) is a former Republican politician who served as a U.S. senator from Kansas (1979–96). She was the first woman elected to the Senate who was not a widow taking her husband's seat.

Nancy Landon is the daughter of Alfred M. Landon, governor of Kansas and Republican candidate for president in 1936. She studied political science at the University of Kansas (B.A., 1954) and diplomatic history at the University of Michigan (M.A., 1956). In 1956 she married Philip Kassebaum and began serving as vice president of Kassebaum Communications, which operated two radio stations. She also served on the Kansas Governmental Ethics Commission and Kansas Committee on the Humanities, as well as the school board in Maize, Kansas (1972–75). After separating from her husband in 1975, Kassebaum moved to Washington, D.C., to work for Sen.

James B. Pearson of Kansas as a caseworker. She was elected to replace Pearson upon his retirement; when she entered office in 1979, she was the only woman in the Senate.

Kassebaum sat on several committees, including the Budget Committee, the Foreign Relations Committee, and the Committee on Labor and Human Resources. She tackled subjects other Republican politicians shied away from and was known for her resoluteness. Early in her career she supported the Equal Rights Amendment, but her later refusal to support the ratification deadline extension lost her the Kansas Women's Political Caucus's support. Kassebaum supported welfare reform, changes in the federal student loan and financial assistance programs, and the National Endowment for the Arts; she also focused on health care issues. In the 1980s she worked toward ending apartheid in South Africa.

In 1996 Kassebaum retired from the Senate and married former senator Howard Baker of Tennessee.

FRANK B. KELLOGG
(b. Dec. 22, 1856, Potsdam, N.Y.—d. Dec. 21, 1937, St. Paul, Minn.)

Frank Billings Kellogg was a politician and government official who served as a U.S. senator from New York (1917–23) and as U.S. secretary of state (1925–29). As a diplomat his most important achievement was the Kellogg-Briand Pact of 1928, a multilateral agreement designed to prohibit war as an instrument of national policy. He was awarded the Nobel Prize for Peace in 1929.

Kellogg studied law and was admitted to the bar in 1877. He achieved prominence as a lawyer representing the U.S. government in antitrust cases and served in the U.S. Senate and as U.S. ambassador to Great Britain (1923–25).

As secretary of state under Pres. Calvin Coolidge, Kellogg generally followed an isolationist policy regarding European affairs, but he helped arrange an international conference at Geneva (1927) that sought unsuccessfully to limit naval armaments.

In 1928 the French foreign minister, Aristide Briand, had evolved a plan for a bilateral pact outlawing war as a tool of national diplomacy. Kellogg delayed for months, partly fearful of a two-nation entanglement. Prodded into action by vocal American proponents of the "outlawry of war" movement, he succeeded in broadening the agreement to include 62 nations, among them all the major powers. Although widely heralded and recognized with the Nobel Prize, the Kellogg-Briand Pact was nevertheless full of loopholes and devoid of means for effective enforcement.

Kellogg later (1930–35) served on the Permanent Court of International Justice.

EDWARD M. KENNEDY

(b. Feb. 22, 1932, Brookline, Mass.— d. Aug. 25, 2009, Hyannis port, Mass.)

Edward Moore Kennedy, also known as Ted Kennedy, was a prominent figure in the Democratic Party and in liberal politics from the 1960s, becoming among the most influential and respected members of the Senate during his 37-year tenure in office.

The youngest child of Rose and Joseph Kennedy, Edward Kennedy was the last surviving brother of Pres. John F. Kennedy. Edward graduated from Harvard University in 1956. He then studied at the International Law School (The Hague) and received a law degree from the University of Virginia (1959). Edward campaigned for his brother John in the 1960 presidential race, and in 1962 he was elected to the president's former U.S. Senate seat representing Massachusetts. Although unable to campaign actively for reelection (1964) for a full term because of an injury, he was swept back into office by a landslide vote.

Early in 1969 he was elected majority whip in the U.S. Senate, and he became an early front-runner for the next Democratic presidential nomination. Then, on the night of July 18, 1969, he accidentally drove his car off an unmarked bridge on Chappaquiddick Island, near Martha's Vineyard, Mass., and his companion in the car, 28-year-old Mary Jo Kopechne, was drowned. Kennedy was found guilty of leaving the scene of an accident. He was reelected to the Senate in 1970 but announced that he would not seek the presidency in 1972.

Kennedy won reelection to a third full term as senator in 1976. He was a serious contender for the 1980 Democratic presidential nomination but withdrew from the race during the convention. He won a fourth term in 1982 and was again reelected to the Senate in 1988, 1994, 2000, and 2006.

Kennedy continued to be a prominent spokesman for the policies that had long been associated with his family name—i.e., support for social welfare legislation and active participation in world affairs. He became a leading advocate in the Senate for many liberal causes, including voting rights, fair housing, consumer protection, and national health insurance. At the same time, he was recognized for his willingness to cooperate with Republicans in the Senate to advance important legislation, such as the No Child Left Behind Act (2001) and other initiatives of the administration of Pres. George W. Bush. In 2008, after being hospitalized for a seizure, Kennedy was diagnosed with a malignant brain tumour. He died in august of the following year, at his home. Pres. Barack Obama eulogized him as the "greatest legislator of our time."

ROBERT F. KENNEDY

(b. Nov. 20, 1925, Brookline, Mass. — d. June 6, 1968, Los Angeles, Calif.)

Robert Francis Kennedy was a Democratic politician and government official who served as U.S. attorney general and adviser during the administration of his brother Pres. John F. Kennedy (1961–63) and as a U.S. senator (1965–68) from Massachusetts. He was assassinated while campaigning for the Democratic presidential nomination.

Robert interrupted his studies at Harvard University to serve in the U.S. Navy during World War II but returned to the university and was graduated in 1948. After receiving his law degree from the University of Virginia Law School in 1951, he began his political career in Massachusetts the next year with the management of his brother John's successful campaign for the U.S. Senate. Robert Kennedy first came into national prominence in 1953, when he was an assistant counsel to the Senate Permanent Subcommittee on Investigations, headed by Sen. Joseph R. McCarthy (Kennedy resigned in mid-1953, returning in 1954 as counsel to the Democratic minority). In 1957 he was chief counsel to the Senate select committee conducting investigations into labour racketeering, which led to his long-standing feud with James R. Hoffa of the Teamsters Union. Kennedy resigned from the committee

Robert F. Kennedy. U.S. News & World Report magazine; photograph, Warren K. Leffler/ Library of congress, Washington, D.C. (digital file no.03685u)

staff in 1960 to conduct his brother's campaign for the U.S. presidency and was subsequently appointed (1961) attorney general in the cabinet of Pres. John F. Kennedy.

On Nov. 22, 1963, the president was assassinated in Dallas, Texas. Robert Kennedy continued to serve as attorney general until he resigned in September 1964. The months after his brother's death were a desperate time for him. He was stooped by grief and spent long periods staring out windows or walking in the Virginia woods. He had presided over the Department of Justice for 44 months. He had emerged as a statesman of the law, improving the lot of many. Learning on May 20, 1961, that a hostile mob threatened the civil rights leader Martin Luther King, Jr., and about 1,200 of his supporters in Montgomery, Ala., Attorney General Kennedy sent 400 federal marshals to protect them. In subsequent racial crises he used long telephone sessions to work out the strategies of peace officers in the South. He also led a tough and imaginative drive against organized crime. One of his proudest achievements was assembling the evidence that convicted Hoffa. On Robert Kennedy's departure from the Department of Justice *The New York Times,* which had criticized his appointment three years earlier, said editorially, "He named excellent men to most key posts, put new vigor into protecting civil rights through administrative action, played a pivotal role in shaping the most comprehensive civil rights law in this country…. Mr. Kennedy has done much to elevate the standard." He was the author of *The Enemy Within* (1960), *Just Friends and Brave Enemies* (1962), and *Pursuit of Justice* (1964).

In November 1964 he was elected U.S. senator from New York. Within two years Kennedy had established himself as a major political figure in his own right. He became the chief spokesman for liberal Democrats and a critic of Pres. Lyndon B. Johnson's Vietnam policy. On

March 16, 1968, he announced his candidacy for the presidency. By June 4 he had won five out of six presidential primaries, including one that day in California. Shortly after midnight on June 5 he spoke to his followers in Los Angeles' Ambassador Hotel. As he left through a kitchen hallway he was fatally wounded by a Palestinian immigrant, Sirhan Bishara Sirhan. Robert Kennedy was buried near his brother at Arlington National Cemetery.

WILLIAM FIFE KNOWLAND
(b. June 26, 1908, Alameda, Calif.—d. Feb. 23, 1974, Monte Rio, Calif.)

William Fife Knowland was a Republican politician who served as leader of his party in the U.S. Senate in the early 1950s. He was best-known for his ardent support of Nationalist China (Taiwan).

The son of a congressman and newspaper publisher, Knowland began his political career at an early age. At 12 he was making speeches for the Harding–Coolidge ticket, and by 25 he held a seat in the California Assembly. Two years later he was in the state senate, and in 1945—when just 37 years old—he was appointed to fill the unexpired term of Sen. Hiram W. Johnson. In the meantime, he acquired a degree from the University of California; worked for the family newspaper, the Oakland *Tribune;* and chaired the executive committee of the Republican National Committee.

While holding some liberal positions on domestic issues, Knowland made his reputation as a leader of the "China Lobby." He decried the loss of mainland China to the Communists in 1949 and advocated the return of Generalissimo Chiang Kai-shek and his Nationalist government to power on the Chinese mainland. He also accused such China experts as John Paton Davies and

Owen Lattimore of being pro-communist, thereby effectively ending their careers in government service.

Overwhelmingly reelected in 1952, Knowland became chairman of the Republican Party's policy committee the following year, and he served as party leader in the Senate following the death of Robert A. Taft. He was a consistent supporter of Sen. Joseph McCarthy, and he opposed the Senate resolution censuring McCarthy and his anticommunist crusade.

Knowland announced that he would run for the Republican presidential nomination in 1956 if Pres. Dwight D. Eisenhower retired in that election year. After Eisenhower was reelected, Knowland decided to run for governor of California in 1958, in preparation for the 1960 presidential race. He lost that contest to Edmund (Pat) Brown, returned to the newspaper business, and never again held elective office. Knowland died in 1974 of a self-inflicted gunshot wound.

ROBERT M. LA FOLLETTE

(b. June 14, 1855, Primrose, Wis.—d. June 18, 1925, Washington, D.C.)

U.S. leader of the Progressive Movement, Robert Marion La Follette was a politician who served as governor of Wisconsin (1901–06) and as a U.S. senator from Wisconsin (1906–25). Noted for his support of reform legislation, he was the unsuccessful presidential candidate of the League for Progressive Political Action (the Progressive Party) in 1924, winning almost 5 million votes, or about one-sixth of the total cast.

As a boy growing up in moderately prosperous rural areas, as a student at the University of Wisconsin (1875–79), as a county district attorney (1880–84), and as a congressman from southwestern Wisconsin, La Follette developed the personality and style that made him a

popular leader. He combined an unusually outgoing personality with an extraordinary flair for zealous oratory. As
an eloquent spokesman for popular causes, La Follette
exalted his constituents' wishes—even when those wishes
ran counter to the desires of party leaders. His principal
concerns in his three terms as congressman were econom-
ical government and protection for his district's farmers.
He married his college sweetheart, Belle Case, on Dec. 31,
1881, after his first year as district attorney.

Defeated for reelection to Congress in a Democratic
landslide in 1890, La Follette returned to Madison to practice law and develop the political organization that within
10 years would elect him governor and allow him to dominate Wisconsin politics until his death. His reputation as
an enemy of political bosses began in 1891 when he
announced that the state Republican boss, Sen. Philetus
Sawyer, had offered him a bribe. For the next six years La
Follette built a competing Republican faction on the support of other party members (Scandinavians, dairy
farmers, young men, disgruntled politicians) with grievances against the dominant "stalwart" faction. His
oratorical talents, combined with his natural charm, organizational skill, and driving ambition to become governor,
made him the leader of his new group of Republicans.

In 1897 La Follette began to advocate programs that
local-level progressives had popularized during the legislative session a few months earlier. Following their lead, he
demanded tax reform, corporation regulation, and political democracy. In particular, he promoted steeper railroad
taxes and a direct primary. Elected governor on this platform in 1900, he was reelected in 1902 and 1904.

As Wisconsin's governor La Follette developed new
political techniques, which he later took to the U.S. Senate.
The first, which received national attention as the

"Wisconsin Idea," was the use of professors from the University of Wisconsin—57 at one point—to draft bills and administer the state regulatory apparatus created by the new laws. The second innovation was his public reading of the "roll call" in districts in which legislators had opposed his reform proposals.

With these new methods he secured the passage of several progressive laws. Believing that the railroads were the principal subverters of the political process, he persuaded the legislature to tax them on the basis of their property (1903) and to regulate them by commission (1905). The legislature enacted the direct primary in 1903 and state civil service reform in 1905. His appointees to the Tax Commission, given new power by the legislature, equalized tax assessments. Wisconsin's leadership in these areas gave La Follette his reputation as a pioneering progressive.

Resigning as governor in 1906, he was elected to the Senate at a time when that institution was widely believed to be a refuge for millionaires. La Follette acquired instant fame as a new type of senator, one who was not controlled by "the interests," and in his first three years there La Follette achieved the passage of laws aimed against the freight rates, labour policies, and financing practices of the railroads.

These laws reflected an emerging ideology that dominated La Follette's Senate activities thereafter. Politics, he believed, was a never-ending struggle between "the people," all men and women in their common roles as consumers and taxpayers, and the "selfish interests" for control of government; law-given privileges allowed "selfish interests" to dominate all facets of American life. He supported labour legislation because unions were battling the same enemies that menaced consumers and because consumers benefited directly from improvements in working conditions. He believed, for example, that his most famous achievement, the La Follette Seaman's Act of 1915, would increase the safety of passengers while it also improved working conditions for sailors. Beginning in 1908, with elaborate documentation during debate on the Aldrich-Vreeland Currency Act, La Follette argued that the nation's entire economy was dominated by fewer than 100 men who were, in turn, controlled by the J.P. Morgan and Standard Oil investment banking groups. Thereafter, he shifted his concern from the power of railroads to the power of their "owners," namely the large banks.

In 1909 La Follette founded *La Follette's Weekly,* later a monthly, and much later called *The Progressive.* The high point of his national popularity came in 1909–11 when he emerged as the leader of newly elected and newly converted progressives in Congress. Having led Republican opposition to the tariff, conservation, and railroad policies of Pres. William Howard Taft, La Follette was widely promoted for the presidency in 1912. Most progressives backed La Follette because their first choice, Theodore Roosevelt, had refused to run; later, when Roosevelt entered the race early in 1912, they deserted La Follette. The bitterness of La Follette's attacks on Roosevelt cost him his reputation as a leader and left him an independent figure in the Senate. Although he had backed Woodrow Wilson in 1912 for the presidency, he was disgusted that the new president ignored the ideas of progressive Republicans and shaped most legislation in the Democratic caucus. While applauding the social justice laws, he believed that most of Wilson's regulatory acts—particularly the Federal Reserve Board—constituted government sponsorship of big business.

Foreign affairs catapulted La Follette back into a leadership position in 1917, this time of the anti-war movement. Since 1910 he had argued that U.S. interventions in the problems of foreign governments were intended to protect the investments of U.S. corporations and to smash revolutions. Now he believed that the United States entered World War I in 1917 because U.S. businessmen needed protection for their investments and because Wilson had become isolated from public opinion. Confident that the majority opposed U.S. involvement, La Follette led the campaign for a popular referendum on war in 1916–17. He led the 1917 Senate filibuster against arming U.S. merchant ships and voted against the war declaration. Once war was declared, he opposed the draft, defended the civil liberties of the war's opponents, and insisted that wealthy individuals and corporations pay the costs of a war that mainly benefited them. Pro-war groups demanded his expulsion from the Senate for treason, but a Senate investigating committee exonerated him. As a martyr to the war hysteria, La Follette once again became a popular hero to millions of Americans.

Believing that the war had given large corporations nearly complete control over the federal government, La Follette concentrated on exposing the most flagrant corruption of the postwar years. His most significant contribution was his major role in publicizing the oil scandals of Pres. Warren Harding's administration.

As labour and farm groups despaired of the conservatism of Democrats and Republicans alike in the 1920s, La Follette was frequently mentioned as a presidential candidate for a third party. Declining the pleas of the Farmer-Labor convention that he run in 1920, La Follette accepted the nomination on the Progressive ticket in 1924. His 1924 candidacy was supported by several farm groups, by organized labour (particularly the railroad brotherhoods, La Follette's oldest friends in the labour movement), by many old progressives, by the Socialist Party, and by the

Scripps-Howard newspaper chain. In the end La Follette carried only the state of Wisconsin, although he placed second in 11 states and polled about one-sixth of the national total. He died in office.

Both of La Follette's sons carried on his work after his death. Robert M. La Follette, Jr. (1895–1953), was elected in 1925 to fill his father's unexpired term in the Senate and was reelected three times thereafter, serving until 1947. He generally supported Pres. Franklin D. Roosevelt's New Deal, and he drafted the congressional reorganization bill of 1946 that streamlined the legislative process in Congress. That same year, though, he was defeated in the Republican senatorial primary by Joseph McCarthy.

Philip Fox La Follette (1897–1965) served as governor of Wisconsin in 1931–33 and 1935–39. In his first term he secured enactment of the first comprehensive unemployment compensation act in any U.S. state. He and his brother Robert organized a separate Progressive Party in Wisconsin in 1934, but it proved short-lived and returned to the Republican ranks in 1946.

HENRY CABOT LODGE

(b. May 12, 1850, Boston, Mass.—d. Nov. 9, 1924, Cambridge, Mass.)

Henry Cabot Lodge was a Republican politician who served as a U.S. senator from Massachusetts for more than 31 years (1893–1924). As a senator he led the successful congressional opposition to his country's participation in the League of Nations following World War I.

Lodge received in 1876 the first Ph.D. in political science to be granted by Harvard University. He remained at Harvard for the next three years as an instructor in American history and retained an active interest in this field throughout his life, editing scholarly journals and writing or editing works on major figures and events in the nation's history. He launched his political career in the state legislature (1880–81) and in the U.S. House of Representatives (1887–93) and then was elected to the U.S. Senate.

With the entrance of the United States into World War I (1917), he called for united support of the war effort. Initially he endorsed an international peacekeeping mechanism in an address before the League to Enforce Peace (May 1916), but, when a world organization with compulsory arbitration was advocated by Pres. Woodrow Wilson, Lodge felt that the nation's sovereignty was at stake and that it would be fatal to bind the nation to international commitments that the United States would not or could not keep. When in 1919 the Republicans gained control of the Senate, Lodge became chairman of the Foreign Relations Committee. He was thus in a position to mastermind the strategy of opposition to adoption of the Treaty of Versailles, including the League of Nations covenant. He adopted a dual course of action: first, delaying tactics to allow enthusiasm for the League to wane; second, introducing a series of amendments (the Lodge reservations) that would require the approval of Congress before the United States would be bound by certain League decisions. Thus, Lodge became the main leader of the U.S. isolationists. Wilson refused to accept the Lodge reservations, feeling that they would destroy the basic intent of the League. The treaty was defeated in the Senate, and the onus of rejection fell on the Wilsonians.

The landslide election of Republican Warren G. Harding in 1920 was considered a vindication of the Lodge position, and with enhanced prestige he went on to serve as one of four U.S. delegates to the Washington Conference on the Limitation of Armaments (1921).

HENRY CABOT LODGE

(b. July 5, 1902, Nahant, Mass.—d. Feb. 27, 1985, Beverly, Mass.)

Henry Cabot Lodge was a Republican politician and government official who served as a U.S. senator from Massachusetts (1937–44, 1947–52). He was a U.S. diplomat who ran unsuccessfully for the vice presidency of the United States in 1960.

He was the grandson of Sen. Henry Cabot Lodge (1850–1924) and a member of a politically dedicated family that included six U.S. senators and a governor of Massachusetts. Lodge began his career in politics after several years as a journalist, with two terms as a Republican in the Massachusetts legislature (1933–36), followed by service in the U.S. Senate. He lost his Senate seat in 1952 to Rep. John F. Kennedy. In that year he had been active in promoting the presidential candidacy of Dwight D. Eisenhower, who subsequently appointed Lodge permanent U.S. representative to the United Nations.

In July 1960 he was nominated for the vice presidency on the unsuccessful Republican ticket headed by Richard M. Nixon. Lodge served as U.S. ambassador to South Vietnam (1963–64, 1965–67), and as such he was the main channel of communication between Washington and the South Vietnamese leadership. After expressing his belief to Pres. Kennedy that the war could not be won while Ngo Dinh Diem remained in power, Lodge, along with agents of the Central Intelligence Agency, notified a cadre of South Vietnamese generals that the United States would make no move to oppose an attempted coup. In November 1963 the plot was carried to fruition, and Diem was deposed. In spite of assurances to Lodge that the lives of Diem and his brother, Ngo Dinh Nhu, would be spared, both were killed during the takeover. Lodge was later named ambassador to West Germany

(1968–69), and he was chief negotiator at the talks in Paris on peace in Vietnam (1969). He then served as special envoy to the Vatican (1970–77). Lodge's writings include *Cult of Weakness* (1932), *The Storm Has Many Eyes* (1973), and *As It Was* (1976).

HUEY (PIERCE) LONG
(b. Aug. 30, 1893, near Winnfield, La.—d. Sept. 10, 1935, Baton Rouge, La.)

Huey Long was the flamboyant and demagogic Democratic governor of Louisiana (1929–32) and a U.S. senator from Louisiana (1933–35). His social reforms and radical welfare proposals were ultimately overshadowed by the unprecedented executive dictatorship that he perpetrated to ensure control of his home state.

In spite of an impoverished background, young Long managed to obtain enough formal schooling to pass the bar examination in 1915. He was politically ambitious and won election to the state railroad commission at age 25. In this post his calls for the equitable regulation of the state utility companies and his attacks on Standard Oil earned him widespread popularity. He ran for the Louisiana governorship in 1924 and was defeated, but in 1928 he won the governorship through the heavy support of the discontented rural districts. His picturesque if irreverent speech, fiery oratory, and unconventional buffoonery soon made him nationally famous, and he was widely known by his nickname, "Kingfish." Long made a genuine contribution with an ambitious program of public works and welfare legislation in a state whose road system and social services had been sadly neglected by the wealthy elite that had long controlled the state government. Always the champion of poor whites, he effected a free-textbook law, launched a massive and very useful program of road and bridge building, expanded state university facilities, and erected a state hospital where free treatment for all was intended. He was opposed to excessive privileges for the rich, and he financed his improvements with increased inheritance and income taxes as well as a severance tax on oil—earning him the bitter enmity of the wealthy and of the oil interests.

Long's folksy manner and sympathy for the underprivileged diverted attention from his ruthless autocratic methods. Surrounding himself with gangsterlike bodyguards, he dictated outright to members of the legislature, using intimidation if necessary. In 1932, when he was about to leave office to serve in the U.S. Senate, he fired the legally elected lieutenant governor and replaced him with two designated successors who would obey him from Washington. In order to fend off local challenges to his control in 1934, he effected radical changes in the Louisiana government, abolishing local government and taking personal control of all educational, police, and fire job appointments throughout the state. He achieved absolute control of the state militia, judiciary, and election and tax-assessing apparatus, while denying citizens any legal or electoral redress.

In the Senate he sought national power with a Share-the-Wealth program ("every man a king"), which was tempting to a depression-shocked public. Had Long been able to unite the various nationwide radical movements, a private poll taken in the spring of 1935 estimated that he would have won up to 4 million votes in the next year's presidential election, thus wielding a balance of power between the two major parties.

Long was at the height of his power when assassinated by Carl Austin Weiss, the son of a man whom he had vilified. The Long political dynasty was carried on by his brother, Earl K. Long, who served as governor (1939–40, 1948–52, 1956–60), and his son, Russell B. Long, who served in the U.S. Senate from 1949 to 1987.

TRENT LOTT
(b. Oct. 9, 1941, Grenada, Miss.)

Trent Lott is a former Republican politician who represented Mississippi in the U.S. House of Representatives (1973–89) and in the U.S. Senate (1989–2007).

The son of a shipyard worker, Lott grew up in the coastal town of Pascagoula, Miss. He earned both bachelor's (1963) and law (1967) degrees from the University of Mississippi. In 1967 he got his start in politics when he worked on the successful gubernatorial campaign of Democrat John Bell Williams, who was openly segregationist. Lott served as an administrative assistant (1968–72) to Rep. William Colmer, also a Democrat and a segregationist, before winning election to the U.S. House of Representatives—to fill Colmer's seat—in 1972.

Lott's election to the House of Representatives was part of a larger shift by Southern voters away from the Democratic Party, to which they had been loyal since the American Civil War (1861–65). Throughout his congressional career, Lott maintained a loyal following in his home state. In the House he served as minority whip from 1981 until his election to the U.S. Senate in 1989.

As a senator, Lott distinguished himself as a conservative Republican and an outspoken opponent of Democratic Pres. Bill Clinton. In 1993 he spoke out against Clinton's cabinet nominee Roberta Achtenberg because of her support for gay rights, and in 1995 he publicly disagreed with Clinton's decision to send American troops to quell violence in Bosnia and Herzegovina. Lott was conservative on social issues such as abortion and gun control, and he was a leading advocate on these and other issues for other conservative senators whose views came to dominate the Republican Party. He served as his party's majority leader (1996–2001) and later minority leader (2001–03).

Lott set off a media firestorm in 2002 at the 100th birthday party of Sen. Strom Thurmond of South Carolina. At the celebration, he alluded to Thurmond's 1948 presidential campaign on a segregationist Dixiecrat platform:

> *I want to say this about my state: When Strom Thurmond ran for president we voted for him. We're proud of it. And if the rest of the country had of followed our lead we wouldn't have had all these problems over all these years, either.*

The remark was construed as racist not only by Lott's critics but also by some members of his own party, including Pres. George W. Bush. Although Lott again won reelection in 2006, he resigned from the Senate in 2007.

Lott is the author of the memoir *Herding Cats: A Life in Politics* (2006).

WILLIAM MAHONE

(b. Dec. 1, 1826, Southampton County, Va.—d. Oct. 8, 1895, Washington, D.C.)

William Mahone was a railroad magnate and general of the Confederacy who led Virginia's "Readjuster" reform movement from 1879 to 1882. He served as a U.S. senator from Virginia from 1881 to 1887.

Born the son of a tavernkeeper in an area of large plantations, Mahone graduated from the Virginia Military Institute in 1847 and then taught while studying engineering. He joined the Norfolk–Petersburg Railroad as an engineer in 1851, and 10 years later he was company president.

With the outbreak of the Civil War, Mahone was appointed quartermaster general of the Confederacy. But during most of the conflict, he served with the Army of Northern Virginia, eventually rising to the rank of major general. A decisive leader, much admired by his troops, Mahone was regarded as a true military hero among Southerners at the conclusion of the war.

He immediately returned to railroading at the cessation of hostilities, becoming president of the Atlantic, Mississippi and Ohio Railroad (later the Norfolk & Western) in 1867. He built a strong political base through railroad patronage, but he lost his line when it went into receivership during the 1870s.

Unable to win the Democratic gubernatorial nomination in 1877—he had never had the support of Virginia's "squirearchy" of wealthy and powerful families—Mahone organized the Readjusters in 1879. This coalition of blacks and poor whites managed to take control of the state government and run it until 1882, reducing Virginia's debt and enacting other reform measures.

After serving in the U.S. Senate, he built a powerful political machine in Virginia, based on his total control of the state's Republican Party. Thoroughly disliked by Southern conservatives, Mahone lost an election for governor in 1889, but he remained a potent political power in Virginia until his death.

MICHAEL MANSFIELD
(b. March 16, 1903, New York, N.Y.—d. Oct. 5, 2001, Washington, D.C.)

Michael Mansfield, also known as Mike Mansfield, was a Democratic politician who was the longest-serving majority leader in the U.S. Senate (1961–77). He also served as U.S. ambassador to Japan from 1977 to 1988.

Reared by relatives in Montana, Mansfield dropped out of school before completing the eighth grade. He enlisted in the U.S. Navy at age 14 and served in military transport during World War I until his age was discovered and he was discharged. He then enlisted in the U.S. Army and later the Marine Corps, serving in several remote outposts, especially in Asia.

Mansfield spent most of the 1920s working in Montana copper mines, but his wife persuaded him to finish school, and in 1933 he earned both his high school and college diplomas (B.A., Montana State University); he obtained his master's degree in 1934. In 1933 he joined the faculty of Montana State University, eventually becoming a professor of Far Eastern and Latin American history.

In 1942 Mansfield was elected to the House of Representatives and became an active member of the Foreign Affairs Committee. He advised presidents Franklin D. Roosevelt and Harry S. Truman on U.S. foreign policy toward China and Japan, and maintained a solidly liberal voting record on domestic issues.

In 1952 Mansfield won a seat in the Senate, despite the accusations of Sen. Joseph R. McCarthy that he was soft on communism. A prominent member of the Foreign Relations Committee, Mansfield in 1957 became majority whip. He succeeded Lyndon B. Johnson as Senate majority leader when Johnson became vice president in 1961.

Reelected to the Senate in 1958, 1964, and 1970, Mansfield refused Johnson's offer to run for vice president in 1964. Throughout the 1960s he became increasingly vocal in his criticism of U.S. involvement in the Vietnam War, and in 1971 he sponsored a bill calling for a cease-fire and the phased withdrawal of U.S. troops from Vietnam. In 1973 he backed the War Powers bill, limiting presidential authority to engage the country in undeclared military conflicts abroad.

Mansfield became a persistent critic of Pres. Richard Nixon, especially during the Watergate investigation. In 1976 he retired from the Senate, but he returned to government service early the next year as part of a commission seeking information about missing U.S. servicemen in

Indochina. In 1977 Pres. Jimmy Carter appointed Mansfield U.S. ambassador to Japan, and he kept the post during both terms of Pres. Ronald Reagan, finally retiring in 1988.

EUGENE J. McCARTHY
(b. March 29, 1916, Watkins, Minn.—d. Dec. 10, 2005, Washington, D.C.)

Eugene Joseph McCarthy was a Democratic politician who served as a U.S. senator from Minnesota (1959–71). His entry into the 1968 race for the Democratic presidential nomination ultimately led Pres. Lyndon B. Johnson to drop his bid for reelection.

McCarthy graduated from St. John's University (Collegeville, Minn.) in 1935, then taught high school while working on a master's degree at the University of Minnesota. He returned as a faculty member to St. John's (1940–43) and subsequently served in the War Department's military intelligence division until the end of World War II. After the war McCarthy again taught school, eventually becoming chairman of the sociology department at the College of St. Thomas in St. Paul, Minn. In 1948 he ran successfully on Minnesota's Democratic-Farmer-Labor Party ticket for the U.S. House of Representatives, where he remained for 10 years, compiling a liberal voting record.

In 1958 McCarthy was elected to the Senate, where he remained a relatively unknown figure nationally until Nov. 30, 1967. On that day, he announced his intention to challenge Johnson in the Democratic presidential primaries. Although in 1964 he had supported the Gulf of Tonkin Resolution (which gave the president broad powers to wage the Vietnam War), by 1967 McCarthy had become an outspoken critic of the war. At first McCarthy's challenge was not taken seriously, but his candidacy soon attracted the growing numbers of Democrats who opposed further American involvement in the Vietnam War. After the Minnesota senator, with his trenchant wit and scholarly, understated manner, captured 42 percent of the vote in the New Hampshire primary in March 1968, Johnson made the dramatic announcement of his withdrawal from the race. McCarthy went on to sweep three primaries but then lost four of the next five to Sen. Robert F. Kennedy. Following Kennedy's assassination, McCarthy lost the nomination at the convention in Chicago to Vice Pres. Hubert H. Humphrey, who had declined to run in the primaries.

In 1970 McCarthy decided not to run for reelection to the Senate. Humphrey won his seat, and McCarthy turned to a career of writing and lecturing. In 1972 he conducted a lacklustre campaign for the Democratic presidential nomination, which was won by Sen. George S. McGovern. Four years later McCarthy made a more vigorous, but again unsuccessful, attempt to win the presidency as an independent; his campaigns in 1988 and 1992 also failed. In 1982 McCarthy made an unsuccessful bid for the Senate seat from Minnesota.

Among his numerous books are *Ground Fog and Night* (1979), a collection of poems; *Complexities and Contraries: Essays of Mild Discontent* (1982); *Up 'Til Now* (1987), a memoir; *1968: War and Democracy* (2000), about the 1968 presidential election; and *Parting Shots from My Brittle Brow* (2004).

JOSEPH R. MCCARTHY

(b. Nov. 14, 1908, near Appleton, Wis.—d. May 2, 1957, Bethesda, Md.)

Joseph Raymond McCarthy was a U.S. senator from Wisconsin who dominated the early 1950s with his sensational but unproved charges of communist subversion in high government circles. In a rare move, he was officially censured for unbecoming conduct by his Senate colleagues (Dec. 2, 1954), thus ending the era of McCarthyism.

A Wisconsin attorney, McCarthy served for three years as a circuit judge (1940–42) before enlisting in the Marines in World War II. In 1946 he won the Republican nomination for the Senate in a stunning upset primary victory over Sen. Robert M. La Follette, Jr.; he was elected that autumn and again in 1952.

McCarthy was a quiet and undistinguished senator until February 1950, when his public charge that 205 communists had infiltrated the State Department created a furor and catapulted him into headlines across the country. Upon subsequently testifying before the Senate Committee on Foreign Relations, he proved unable to produce the name of a single "card-carrying communist" in any government department. Nevertheless, he gained increasing popular support for his campaign of accusations by capitalizing on the fears and frustrations of a nation weary of the Korean War and appalled by communist advances in eastern Europe and China. McCarthy proceeded to instigate a nationwide, militant anti communist "crusade"; to his supporters, he appeared as a dedicated patriot and guardian of genuine Americanism, to his detractors, as an irresponsible, self-seeking witch-hunter who was undermining the nation's traditions of civil liberties.

McCarthy was reelected in 1952 and obtained the chairmanship of the Government Committee on Operations of the Senate and of its permanent subcommittee on investigations. For the next two years he was constantly in the spotlight, investigating various government departments and questioning innumerable witnesses about their suspected communist affiliations. Although he failed to make a plausible case against anyone, his colourful and cleverly presented accusations drove some persons out of their jobs and brought popular condemnation to others. The persecution of innocent persons on the charge of being communists and the forced conformity that this practice engendered in American public life came to be known as McCarthyism. Meanwhile, less flamboyant government agencies actually did identify and prosecute cases of communist infiltration.

McCarthy's increasingly irresponsible attacks came to include Pres. Dwight D. Eisenhower and other Republican and Democratic leaders. His influence waned in 1954 as a result of the sensational, nationally televised, 36-day hearing on his charges of subversion by U.S. Army officers and civilian officials. This detailed television exposure of his brutal and truculent interrogative tactics—which famously prompted Joseph Nye Welch, special counsel for the army, to ask McCarthy, "Have you no sense of decency, sir, at long last? Have you left no sense of decency?"—discredited him and helped to turn the tide of public opinion against him.

When the Republicans lost control of the Senate in the midterm elections that November, McCarthy was replaced as chairman of the investigating committee. Soon after, the Senate felt secure enough to formally condemn him on a vote of 67 to 22 for conduct "contrary to Senate traditions," and McCarthy was largely ignored by his colleagues and by the media thereafter.

George S. McGovern

(b. July 19, 1922, Avon, S.D.)

George Stanley McGovern is a former U.S. senator from South Dakota who was an unsuccessful reformist

Democratic candidate for the presidency in 1972. He campaigned on a platform advocating an immediate end to the Vietnam War and for a broad program of liberal social and economic reforms at home.

After service as a pilot in World War II, for which he was awarded the Distinguished Flying Cross, McGovern earned a Ph.D. in history at Northwestern University in Evanston, Ill., and later taught at Dakota Wesleyan University in Mitchell, S.D. He was active in Democratic politics, beginning in 1948, and served in the U.S. House of Representatives (1957–60). After losing an election for a Senate seat in South Dakota in 1960, he served for two years as the director of the Food for Peace Program under Pres. John F. Kennedy. Stressing farm-support programs, McGovern won election to the U.S. Senate in 1962 and was reelected in 1968. By then he had emerged as one of the leading opponents to the United States' continued military involvement in Indochina.

As chairman of a Commission on Party Structure and Delegate Selection prior to the Democratic National Convention in 1972, McGovern helped enact party reforms that gave increased representation to minority groups at the convention. Supported by these groups, he won the presidential nomination but alienated many of the more traditional elements in the Democratic Party. McGovern was unable to unify the party sufficiently to offer an effective challenge to the incumbent Republican president, Richard M. Nixon, who defeated him by an overwhelming margin.

McGovern was reelected to the Senate in 1974, but lost his seat in 1980 to a Republican opponent supported by right-wing groups. After lecturing as a visiting professor in foreign policy at several universities, including Northwestern University, McGovern declared himself a candidate for the 1984 Democratic presidential nomination, but decided to drop out of the race after a third-place finish in the Massachusetts primary—the only state that he had carried in the 1972 election. Although unsuccessful, his 1984 bid for the nomination did serve to reassert his status as a noted American spokesman for liberal causes.

McGovern's autobiography, entitled *Grassroots*, was published in 1978.

GEORGE MITCHELL
(b. Aug. 20, 1933, Waterville, Maine)

George Mitchell is a Democratic politician and diplomat who served as a member of the U.S. Senate (1980–95),

including service as majority leader (1989–95), and who later was special adviser to the peace process in Northern Ireland under U.S. Pres. Bill Clinton (1995–2000). In 2009 he was appointed special envoy to the Middle East by Pres. Barack Obama.

Mitchell earned a B.A. from Bowdoin College in Brunswick, Maine (1954), before enlisting in the U.S. Army, where he served as a counterintelligence officer in Berlin. After completing his service in 1956, he returned to the United States and earned a law degree from Georgetown University in Washington, D.C. (1960). Mitchell remained

George Mitchell speaking at the King David Hotel, Jerusalem, January 28, 2009. Matty Stern—U.S. Embassy Tel Aviv/ U.S. Department of State

in Washington, working as an attorney for the Department of Justice's antitrust division (1960–62) and as an assistant to U.S. Sen. Edmund Muskie (1962–65). Mitchell left Washington to work for a law firm in Maine, but he maintained his political ties. He chaired the Maine Democratic Party (1966–68) and worked on Muskie's 1968 vice presidential campaign, as well as Muskie's bid for the Democratic presidential nomination four years later. Mitchell ran for governor of Maine in 1974 but was narrowly defeated by independent candidate James Longley. In 1977 Mitchell was named U.S. attorney for Maine, a position he held until he was appointed to the U.S. District Court of Maine by Pres. Jimmy Carter in 1979.

When Muskie was named secretary of state in 1980, Mitchell was chosen to complete the final two years of Muskie's term in the Senate. He won the seat outright in 1982 and rose to national prominence in 1987 with his incisive criticism of Oliver North at the Senate hearings over the Iran-Contra Affair. The following year Mitchell was

George Mitchell, 1985. PH2 Carlos Drake—U.S. Navy/U.S. Department of Defense

George Mitchell arriving in Israel as special envoy to the Middle East, January 28, 2009. Matty Stern—U.S. Embassy Tel Aviv/U.S. Department of State

elected Senate majority leader, and he assumed that role when the 101st Congress began its session in January 1989. A moderate liberal on most issues, he was respected by lawmakers on both sides of the political aisle. In 1994 Mitchell was offered the U.S. Supreme Court seat vacated by retiring justice Harry A. Blackmun, but he declined the nomination, stating that he wished to devote his time to health care reform. Mitchell retired from the Senate in 1995.

In late 1995 Mitchell accepted a position as special adviser to Pres. Bill Clinton on the conflict in Northern Ireland. Over the next five years, Mitchell crossed the Atlantic more than 100 times, mediating a conclusion to the hostilities that had plagued the region for generations. His work culminated in the Belfast Agreement (1998) and, ultimately, the decommissioning of the Irish Republican Army. For his efforts, Mitchell in 1999 received the Presidential Medal of Freedom, the UNESCO Peace Prize, and an honorary knighthood in the Order of the British Empire. In 2000 he was selected to chair an international committee on the Israeli-Palestinian conflict. The group's analysis, completed in 2001, called for concessions from both sides, and it provided a framework for future negotiations.

Mitchell lent his diplomatic skills to the corporate sphere, where, as chairman of the Disney Company (2004–07), he averted a stockholder rebellion and helped guide the entertainment giant through a contentious leadership transition. In 2006 Bud Selig, the commissioner of Major League Baseball, asked him to lead an investigation of the illegal use of performance-enhancing drugs by players. Mitchell's report, issued in December 2007, stated that drug abuse was pervasive throughout the league, and it identified 89 current and former players, including marquee names such as Barry Bonds and Roger Clemens, as users of banned substances. The report led to the creation of a permanent substance-abuse investigations department within Major League Baseball. Mitchell returned to public service in January 2009, when Pres. Barack Obama named him special envoy to the Middle East.

Justin S. Morrill
(b. April 14, 1810, Strafford, Vt.—d. Dec. 28, 1898, Washington, D.C.)

Justin Smith Morrill was a Republican legislator who established a record for longevity by serving 43 years in both houses of the Congress; his name is particularly associated with the first high protective tariff and with federal support of land-grant colleges.

Following a modest career in local business, Morrill became active in Whig politics in the 1850s. Struck by the internal dissension within the party, he devoted himself afterward to preserving harmony within the Republican Party, which he helped found in Vermont (1855). He then went on to serve 12 years in the House of Representatives (1855–67) and 31 years in the Senate (1867–98).

A financial conservative, Morrill sponsored the Tariff Act of 1861 and succeeding years, usually referred to as the

Morrill tariffs, which introduced high import duties not for the traditional purpose of national revenue but to protect American industry from overseas competition. A consistent champion of "sound" currency, he opposed the resort to paper money during and after the U.S. Civil War (1861–65). He also opposed the various proposals for the use of silver as a monetary standard.

Many considered that Morrill's most important legislative contribution was the Morrill Act of 1862, which provided grants of land to state colleges, whose "leading object" would be to teach subjects "related to agriculture and the mechanic arts," without excluding the general sciences and classical studies. Morrill was henceforth called the "Father of the Agricultural Colleges," many of which have become leading educational institutions.

Gouverneur Morris

(b. Jan. 31, 1752, New York, N.Y.—d. Nov. 6, 1816, New York, N.Y.)

Gouverneur Morris was a statesman, diplomat, and financial expert who represented New York in the U.S. Senate (1800–03). He helped to plan the U.S. decimal coinage system.

Morris graduated from King's College (later Columbia University) in 1768, studied law, and was admitted to the bar in 1771. An extreme conservative in his political views, he distrusted the democratic tendencies of colonists who wanted to break with England, but his belief in independence led him to join their ranks. He served in the New York Provincial Congress (1775–77), where he led a successful fight to include a provision for religious toleration in the first state constitution. He then sat in the Continental Congress (1778–79).

Following his defeat for reelection to Congress in 1779, Morris settled in Philadelphia as a lawyer. His series of essays on finance (published in the *Pennsylvania Packet,*

1780) led to his appointment, under the Articles of Confederation, as assistant to the superintendent of finance, Robert Morris (to whom he was not related). During his tenure (1781–85) he proposed the decimal coinage system that, with some modifications by Thomas Jefferson, forms the basis of the present U.S. monetary system. During the Constitutional Convention (1787), Morris advocated a strong central government, with life tenure for the president and presidential appointment of senators. As a member of the Committee of Style, he was largely responsible for the final wording of the Constitution.

Morris was appointed minister to France in 1792; he openly disapproved of the French Revolution and sought to aid King Louis XVI in fleeing the country. His hostility led the French Revolutionary government to request his recall in 1794. In 1803, after a brief term in the U.S. Senate, he ended his public career. Unsympathetic to the forces of republicanism, he allied himself with the extreme Federalists, who hoped to create a northern confederation during the War of 1812. From 1810 he was chairman of the commission in charge of the construction of the Erie Canal.

CAROL MOSELEY BRAUN
(b. Aug. 16, 1947, Chicago, Ill.)

Carol Moseley Braun (née Carol Moseley) is a former Democratic politician from Illinois who in 1992 became the first African American woman elected to the U.S. Senate.

Carol Moseley attended the University of Illinois at Chicago (B.A., 1969) and received a law degree from the University of Chicago (1972). She married Michael Braun in 1973 (divorced 1986) and worked as an assistant U.S. attorney before her election to the Illinois House of Representatives in 1978. During her 10 years there she became known for her advocacy of health care and education reform and gun control. She was named assistant leader for the Democratic majority.

From 1988 to 1992 Moseley Braun served as Cook County (Illinois) recorder of deeds. Displeased with U.S. Sen. Alan Dixon's support of U.S. Supreme Court nominee Clarence Thomas, she ran against Dixon in the 1992 Democratic primary. Though poorly financed, she won an upset victory over Dixon on her way to capturing a seat in the Senate.

Shortly after becoming senator, Moseley Braun won clashes with Southern senators over a patent for a Confederate insignia. She was noted for her support of individual retirement accounts for homemakers and for filibustering to restore budget monies for youth job training and for senior citizens. Her record was tarnished, however, by her helping to ease legal restrictions on the sale of two television broadcasting companies, by lavish personal spending of campaign money, and by her favouring legislation to benefit a corporate campaign donor. She also was criticized for associating with two Nigerian military dictators.

In 1998 Moseley Braun lost her seat to her Republican challenger, Peter Fitzgerald. From 1999 to 2001 she served as U.S. ambassador to New Zealand. She unsuccessfully sought the Democratic Party presidential nomination in 2004.

DANIEL PATRICK MOYNIHAN

(b. March 16, 1927, Tulsa, Okla. — d. March 26, 2003, Washington, D.C.)

Daniel Patrick Moynihan was a scholar and Democratic Party politician who served as a U.S. senator from New York from 1977 to 2001.

Moynihan grew up in poverty in New York and, after service in the U.S. Navy in World War II, attended Tufts University (Medford, Mass.) on the GI Bill of Rights (B.A., 1948) and Tufts's Fletcher School of Law and Diplomacy (M.A., 1949), later receiving a Ph.D. from Fletcher (1961). His first taste of politics came in 1953 as a Democratic campaign worker in New York, and he held various public and party posts in New York state in the 1950s.

During the 1960s Moynihan was in Washington, D.C., and, while serving in the Department of Labor, cowrote *The Negro Family: The Case for National Action*, popularly called the Moynihan Report, which held that many of the educational problems of American blacks resulted from the instability of black urban families. The report caused a storm of controversy and made Moynihan famous. He became a professor at Harvard in 1966, held advisory posts in the Richard M. Nixon administration, and served as U.S. ambassador to India (1973–75) and permanent representative to the United Nations (1975–76). Moynihan's political stance defied easy characterization. He campaigned vigorously for Sen. Henry Jackson's ill-fated presidential bid in 1976; when that bid failed, Moynihan put himself into the race for U.S. senator in New York. He won the election despite the opposition of liberal Democrats, and he was reelected in 1982, 1988, and 1994. After serving four terms as senator, Moynihan decided not to run for reelection in 2000; he was succeeded by Hillary Rodham Clinton. Moynihan remained active in politics, and in 2001 he became cochairman of a presidential committee studying possible reforms to the Social Security retirement system. Among his numerous honours is the Presidential Medal of Freedom (2000). He is buried at Arlington National Cemetery.

GEORGE LLOYD MURPHY

(b. July 4, 1902, New Haven, Conn.—d. May 3, 1992, Palm Beach, Fla.)

George Lloyd Murphy was a politician and actor who served as a U.S. senator from California (1965–71). In the 1930s and 1940s he was an amiable song-and-dance man in a succession of Hollywood musicals.

Murphy attended Yale University but dropped out in his junior year and began working at a series of jobs—as a Wall Street messenger, a miner, a toolmaker, and a night-club dancer. He made his Broadway debut as a member of the chorus in *Good News* (1927) and performed in three other Broadway shows—*Hold Everything!, Of Thee I Sing,* and *Roberta*—before making his Hollywood debut in *Kid Millions* (1934). He appeared with Shirley Temple in *Little Miss Broadway* (1938), with Judy Garland in *Little Nellie Kelly* (1940), and with Fred Astaire in *Broadway Melody of 1940* (1940). After switching from the Democratic Party to the Republican Party in 1939, he became a close political ally of Ronald Reagan, with whom he appeared in *This Is the Army* (1943).

Among Murphy's other films were *Hold That Co-ed* (1938), *The Navy Comes Through* (1942), *Bataan* (1943), and *Walk East on Beacon* (1952), his final film. He served on the board of directors of the Screen Actors Guild (1937–53) and was its president (1944–46); in 1950 he won an Academy Award for career achievement. After retiring from acting, he worked as a motion-picture executive and won election to the U.S. Senate, defeating Pierre Salinger. His 1970 reelection bid failed after it was revealed that he had continued to receive a salary from a film company while serving in the Senate. His autobiography, *Say...Didn't You Used to Be George Murphy?,* was published in 1970.

EDMUND SIXTUS MUSKIE

(b. March 28, 1914, Rumford, Maine—d. March 26, 1996,
Washington, D.C.)

Edmund Muskie was a Democratic politician who served
as governor, U.S. senator, and U.S. secretary of state during a long career and was the Democratic Party's
vice-presidential candidate in 1968. He was perhaps better remembered for his failure to win the Democratic
presidential nomination in 1972. While campaigning in
New Hampshire and angrily denouncing *Manchester Union
Leader* attacks on his wife, he seemed to some to be cry-
ing. Though he said that what appeared to be tears on his
face was really melting snow, Muskie could not shake an
image of weakness.

After graduating cum laude from Bates College in
Lewiston, Maine (1936) and from Cornell Law School in
Ithaca, N.Y. (1939), Muskie began practicing law in
Waterville, Maine. He served in the navy during World
War II and then returned to his practice in Waterville. His
political career began in the state legislature, and in 1954
he became the first Democrat in 20 years to be elected
Maine's governor. In that post Muskie stressed environmental concerns, supporting clean air and water legislation.
His continued support of environmental issues during his
years in the U.S. Senate (1959–80) earned him the nickname "Mr. Clean." Laws regarding water quality, regional
clean air standards, and a model cities program were
among his successes.

Muskie first gained nationwide public recognition
when Hubert Humphrey selected him as his running
mate in the 1968 presidential election campaign. In a
close contest, the Democrats lost to the Richard Nixon-
Spiro Agnew ticket. In 1980 Muskie left the Senate to

serve as secretary of state during the last months of Jimmy Carter's administration. After Carter left office in 1981, Muskie returned to law. He was a senior partner in the Washington, D.C., office of a New York law firm at the time of his death.

George W. Norris

(b. July 11, 1861, Sandusky, Ohio—d. Sept. 2, 1944, McCook, Neb.)

George William Norris was a Republican politician who served as a U.S. senator from Nebraska (1913–43). He was noted for his advocacy of political reform and of public ownership of hydroelectric-power plants.

After attending Baldwin University (now Baldwin-Wallace College), Norris taught school and studied law at Northern Indiana Normal School (now Valparaiso University). He was admitted to the bar in 1883 and two years later moved to Nebraska to begin practice. In 1902 he was elected to Congress as a Republican and was reelected four times in succession, becoming leader of an insurgent group that in 1910 forced reforms in the House rules to reduce the autocratic control of the speaker.

Elected in 1912 to the Senate, Norris became known as an independent, saying he "would rather be right than regular." His strong antiwar convictions led him to vote against U.S. entry into World War I, and he denounced the Treaty of Versailles that followed it. He was the author of the 20th Amendment to the Constitution, which abolished the so-called lame-duck sessions of Congress. He fought for the introduction of presidential primaries and for direct election of U.S. senators. One of his most significant contributions was his introduction of the bill establishing the Tennessee Valley Authority. He was coauthor of the Norris–La Guardia Act, which restricted the use of injunctions in labour disputes.

Though always a Republican, Norris felt his party ties lightly; he endorsed Progressives Theodore Roosevelt in 1912 and Robert M. La Follette in 1924, and Democrats Alfred E. Smith in 1928 and Franklin D. Roosevelt in each of his campaigns for the presidency. In 1945 his book *Fighting Liberal* was published.

GEORGE PENDLETON
(b. July 29, 1825, Cincinnati, Ohio—d. Nov. 24, 1889, Brussels, Belg.)

George Pendleton was a Democratic politician who served as a representative from Ohio in the U.S. House of Representatives (1857–65) and as a U.S. senator from Ohio (1879–85). An advocate of civil service reform, he sponsored the Pendleton Civil Service Act (1883), which created the modern civil service system.

Admitted to the bar in 1847, Pendleton practiced law in Cincinnati and in 1853 was elected to the state senate. As a member of the U.S. House of Representatives (1857–65), he opposed suspension of *habeas corpus* and other extraordinary measures taken by Pres. Abraham Lincoln during the Civil War. In 1864 he was the Democratic vice presidential nominee, sharing the ticket with the former Union Army general George B. McClellan. The Democrats, who made peace their primary issue, were soundly defeated.

After the war Pendleton was a Greenbacker and a principal advocate of the Ohio Idea, a proposal for redeeming certain Civil War bonds in paper currency (greenbacks) instead of in gold. On this issue he alienated Eastern Democrats, who in turn deprived him of the 1868 Democratic presidential nomination. As a U.S. senator from Ohio (1879–85), he sponsored the Pendleton Civil Service Act (1883), which provided for a federal civil service commission and a corps of professional civil servants recruited by means of competitive examinations. Appointed minister to Germany by Pres. Grover Cleveland in 1885, Pendleton served abroad until his death.

BOIES PENROSE

(b. Nov. 1, 1860, Philadelphia, Pa.—d. Dec. 31, 1921, Washington, D.C.)

Boies Penrose was a Republican politician who was a long-time party boss of Pennsylvania and a U.S. senator from Pennsylvania (1897–1921).

Penrose was a member of a socially prominent Philadelphia family. He graduated from Harvard University in 1881 and was admitted to the Pennsylvania bar in 1883. Penrose began to practice law in Philadelphia and soon became interested in government and politics. He was elected as a Republican to the state legislature in 1884 and to the state senate in 1887. In that year he also published *The City Government of Philadelphia,* a study prepared in collaboration with law partner Edward P. Allinson, which advocated certain municipal reforms. The politics of reform did not long hold his interest, however, as he became associated with state party boss Matthew S. Quay. In 1895 Penrose ran unsuccessfully for the Republican nomination for mayor of Philadelphia. Two years later he was elected to the U.S. Senate and was successively reelected until his death.

Succeeding Quay as Republican boss of Pennsylvania in 1904, Penrose thereafter maintained a firm grip on state affairs that was broken only temporarily in 1912, when Progressives, led by former President Theodore Roosevelt on the national level, succeeded in challenging his authority. In a dispute over campaign funds, Roosevelt and others stepped up their attacks, characterizing Penrose as the archetypal political boss whose corrupting influence stood in the way of clean, honest government. Although never charged with bribery or otherwise profiting financially from his role in politics (he was independently wealthy), Penrose was undisputedly the chief power broker in Pennsylvania in the first decades of the century and used that power freely. In the Senate he rose to the post of chairman of the Finance Committee in 1911 and again in 1919. He held the position until his death. He opposed virtually all measures that the Progressives brought forth during this period, including liquor prohibition and women's suffrage.

HIRAM R. REVELS

(b. Sept. 1, 1822, Fayetteville, N.C.—d. Jan. 16, 1901, Aberdeen, Miss.)

Hiram Rhoades Revels was a clergyman and educator who became the first African American citizen to be elected to the U.S. Senate (1870–71), during Reconstruction.

Born of free parents, young Revels traveled to Indiana and Illinois to receive the education that was denied him in the South. He was ordained a minister in the African Methodist Episcopal Church in 1845 and eventually settled in Baltimore, Md., where he served as a church pastor and principal of a school for African Americans. Soon after the Civil War began (1861), he helped organize two volunteer regiments of blacks for service in the Union Army. Two years later he joined the Federal forces to serve as a chaplain to a black regiment stationed in Mississippi.

After the war Revels settled in Natchez, Miss., to preach to a large congregation. Despite some misgivings about entering politics, he accepted appointment by the military governor as alderman (1868) and was later (1869) elected to the state senate. Although Revels was a Republican, he was anxious not to encourage race friction with white Southerners; he therefore supported legislation that would have restored the power to vote and to hold office to disenfranchised members of the former Confederacy. In January 1870 he was elected to the U.S. Senate to fill the unexpired term of the former Confederate president, Jefferson Davis. He performed competently in office, advocating desegregation in the schools and on the railroads.

On leaving the Senate, Revels became president of Alcorn Agricultural and Mechanical College, a recently opened institution of higher education for blacks, near Lorman, Miss. In 1874, however, he was dismissed from the college presidency. In 1875 he helped overturn the Republican (Carpetbag) government of Mississippi, defending his action on the grounds that too many politicians in that party were corrupt. He was rewarded by the Democratic administration, which returned him to the chief post at Alcorn in 1876, where he remained until his retirement.

JOSEPH T. ROBINSON

(b. Aug. 26, 1872, near Lonoke, Ark. — d. July 14, 1937, Washington, D.C.)

Joseph Taylor Robinson was a Democratic politician who served as a representative of Arkansas in the U.S. House of Representatives (1903–13) and as a U.S. senator from Arkansas (1913–37). He was lawyer and legislator, a major figure in the enactment of New Deal legislation.

Admitted to the bar in 1895, Robinson practiced law in Lonoke. In 1902 he was elected to the U.S. House of Representatives, where he served for 10 years. Elected governor of Arkansas in 1912, he resigned a few months later to assume the U.S. Senate seat left vacant by the death of Jeff Davis, himself a former Arkansas governor. Robinson was successively reelected until his death, eventually becoming Senate majority leader under Pres. Franklin D. Roosevelt. In 1928 Robinson ran as the

Democratic vice presidential candidate on the losing ticket with Al Smith. As minority leader in the Senate, Robinson in 1929 pledged to cooperate with Hoover's economic program; he soon found himself at odds with the new president, however, and tried to convince him to step up relief efforts and public-works projects.

With the Democratic takeover of Congress in 1933, Robinson became majority leader and thus was responsible for steering through the upper chamber much of Roosevelt's New Deal program. In his final effort, Robinson worked tirelessly on behalf of the president's ill-fated court-packing plan, having received assurances from Roosevelt that he would be appointed to one of the new Supreme Court seats to be created by the bill. Roosevelt's court-packing plan was unpopular in the Senate—even among leading Democrats—and during the legislative battle, Robinson suffered a fatal stroke. He was considered an able and effective legislator, active in the drafting and passage of numerous bills, although only one, the Robinson-Patman Act of 1936, a fair-trade bill, bears his name.

Elihu Root

(b. Feb. 15, 1845, Clinton, N.Y.—d. Feb. 7, 1937, New York, N.Y.)

Elihu Root was a Republican politician and statesman who served as a U.S. senator from New York (1909–15). For his diplomatic contributions to world peace he was awarded the Nobel Prize for Peace in 1912.

Root received his law degree from New York University in 1867 and became a leading corporation lawyer. As U.S. attorney for the southern district of New York (1883–85) he came into close contact with Theodore Roosevelt, then a leader in New York Republican politics, and became Roosevelt's friend and legal advisor.

As secretary of war in Pres. William McKinley's (and, after McKinley's assassination, Roosevelt's) cabinet (1899–1903), Root worked out governmental arrangements for the former Spanish areas then under U.S. control as a result of the Spanish-American War. He was the primary author of the Foraker Act (1900), which provided for civil government in Puerto Rico. He established U.S. authority in the Philippines and wrote the instructions for an American governing commission sent there in 1900. He also effected a reorganization of the U.S. Army, established the principle of rotation of officers from staff to line, and created the Army War College in 1901.

Root left the cabinet in 1904 but returned as secretary of state the following year during Roosevelt's second term and remained until 1909. On a tour of South America (1906) he persuaded Latin American states to participate in the Second Hague Peace Conference, and he negotiated agreements by which Japan undertook to control its immigration to the United States and to arbitrate certain kinds of disputes. With the Japanese ambassador to the United States, Takahira Kogoro, Root negotiated the Root-Takahira Agreement (1908), under whose terms Japan promised to respect the Open Door Policy in China. Root also concluded treaties of arbitration with more than 20 nations. Later, as chief counsel for the United States before the Hague Tribunal, he settled the controversy between the United States and Great Britain over the North Atlantic coast fisheries. For these and other contributions to peace and general world harmony he was awarded the Nobel Prize for Peace.

From 1909 to 1915, as a Republican senator from New York, Root sided with the William Howard Taft wing of the party. After the outbreak of World War I in Europe, he openly supported the Allies and was critical of Pres. Woodrow Wilson's policy of neutrality. He was a leading

Republican supporter of international law and served on the commission of jurists that established the Permanent Court of International Justice (1920–21). Pres. Warren Harding appointed him one of four U.S. delegates to the International Conference on the Limitation of Armaments (1921–22). In his later years Root worked closely with Andrew Carnegie on programs for international peace and for the advancement of science.

Carl Schurz

(b. March 2, 1829, Liblar, near Cologne, Prussia [now in Germany]—d. May 14, 1906, New York, N.Y.)

Carl Schurz was a German-American political leader, journalist, orator, and dedicated reformer who pressed for high moral standards in government in a period of notorious public laxity. He served as a Republican U.S. senator from Missouri from 1869 to 1875.

As a student at the University of Bonn, Schurz participated in the abortive German revolution of 1848, was imprisoned, escaped, and eventually came to the United States (1852). He settled in Wisconsin (1856), quickly became active in the antislavery movement, and, as a delegate to the Republican National Convention of 1860, worked for the nomination of Abraham Lincoln for president.

Schurz joined the Union army in 1862 and was made brigadier general of volunteers. In the next year and a half he commanded troops at the Second Battle of Bull Run (August 1862) and at the battles of Chancellorsville, Gettysburg, and Chattanooga (all 1863). The conduct of his troops at Chancellorsville and Gettysburg was criticized, but he apparently retained the respect of his fellow officers.

After the war Schurz toured the South to report on conditions for Pres. Andrew Johnson. Strongly advocating support of rights for blacks, the report emphasized granting the franchise to freedmen as a condition of the Southern states' readmission to the Union. Johnson, however, resisted these views and shelved the report. In 1866 Schurz became editor of the *Detroit Post* and then editor and part owner of the German-language *St. Louis Westliche Post.*

In Missouri he won election in 1869 to the U.S. Senate, his only elective office. During his single term as senator he broke with Pres. Ulysses S. Grant on the issue of political corruption, on Reconstruction policy, and on the proposed annexation of Santo Domingo. These conflicts led him in 1872 to help organize the Liberal Republican Party, opposing Grant's renomination. Four years later, however, he rejoined the regular Republicans, supporting Rutherford B. Hayes on the issues of good government and hard money. In return, he served as Pres. Hayes's secretary of the interior (1877–81), promoting civil-service reform and an improved Indian policy.

Returning to journalism and writing, Schurz edited the *New York Evening Post* and *The Nation* in the early 1880s and wrote biographies. Pursuing his advocacy of honest government, he headed the National Civil Service Reform League from 1892 to 1901. He encouraged reform-minded Republicans, commonly referred to as Mugwumps, to support the presidential candidacy of Democrat Grover Cleveland in 1884.

WILLIAM H. SEWARD
(b. May 16, 1801, Florida, N.Y.—d. Oct. 10, 1872, Auburn, N.Y.)

William Henry Seward was a U.S. senator from New York (1849–61), an antislavery activist in the Whig and Republican parties before the American Civil War, and

U.S. secretary of state from 1861 to 1869. He is also remembered for the purchase of Alaska in 1867 — referred to at that time as "Seward's Folly."

Admitted to the New York state bar in 1822, Seward began the practice of law the following year at Auburn. He gradually developed a taste for politics and became active in the Antimasonic Party in 1828, serving in the New York senate from 1830 to 1834. At about this time he allied himself with other opponents of the Jacksonian Democrats in forming the new Whig Party. Under this banner Seward served as governor of New York for four years (1839–43), soon becoming recognized as leader of the antislavery wing of the party.

In 1848 Seward was elected to the U.S. Senate, where the antagonism between free and slave labour became the theme of many of his speeches. During the turbulent 1850s he increasingly resisted the Whig attempt to compromise on the slavery issue, and when the party collapsed (1854–55), Seward joined the newly organized Republican Party, which took a firm stand against expansion of slavery into the territories. Although Seward was the recognized Republican leader, he was twice thwarted (1856, 1860) in his wish to be nominated for the presidency.

When Abraham Lincoln took office as president on the eve of the Civil War (March 1861), he promptly named Seward secretary of state. On most issues he was Lincoln's closest and most influential adviser, despite early differences over the reinforcement of Ft. Sumter, S.C., and Seward's irresponsible suggestion that a foreign war be provoked to distract the country from its civil conflict at home. Seward gradually rose to the challenge of the office and was particularly successful in preventing foreign governments from giving official recognition to the Confederacy. While

he did not succeed in preventing the French occupation of
Mexico or the acquisition by the Confederacy of the war-
ship *Alabama* from England, his diplomacy prepared the
way for a satisfactory adjustment of the difficulties with
these powers at a later date. Although a treaty in 1862 for
the suppression of the slave trade conceded to England the
right to search U.S. vessels for slaves in African and Cuban
waters, he secured a similar concession for U.S. war vessels
from the British government. By his course in the "Trent"
Affair, concerning the capture and imprisonment of two
Confederate agents from a British ship, he virtually committed Great Britain to the U.S. attitude concerning the
right of search of vessels on the high seas.

On April 14, 1865, nine days after he was severely
injured in a carriage accident, the bedridden Seward was
stabbed in the throat by Lewis Powell (alias Lewis Payne),
a fellow conspirator of John Wilkes Booth, who had that
night assassinated Lincoln. Seward made a remarkable
recovery and retained his cabinet post under Pres. Andrew
Johnson until 1869. He chose to support Johnson's unpopular Reconstruction policies and had to share some of the
bitter congressional obloquy bestowed upon his chief.
Seward's last act of public renown was the purchase of
Alaska from Russia for $7,200,000 in 1867.

John Sherman

(b. May 10, 1823, Lancaster, Ohio—d. Oct. 22, 1900, Washington, D.C.)

John Sherman was a Republican statesman, financial
administrator, and author of major legislation concerning
currency and regulation of commerce. He served as a representative from Ohio in the U.S. House of Representatives
(1855–61) and as a U.S. senator from Ohio (1861–77, 1881–
97). He was also secretary of the Treasury under Pres.

Rutherford B. Hayes (1877–81) and secretary of state under Pres. William McKinley (1897–98).

A younger brother of Gen. William Tecumseh Sherman, he practiced law in Ohio before entering politics. Early in his congressional career Sherman gained a reputation as a fiscal expert. He was chairman of the House Ways and Means Committee (1859–61) and of the Senate Finance Committee (1867–77). He consistently preferred conservative financial policies but was often forced to balance his own convictions with the preferences of his constituents, many of whom favoured inflationary measures. He played a leading role in the establishment of the national banking system (1863), in the enactment of the bill (1873) that discontinued the coinage of silver dollars (denounced by critics as "the crime of '73") and of the Specie Payment Resumption Act (1875), which provided for the redemption of Civil War greenbacks in gold. It was thus largely through his efforts that the United States returned to the gold standard. During the administration of Pres. Benjamin Harrison, the Antitrust Act of 1890 and the Silver Purchase Act of the same year bore his name, but both represented compromises that had only his qualified approval.

Sherman's name was presented as a presidential consideration to three Republican national conventions (1880, 1884, and 1888). His lack of popular appeal, however, and his middle-of-the-road course on monetary policies, which suited neither the inflationist West nor the conservative East, prevented his winning the nomination.

In 1897 Pres. William McKinley appointed Sherman secretary of state, but partly for reasons of health and partly for reasons of principle he resigned on April 25, 1898, the day Congress declared war against Spain.

MARGARET CHASE SMITH

(b. Dec. 14, 1897, Skowhegan, Maine—d. May 29, 1995, Skowhegan)

Margaret Chase Smith (née Margaret Madeline Chase) was a public official who became the first woman to serve in both U.S. houses of Congress.

Margaret Chase attended high school in her native Skowhegan, Maine, graduating in 1916. She then taught school briefly, held a series of other jobs, and served as president of the Maine Federation of Business and Professional Women's Clubs from 1926 to 1928. In 1930 she married Clyde H. Smith, a local political figure and co-owner of the Skowhegan *Independent Reporter,* for which she had earlier worked. From 1930 to 1936 she was a member of the state Republican committee, and after her husband's election to the U.S. House of Representatives in 1936 she worked as his secretary. When he suffered a heart attack in 1940, he urged her to run in his stead in the election that year. He died in April, and two months later she was chosen in a special election to complete his term. Almost immediately she displayed the independent judgment that became characteristic of her political career by breaking with her Republican colleagues to vote in September in favour of the Selective Service Act. In that month she was elected to a full term, and she was returned to her seat three more times.

During her eight years in the House of Representatives, Smith served on the Naval Affairs Committee and later on the Armed Services Committee and concerned herself particularly with the status of women in the armed forces. She played a major role in the passage of the Women's Armed Services Integration Act of June 1948, which gave women equal pay, rank, and privileges. In 1948 she ran successfully for a seat in the Senate, winning it by a record plurality in Maine. She quickly established

herself as an outspoken legislator of high integrity and
considerable influence.

Smith was generally liberal
on domestic issues, often
backing New Deal legislation
proposed by Democratic Pres.
Franklin D. Roosevelt, and she
was a strong supporter of
national defense and security.
Although a staunch anticommunist, she was nevertheless
the first Republican senator to
condemn Sen. Joseph R.
McCarthy's anticommunist
witch-hunts, delivering a
memorable "Declaration of
Conscience" on the Senate
floor in 1950. Her opinion that
Pres. John F. Kennedy should

Margaret Chase Smith. Library
of Congress, Washington,
D.C.; neg. no. LC USZ 62
42661

use nuclear weapons against the Soviet Union prompted
Soviet leader Nikita Khrushchev to dub her "the devil in
disguise of a woman."

Reelected by large majorities in 1954, 1960, and 1966,
Smith served in the Senate longer than any other woman.
She was considered as a vice-presidential candidate in 1952
and received several votes for the presidential nomination
at the 1964 Republican National Convention. Her defeat
for reelection to the Senate in 1972 by William D. Hathaway
turned mainly on the question of her age and health; she
had campaigned little.

Among the many honours Smith received were several
citations as woman of the year, the *Newsweek* magazine
press poll rating as Most Valuable Senator for 1960, and the
Presidential Medal of Freedom in 1989.

SAMUEL SMITH

(b. July 27, 1752, Carlisle, Pa.—d. April 22, 1839, Baltimore, Md.)

Samuel Smith was a U.S. soldier and politician best known as the commander of land and sea forces that defended Baltimore from the British during the War of 1812. He served in both the U.S. House of Representatives (1793–1803, 1817–23) and the U.S. Senate (1803–15, 1823–33).

Smith grew up in Baltimore, to which his family had moved in 1760. The son of a wealthy merchant, he joined the family business after lengthy travels in Europe.

Smith fought in the American Revolution, participating in the Battle of Long Island and spending the winter with George Washington at Valley Forge. As commander of Fort Mifflin, he helped prevent Gen. William Howe's fleet from coming to the aid of Gen. John Burgoyne, contributing to the crucial American victory at Saratoga in 1777.

After the Revolution, Smith returned to Baltimore, where he became quite wealthy through land speculation as well as the family mercantile concerns. His main interest turning to politics, he served 10 years in the U.S. House of Representatives and 12 years in the U.S. Senate.

During the British invasion of Maryland in 1814, Smith led about 13,000 troops in defending Baltimore. The Americans repulsed the invaders and inflicted heavy losses on them. The American-held citadel Fort McHenry withstood a two-day bombardment (inspiring Francis Scott Key to compose "The Star-Spangled Banner") before the British finally withdrew.

Two years later he resumed his political career, serving six years in the House and 10 in the Senate. In 1835—at the age of 83—he took command of the state militia and put down riots in Baltimore. The grateful city elected Smith mayor, and he served in that capacity until 1838, one year before his death.

John Cornelius Stennis
(b. Aug. 3, 1901, De Kalb, Miss.—d. April 23, 1995, Jackson, Miss.)

John Cornelius Stennis was a Democratic U.S. senator from Mississippi (1947–89) who became the second longest-serving U.S. senator, after Carl Hayden of Arizona. In the Senate,Stennis exerted vast influence over the U.S. military while serving as chairman of both the Armed Services Committee and the defense subcommittee of the Appropriations Committee during the 1970s; he was especially admired for his sterling integrity, a trait that led colleagues to select him to head numerous political inquiries.

One year after earning a law degree from the University of Virginia (1927), Stennis was elected to the Mississippi legislature. He served as a district attorney and circuit judge before winning the Senate seat left vacant by the death of Theodore Bilbo. Stennis's Senate record also was marked by his opposition to integration, although late in his career he supported some civil rights measures. The indomitable Stennis, who was nicknamed the "conscience of the Senate" for his work on the Senate's ethics code, exhibited personal fortitude in 1973 when he made a remarkably swift recovery after being shot by robbers and left bleeding on the sidewalk in front of his home. In 1984, after losing a leg to cancer, Stennis returned to his desk sooner than expected. He remained a staunch advocate of a strong military throughout his career and during the final years of his tenure became a mentor to junior senators.

Ted Stevens
(b. Nov. 18, 1923, Indianapolis, Ind.)

Ted Stevens is a Republican politician who served as a U.S. senator from Alaska (1968–2009). In October 2008, just eight days before his reelection bid, Stevens was convicted of making false statements on financial disclosure forms; he narrowly lost reelection, and the following year the conviction was reversed.

Stevens served in the U.S. Army Air Corps during World War II. He graduated from the University of California at Los Angeles with a bachelor's degree in political science in 1947 and from Harvard Law School in 1950. After working for the Department of the Interior (1956–61) in Washington, D.C., he moved to Anchorage, Alaska, to practice law. He was twice defeated (1962, 1968) in bids for the U.S. Senate. Elected to the Alaska State House of Representatives in 1964, he became majority leader in 1966. On Dec. 24, 1968, he was appointed to the U.S. Senate to fill the seat left vacant by the death of Sen. E.L. Bartlett.

In his 40 years as senator, Stevens earned a reputation as a powerful advocate for Alaskan industry. In 1971 he helped to draft the Alaska Native Claims Settlement Act, which enabled construction of the Trans-Alaska Pipeline (completed 1977). Despite concerns voiced by environmentalists, in the early 1980s he brokered legislation that opened the Tongass National Forest to logging and mandated millions of dollars in federal payments to Alaska for prohibiting development in other large wilderness areas. (The federal government cut the earmark in 2009.) After the tanker *Exxon Valdez* spilled some 10.9 million gallons of crude oil into Alaska's Prince William Sound in 1989, Stevens introduced a bill to allocate more federal money to cleanup efforts, arguing that Exxon Corporation had not done enough. In 1993 Stevens convinced Congress to allot $10 million for research to determine the effects of large amounts of nuclear waste reportedly dumped into the oceans by the former Soviet Union. Stevens was a fierce advocate of allowing oil drilling in the Arctic National Wildlife Refuge, though his efforts did not meet success. In a passionate speech on the Senate floor, Stevens warned his colleagues: "People who vote against this today are voting against me. I will not forget it." He was more successful in directing federal funds toward his state, particularly as chair of the Senate Appropriations Committee (1997–01, 2003–05), funneling more than $3 billion to Alaska between 1995 and 2008.

In 2003 an article in the *Los Angeles Times* suggested that Stevens had invested his own money in Alaskan companies that benefited from legislation he sponsored and from earmarks he obtained. Stevens responded by insisting that his actions had not violated any Senate rules. In 2007 the Justice Department announced that it was investigating the senator's ties to Bill J. Allen, a former oil-service company executive who had been accused of bribing members of the state legislature. After Allen claimed that he had paid for renovations to Stevens's home in Girdwood, Alaska, and even had provided workers for the job, Stevens was indicted in July 2008 for failing to disclose those gifts. The ensuing corruption trial cast a shadow not only on Stevens's own 2008 reelection campaign—which he lost—but also on the vice-presidential campaign of Alaska Gov. Sarah Palin, the running mate of Republican Sen. John McCain in the 2008 presidential election. Although jurors returned a guilty verdict in Stevens's trial, in 2009 a federal judge overruled the conviction, citing prosecutorial misconduct.

ADLAI STEVENSON

(b. Oct. 23, 1835, Christian County, Ky.—d. June 14, 1914, Chicago, Ill.)

Adlai Stevenson was the 23rd vice president of the United States (1893–97) in the Democratic administration of Pres. Grover Cleveland and Democratic representative from Illinois in the U.S. House of Representatives (1875–77, 1879–81).

Stevenson was the son of John Turner Stevenson, a tobacco farmer, and Eliza Ann Ewing. After studying law, he began his practice in Metamora, Ill. Stimulated by the famous Lincoln–Douglas Debates, which took place during the Illinois senatorial campaign of 1858, he became active in local and national politics and was appointed to his first public office as a master in chancery of Woodford County's circuit court in 1860, a position he held throughout the American Civil War. He served as a presidential elector for Gen. George McClellan, the failed Democratic Party candidate in the 1864 presidential election. In 1865 he was elected state's attorney, and 10 years later he entered the House of Representatives, where he favoured low tariffs and a soft-money policy. He also played a conspicuous role in the congressional debate over the disputed presidential election of 1876 between Rutherford B. Hayes and Samuel J. Tilden, which was decided by a special Electoral Commission.

As first assistant postmaster general under Pres. Cleveland (1885–89), Stevenson received the enmity of the Republican Party for his removal of thousands of Republican postmasters throughout the country. After unsuccessfully seeking the vice presidential nomination in 1888, Stevenson was named associate justice of the Supreme Court for the District of Columbia, though the Republican-controlled Senate blocked his nomination. When Cleveland was renominated in 1892, Stevenson was selected as the vice presidential candidate who could best unite all factions of the party. As vice president, he strongly supported Cleveland's policies and won wide admiration for his impartiality as presiding officer of the Senate. After failing to capture the Democratic nomination in 1896, he was appointed by Pres. William McKinley to serve as chairman of a commission sent to Europe to work for international bimetallism. Afterward he ran unsuccessfully for vice president (1900) and for governor of Illinois (1908). His grandson, Adlai Ewing Stevenson II, served as a governor of Illinois and was twice an unsuccessful candidate for president (1952 and 1956).

CHARLES SUMNER

(b. Jan. 6, 1811, Boston, Mass. — d. March 11, 1874, Washington, D.C.)

Charles Sumner was a politician and statesman who served as a U.S. senator from Massachusetts (1852–74). He was remembered for his dedication to human equality and to the abolition of slavery.

A graduate of Harvard Law School (1833), Sumner crusaded for many causes, including prison reform, world peace, and Horace Mann's educational reforms. It was in his long service as a U.S. senator from Massachusetts, however, that he exercised his major influence on history. He bitterly attacked the Compromise of 1850, which attempted to balance the demands of North against South. On May 19–20, 1856, he denounced the "Crime against Kansas" (the Kansas–Nebraska Act) as "in every respect a swindle" and characterized its authors, Senators Andrew P. Butler and Stephen A. Douglas, as myrmidons (followers) of slavery. Two days later Congressman Preston S. Brooks of South Carolina invaded the Senate, labelled the speech a libel on his state and on his uncle, Sen. Butler, and then severely beat Sumner with a cane. It took three years for Sumner to recover from the beating.

Sumner was chairman of the Senate Foreign Relations Committee from March 1861 to March 1871. Close acquaintanceships with prominent Englishmen such as Richard Cobden, John Bright, William Ewart Gladstone, and other European leaders — gained during his several European sojourns (1837–40)—afforded him unusual understanding of and influence in international affairs. He helped preserve peace between Britain and the United States by persuading Pres. Abraham Lincoln to give up Confederate commissioners James M. Mason and John Slidell after their capture aboard the *Trent* in November 1861.

Sumner opposed President Lincoln and later Pres. Andrew Johnson on post-war Reconstruction policy. He took the position that the defeated South was a conquered province outside the protection of the Constitution, and that the Confederate states should provide constitutional guarantees of equal voting rights to blacks before those states could be readmitted to the Union.

In 1870 Sumner helped defeat Pres. Ulysses S. Grant's proposal to annex Santo Domingo. As a result, Grant apparently brought about Sumner's removal from the chairmanship of the Foreign Relations Committee, a blow that almost broke Sumner.

In a move for magnanimity toward the defeated South, Sumner introduced a Senate resolution (1872) providing that the names of battles between fellow citizens should not be placed on the regimental colours of the U.S. Army. Reaction in his home state was immediate and bitter. The Massachusetts legislature censured the resolution as "an insult to the loyal soldiery of the nation" and as meeting "the unqualified condemnation of the people of the Commonwealth." Two years later, however, the legislature rescinded its action. Shortly after receiving news that he had been exonerated, Sumner suffered a fatal heart attack.

ROBERT A. TAFT

(b. Sept. 8, 1889, Cincinnati, Ohio—d. July 31, 1953, New York, N.Y.)

Robert Alphonso Taft was a Republican leader in the U.S. Senate for 14 years (1939–53) whose espousal of traditional conservatism won him the sobriquet "Mr. Republican"; his failure to receive the presidential nomination in 1948 and 1952 was indicative of the defeat of isolationism by the internationalist wing of the party.

The son of William Howard Taft, 27th president of the United States (1909–13), Taft was admitted to the Ohio bar in 1913. Specializing in trust and utility cases, he also became a director of several successful businesses. During World War I he served as assistant counsel for the U.S. Food Administration (1917–18) and counsel for the American Relief Administration (1919). He then served in the Ohio House of Representatives (1921–26) and in the state senate (1931–32).

Elected to the U.S. Senate in 1938, Taft soon established himself as a powerful influence in Washington D.C., denouncing the "socialist trends" of the New Deal and calling for economy in government, a balanced budget, and less centralization of power in the nation's capital. Before the Japanese attack on Pearl Harbor (December 1941), he was an outspoken anti-interventionist; afterward, he threw his weight behind the war effort but was often critical of Pres. Franklin D. Roosevelt's war policies.

With the election of a Republican majority to Congress in 1946, Taft entered a new phase of power and prestige. He was tireless as chairman of the Republican Senate Policy Committee and well informed on the whole range of legislation before Congress. His most notable achievement was the enactment of the Taft-Hartley Labor Relations Act (1947), which placed restrictions on organized labour and, according to its sponsors, sought to balance the bargaining rights of management and labour. Although he sponsored modified social welfare measures in housing, health, and education, he continued to oppose centralization of power in the federal government.

A steadfast isolationist, Taft opposed U.S. post–World War II involvement in world affairs through such international organizations as the North Atlantic Treaty Organization (NATO), founded in 1949. Rather, he joined former president Herbert Hoover in calling for "fortress America" and the "principle of the free hand." It was on these grounds that Taft was most determinedly opposed for the nomination to the presidency. Already a favourite-son candidate at every national convention since 1936, he came to the 1948 convention with considerable nation-wide support but lost to the well-organized forces of the internationalist Thomas E. Dewey. Again in 1952 the nom-ination was denied him by the strong internationalist coalition, which rallied around the popular wartime gen-eral Dwight D. Eisenhower. After his party's victory at the polls Taft became majority leader and Eisenhower's chief adviser in the Senate.

JOHN TAYLOR

(b. Dec. 19?, 1753, Caroline County, Va.—d. Aug. 21, 1824, Caroline county)

John Taylor was a politician and one of the leading American philosophers of the liberal agrarian political movement—commonly known as Jeffersonian democ-racy—during the early national period. He also served as a U.S. senator from Virginia (1792–94, 1822–24).

Orphaned as a child, Taylor grew up in the home of his uncle, Edmund Pendleton. He received his education from private tutors, a private academy, and the College of William and Mary. Early in the 1770s he began studying law in Pendleton's office, and in 1774 Taylor received his license to practice.

At the outbreak of the American Revolution, Taylor joined the Continental Army. He served until resigning in

1779, after which he fought with the Virginia militia. Elected in 1779 to the Virginia House of Delegates, Taylor emerged as a leader in the movement for religious disestablishment, broader voting rights, and more equitable representation. He served in the House of Delegates from 1779 to 1781 and again from 1783 to 1785.

Taylor was dismayed at the prospect of a strong central government and opposed the ratification of the Constitution. From 1796 to 1800, he was again in the Virginia House of Delegates after filling an unexpired U.S. Senate term from 1792 to 1794. It was while in the Virginia legislature in 1798 that he introduced James Madison's Virginia Resolutions, the states' rights document drawn up in reaction to the passage of the Alien and Sedition Acts. Taylor was a vigorous backer of Pres. Thomas Jefferson. He again filled an unexpired Senate term in 1803.

Except for filling yet another unexpired Senate term, from 1822 to 1824, Taylor devoted the remainder of his life to political writing. *An Inquiry into the Principles and Policy of the Government of the United States* (1814) and *Construction Construed and Constitutions Vindicated* (1820) were highly prolix works but important as defenses of agrarian democracy against the assaults of a too-powerful central government and the monied mercantile classes. Taylor attacked the notion that the Supreme Court could negate state actions and that Congress could restrict the expansion of slavery into the territories. Like most of his fellow Southern critics of centralization, he provided slavery's defenders with an arsenal of high-minded abstractions to invoke.

Taylor's other writings dealt with his experiments in scientific agriculture, and in 1813 he published a collection of his essays under the title *The Arator.* He always thought of himself as a farmer, and he spent most of his life on his plantation—"Hazelwood"—in Caroline County.

Fred Thompson

(b. Aug. 19, 1942, Sheffield, Ala.)

Fred Thompson is an actor and politician who served as a member of the U.S. Senate (1994–2003) and who unsuccessfully sought the Republican nomination for president in 2008.

Thompson was raised in Lawrenceburg, Tenn. He received a bachelor's degree in philosophy and political science from Memphis State University in 1964 and earned a law degree from Vanderbilt University in Nashville in 1967. He wasted no time in exploring the political arena, and he modeled his views on those of Ronald Reagan, who was then governor of California. In 1969 he was named assistant U.S. attorney, though he left that position in 1972 to serve as the campaign manager for Sen. Howard Baker's successful reelection bid. In 1973 Thompson made head-lines as the minority (Republican) counsel at the Senate Select Committee on Presidential Campaign Activities (the Watergate Committee) when he asked former White House staffer Alexander Butterfield about the existence of recording devices in the Oval Office. This question triggered a series of events that led to Pres. Richard M. Nixon's resignation the following year.

In 1974 Thompson returned to private law practice in Nashville, where a wrongful termination suit paved the way for his second career. He represented the former chairperson of the state parole board, Marie Ragghianti, after Ragghianti was fired by Gov. Ray Blanton for refusing to grant early releases to inmates who had bribed members of Blanton's staff. The story was made into the film *Marie* (1985), and Thompson was cast to play himself. This launched an acting career that included such films as *The Hunt for Red October* (1990), *Die Hard 2* (1990), and *Cape Fear* (1991).

Thompson returned to politics in 1994 with a successful run for the U.S. Senate, filling the seat vacated by Al Gore when the latter became vice president. Thompson was reelected in 1996 but declined to run again in 2002, instead resuming his acting career as a regular on the television series *Law & Order* and its related spin-offs. In 2007 he quit the show in order to explore a presidential run. Among the issues he supported were lower taxes, a smaller federal government, and increased defense spending. Thompson withdrew from the race in January 2008 after finishing third in the South Carolina primary.

STROM THURMOND
(b. Dec. 5, 1902, Edgefield, S.C.—d. June 26, 2003, Edgefield)

Strom Thurmond was a politician who was a prominent advocate of states' rights and segregation. He ran for the U.S. presidency in 1948 on the Dixiecrat ticket and was one of the longest-serving senators in U.S. history (1954–2003).

After graduating from Clemson College (now Clemson University) in South Carolina (1923), Thurmond taught school until 1929, when he became superintendent of education for Edgefield County. During this time he also began studying law and in 1930 was admitted to the bar. He then served as a city and county attorney until 1938 and was also a state senator (1933–38) and a circuit court judge (1938–41). Thurmond emerged from his military service in World War II a highly decorated lieutenant colonel. He was elected governor of South Carolina in 1946 and proceeded to initiate several liberal reforms, including a notable expansion of the state educational system. At the Democratic National Convention of 1948, however, Thurmond led the bolt of Southern delegates angry over the civil rights plank in the party platform.

The Southerners formed the States' Rights Democratic Party—popularly known as the Dixiecrats—and nominated Thurmond as their presidential candidate. He won 39 electoral votes.

Elected by write-in vote to the Senate in 1954, Thurmond quickly established himself in the Southern conservative mold as a vigorous champion of increased military power and spending and an archfoe of civil rights legislation. He was reelected in 1960, but in 1964 he again left the Democratic Party in support of the conservative Republican presidential nominee, Barry Goldwater. Reelected as a Republican to seven consecutive terms, Thurmond continued to seek Southern conservative support for the GOP. In 1996 he became the oldest person to serve in Congress and the following year became the longest-serving U.S. senator; he held the latter distinction until 2006, when he was surpassed by Robert C. Byrd of West Virginia.

Soon after Thurmond's death it was revealed that at the age of 22 he had fathered a daughter out of wedlock. The mother was a 16-year-old African American maid who worked for his family.

BENJAMIN R. TILLMAN

(b. Aug. 11, 1847, Edgefield County, S.C.—d. July 3, 1918, Washington, D.C.)

Benjamin Ryan Tillman was a Democratic politician who was an outspoken populist and a champion of both agrarian reform and white supremacy. He served as governor of South Carolina (1890–94) and was a member of the U.S. Senate (1895–1918).

A farmer prior to his entry into politics, Tillman emerged during the 1880s as a spokesman for poor rural whites in South Carolina in their conflict against both the ruling white aristocracy and the impoverished African American population. The rise of Tillman marked the decline of the former Confederate general Wade Hampton as a political force in the state. Elected governor in 1890, Tillman translated his populist rhetoric into concrete reforms. He shifted the tax burden to the wealthy, improved public education, founded the agricultural college later to be known as Clemson University, and regulated the railroads. He also helped write the state constitution to disfranchise African Americans and circumvent the Fifteenth Amendment with a patchwork

Benjamin R. Tillman, c. 1905. Library of Congress, Washington, D.C. (digital file number 3c04434)

of Jim Crow laws (i.e., laws enforcing racial segregation). An unabashed bigot, he considered lynching an acceptable law-enforcement measure.

Elected to the U.S. Senate in 1894, Tillman served until his death, continuing to press for agrarian reform on the national level. He bitterly assailed Pres. Grover Cleveland for his hard-money policy, supporting instead the free-silver program of William Jennings Bryan. In most instances he opposed the administration of Pres. Theodore Roosevelt. In fact, the two became such bitter enemies that at one point the president barred Tillman from the White House. They put aside their differences long enough, however, to collaborate in securing passage of the Hepburn Act (1906), extending the Interstate Commerce Commission's regulatory powers over the railroads. Tillman was floor leader for the bill. He generally supported Pres. Woodrow Wilson and, as chairman of the Senate Naval Affairs Committee, promoted the administration's program to strengthen the navy. His vituperative and often profane attacks on his political opponents earned him the nickname "Pitchfork Ben"; he once had a fistfight with his South Carolina colleague on the floor of the Senate.

ROBERT A. TOOMBS
(b. July 2, 1810, Wilkes County, Ga.—d. Dec. 15, 1885, Washington, Ga.)

Robert Augustus Toombs was an American Southern antebellum politician who served as a representative from Georgia in the U.S. House of Representatives (1845–53) and as a U.S. senator from Georgia (1853–61). He served briefly as Confederate secretary of state and later sought to restore white supremacy in Georgia during and after Reconstruction.

Born into a wealthy planter family, Toombs entered and withdrew from the University of Georgia before graduating in 1828 from Union College in Schenectady, N.Y. Admitted to the bar in 1830, he quickly developed a lucrative legal practice in Washington, Ga. In addition, he owned a plantation and many slaves in southwestern Georgia.

From 1837 to 1840 and again from 1842 to 1843, Toombs served in the Georgia legislature, establishing himself as an expert in fiscal matters. A Whig, he joined the U.S. House of Representatives in 1845. He was reelected to the House in 1846, 1848, and 1850.

In 1850 Toombs began to emerge as an advocate of states' rights, and ultimately secession, advocate. In his "Hamilcar" speech, he demanded that the South not be denied its rights in the newly acquired territories. Yet he worked for passage of the Compromise of 1850 and its acceptance in Georgia, and he helped organize the Constitutional Union Party in Georgia as a political vehicle for conservatives unhappy with the Whigs but not ready to support the secession-minded Democrats.

Running on the Constitutional Union ticket in 1852, Toombs won election to the U.S. Senate. Shortly thereafter he joined the Democrats, but he remained a moderate on the states' rights issue until 1860.

Not until Abraham Lincoln's election as president and the failure of the Crittenden Compromise of 1860 did Toombs publicly call for secession. He led the movement for a Georgia convention to vote to secede from the Union. In 1861 he resigned from the Senate and was a delegate to the Montgomery convention that established the Confederacy. Severely disappointed at not being selected president of the Confederate States of America, he nonetheless accepted appointment by Jefferson Davis to become secretary of state. Within a few months, however, he broke with Davis and left the government.

In July 1861 Toombs took command of a Georgia brigade as a brigadier general. His military experience was undistinguished, though he did take a bullet in his left hand at Antietam. When no promotion followed, Toombs angrily resigned his commission. He stayed out of the war until near the end, and he continually criticized Davis' s leadership and Confederate policies—especially conscription, suspension of habeas corpus, and reliance upon credit to finance the war effort.

In May 1865 Toombs fled—by way of New Orleans and Havana—to London. He returned to Georgia in 1867, but he refused to seek a pardon or take the oath of allegiance. Instead, he devoted himself to rebuilding his law practice and to overthrowing Radical Reconstruction in Georgia.

In 1877 he broke with other Democrats in welcoming Pres. Rutherford Hayes's plans to end Reconstruction, and the same year, he played a prominent role at the convention that revised the state constitution in favour of white supremacy.

Toombs's last major public activity was to seek legislation that would give the state control over railroads and corporations.

OSCAR W. UNDERWOOD

(b. May 6, 1862, Louisville, Ky.—d. Jan. 25, 1929, Fairfax County, Va.)

Oscar Wilder Underwood was a Democratic politician who served as a representative from Alabama in the U.S. House of Representatives (1895–96, 1897–1915) and as a U.S. senator from Alabama (1915–27). He is best known for drafting the Underwood Tariff Act of 1913.

Oscar W. Underwood. Encyclopædia Britannica, Inc.

After studying law at the University of Virginia he was admitted to the bar in 1884. Underwood settled in Birmingham, Ala., and in 1894 was elected to the U.S. House of Representatives, rising to chairman of the Ways and Means Committee and becoming an expert on trade and tariffs. He ran successfully for the Senate in 1914 and served two terms.

Underwood decided to seek the Democratic presidential nomination in 1912. He lost the nomination to Woodrow Wilson, but the winning candidate was for the most part receptive to his views on the subject of protective tariffs, and it was under the Wilson administration that Underwood was able to enact the tariff legislation that bears his name. The bill, passed in 1913, sought to promote international trade by lowering import duties (and, to make up for the expected loss of revenue, levied the first federal income tax). Underwood generally supported Wilson's programs, promoting passage of the Federal Reserve Act (1913) and advocating U.S. participation in the League of Nations.

He was a member of the U.S. delegation to the Washington conference on arms limitations (1921–22) under the administration of Warren G. Harding and reportedly refused Harding's offer of an appointment to the Supreme Court. He sought the Democratic presidential nomination once again in 1924, but his denunciation of the Ku Klux Klan—which alienated his Southern colleagues—and his opposition to Prohibition were largely responsible for his failure to win the party's support.

Arthur H. Vandenberg

(b. March 22, 1884, Grand Rapids, Mich.—d. April 18, 1951, Grand Rapids)

Arthur Hendrick Vandenberg was a Republican politician who served as a U.S. senator from Michigan (1928–51). He was largely responsible for bipartisan congressional support of international cooperation and of Pres. Harry S. Truman's anticommunist foreign policy after World War II.

Editor of the *Grand Rapids Herald* from 1906, Vandenberg became active in Republican politics and was appointed U.S. senator in 1928, a post he retained through election until his death. While supporting conservative policies in the domestic field, he grew interested chiefly in foreign relations. During the 1930s, he was a spokesman for isolationist sentiment and a bitter critic of Pres.

Franklin D. Roosevelt. After the Japanese attack on Pearl Harbor (Dec. 7, 1941), however, he began to revise his picture of world relations and by the war's end had come around to the view that the United States should participate actively in an effective international organization. He expressed this opinion in a notable Senate speech (January 1945) and thus provided valuable Republican support for the United Nations. In the same year, Roosevelt appointed him a delegate to the United Nations Conference on International Organization that met in San Francisco.

As chairman of the Senate Foreign Relations Committee (1946–48), Vandenberg marshaled congressional support for the Truman Doctrine of aid to Greece and Turkey (1947), the Marshall Plan of aid to Europe (1948), and the North Atlantic Treaty Organization (1949), all of which sought to prevent the spread of communism in Europe. Furthermore, in the spring of 1948 he helped defeat a Republican-sponsored measure to inhibit the Reciprocal Trade Agreements program, substituting instead a provision for independent action on the part of the Tariff Commission.

BENJAMIN F. WADE

(b. Oct. 27, 1800, Springfield, Mass. —d. March 2, 1878, Jefferson, Ohio)

Benjamin Franklin Wade was a politician who served as a U.S. senator from Ohio during the Civil War. His radical views brought him into conflict with presidents Abraham Lincoln and Andrew Johnson.

In 1821 Wade's family moved to Andover, Ohio. He studied law, was admitted to the bar, and formed a successful partnership in 1831 with the outspoken antislavery advocate Joshua R. Giddings. After a term as prosecuting attorney, Wade was elected in 1837 to the state Senate as a Whig. His determined antislavery stand cost him reelection in 1839, but he won another term in 1841. In 1847 he was elected by the legislature as president judge of the third judicial district. His businesslike, forceful methods won him popular attention, and the Whig-controlled legislature in 1851 elected him to the U.S. Senate. He was reelected to the Senate as a Republican in 1857 and 1863.

In the Senate during the 1850s Wade was an uncompromising foe of the extension of slavery and vigorously opposed the passage of the Kansas-Nebraska Act (1854), which opened the door to the spread of slavery in the West. During the Civil War he took his stand with the Radical Republicans, a congressional group that favoured vigorous prosecution of the war, emancipation of the slaves, and severe punishment for the South. As chairman of the Joint Congressional Committee on the Conduct of the War, Wade played a prominent but controversial role in investigating all aspects of the Union military effort. In 1864, as cosponsor of the Wade-Davis Bill, which declared that reconstruction of the Southern state governments was a legislative rather than an executive concern, he came into direct conflict with Pres. Lincoln.

When Andrew Johnson became president after Lincoln's assassination, Wade at first cooperated with him. But when Johnson made it clear that he favoured a lenient plan of reconstruction, Wade became his caustic critic. Elected president pro tempore of the Senate on March 2, 1867, Wade would have succeeded to the presidency had Johnson been removed by the Senate in the impeachment trial of May 1868. Certain of success, Wade actually began to select his cabinet, and Johnson's acquittal bitterly disappointed him. When the Democratic majority in the Ohio legislature denied him a fourth senatorial term, Wade retired to his Ohio law practice in 1869.

Robert F. Wagner

(b. June 8, 1877, Nastätten, Hesse-Nassau, Ger.—d. May 4, 1953, New York, N.Y.)

Robert Ferdinand Wagner was a Democratic politician who served as a U.S. senator from New York (1927–49). He was a leading architect of the modern welfare state.

Wagner arrived in the United States at the age of eight and settled with his parents in a New York tenement neighborhood. After graduating from the City College of New York in 1898, he went on to obtain a law degree from New York Law School in 1900. Later that year he was admitted to the bar and opened a practice.

But Wagner quickly abandoned law for Democratic Party politics. Starting as a ward heeler for Tammany Hall, he moved up the ranks until in 1904 he won a seat in the New York State Assembly. Four years later he was elected to the state senate. It was in the New York Senate—especially as an outgrowth of his investigation into industrial working conditions in New York—that Wagner first won renown as a leader in formulating social legislation.

From 1919 to 1926 Wagner served as a justice of the New York Supreme Court. In 1926 he ran successfully for the U.S. Senate, a position to which he would be reelected three times. During his first term Wagner introduced legislation to assist labour and the unemployed, but his initiatives were rebuffed.

Not until the advent of the New Deal did Wagner's legislative proposals become law. He helped draft the National Industrial Recovery Act (1933), the Federal Emergency Relief Administration bill (1933), and the law establishing the Civilian Conservation Corps (1933). An ally of Pres. Franklin Roosevelt, Wagner firmly believed in the government's duty to take an active role in promoting the public good.

In 1935 Wagner sponsored two major pieces of New Deal legislation: the Social Security Act (enacted 1936) and the National Labor Relations Act (better known as the Wagner Act). The latter bill established the National Labor Relations Board, guaranteed workers the right to bargain collectively without jeopardizing their jobs, and outlawed a number of unfair labour practices. In 1937 the Wagner-Steagall Act created the United States Housing Authority, an agency to provide loans for low-cost public housing.

As the New Deal lost momentum, Wagner persisted. He presented national health care and anti-lynching legislation, but both measures failed to gain passage. More successful were his drives to expand housing and social security programs, and in 1945 a weakened version of his full-employment bill became law. Wagner resigned from the Senate for health reasons in 1949. He lived out his last years at his home in New York, devoting much of his time to supporting the creation of the new nation of Israel. His son, Robert F. Wagner, Jr. (1910–91), served as mayor of New York from 1954 to 1965.

PAUL DAVID WELLSTONE

(b. July 21, 1944, Washington, D.C. — d. Oct. 25, 2002, near Eveleth, Minn.)

Paul David Wellstone was a Democratic politician who served as a U.S. senator from Minnesota (1991–2002). Often referred to as the most liberal member of the Senate, he was respected as a man of principle who did not forsake his convictions for political expediency.

Wellstone's father was an immigrant Russian Jew, and his mother was the daughter of Russian immigrants. He was educated in political science at the University of North Carolina at Chapel Hill (B.A., 1965; Ph.D., 1969) and then began teaching at Carleton College in Northfield, Minn., where his involvement in political causes sometimes created problems with the school administration. In 1990 he was the candidate of the Democratic-Farmer-Labor Party for the U.S. Senate and, with only a small amount of money, pulled off a surprise victory over the incumbent.

Over the years, Wellstone worked with senators whose views were much more conservative than his, but he consistently championed the interests of the poor, the farmers, and the union workers against large banks, agribusiness, and multinational corporations. Among other things, he advocated increases in the minimum wage, protections for consumers, the strengthening of Social Security, and the expansion of Medicare to include drug benefits, and he pushed for mental health coverage by insurance companies. In 1990–91 Wellstone opposed the Persian Gulf War, and he was one of a small minority of senators who in 2002 voted against giving Pres. George W. Bush authorization for military action against Iraq. In 2001 Wellstone published *The Conscience of a Liberal: Reclaiming the Compassionate Agenda*. Along with his wife, his daughter, three campaign aides, and two pilots, he was killed in a plane crash 11 days before the 2002 election.

Historic Laws and Resolutions

Chapter 4

In its more than 200-year existence the U.S. Congress has passed countless laws and resolutions. The measures discussed in this chapter are notable for the profound impact they achieved (or were intended to achieve) in a number of areas, including civil rights and civil liberties, the powers of the executive, the organization of the federal government, western territorial expansion, foreign relations, the administration of overseas territories, immigration, national security, property law, antitrust law, labour standards and worker's rights, and social welfare.

JUDICIARY ACT OF 1789

The Judiciary Act of 1789 established the organization of the U.S. federal court system, which had been sketched only in general terms in the U.S. Constitution. The act established a three-part judiciary—made up of district courts, circuit courts, and the Supreme Court—and outlined the structure and jurisdiction of each branch.

The act, officially titled "An Act to Establish the Judicial Courts of the United States," was principally authored by senators Oliver Ellsworth and William Paterson and signed into law by Pres. George Washington on Sept. 24, 1789. The law's creators, by essentially all accounts, viewed it as a work in progress. However, although indeed amended throughout the years, the basic outline it provided has remained largely intact.

The act divided the country into districts with one court and one judge in each, along with attorneys responsible for civil and criminal actions in their districts. The act also created the office of attorney general of the United States; the attorney general, a member of the cabinet, is appointed by the president and is head of the Department of Justice.

Circuit courts—which make up the middle tier of the federal court system—were created to serve as principal trial courts, which also exercise limited appellate jurisdiction. A local district judge and two Supreme Court justices preside over the circuit courts.

The act established that the Supreme Court would be composed of one chief justice and five associate justices, and any decision rendered would be final. The act also held that the Supreme Court could settle disputes between states and provided for mandatory Supreme Court review of the final judgments of the highest court of any state in cases "where is drawn in question the validity of a treaty or statute of the United States and the decision is against its validity" or "where is drawn in question the validity of a statute of any state on the ground of its being repugnant to the Constitution, treaties or laws of the United States, and the decision is in favor of its validity." In *Cohens v. Virginia* (1821), the Supreme Court reaffirmed its right under the Judiciary Act to review all state court judgments in cases arising under the federal Constitution or a law of the United States.

FUGITIVE SLAVE ACTS (1793, 1850)

The Fugitive Slave Acts, passed by Congress in 1793 and 1850 (and repealed in 1864), provided for the seizure and return of runaway slaves who escaped from one state into another or into a federal territory. The 1793 law enforced Article IV, Section 2, of the U.S. Constitution in authorizing any federal district judge or circuit court judge, or any state magistrate, to decide finally and without a jury trial the status of an alleged fugitive slave.

The measure met with strong opposition in the Northern states, some of which enacted personal-liberty laws to hamper the execution of the federal law; these laws provided that fugitives who appealed from an original decision against them were entitled to a jury trial. As early as 1810 individual dissatisfaction with the law of 1793 had taken the form of systematic assistance rendered to slaves escaping from the South to New England or Canada—via the Underground Railroad.

The demand from the South for more effective legislation resulted in enactment of a second Fugitive Slave Act in 1850. Under this law fugitives could not testify on their own behalf, nor were they permitted a trial by jury. Heavy penalties were imposed upon federal marshals who refused to enforce the law or from whom a fugitive escaped; penalties were also imposed on individuals who helped slaves to escape. Finally, under the 1850 act, special commissioners were to have concurrent jurisdiction with the U.S. courts in enforcing the law. The severity of the 1850 measure led to abuses and defeated its purpose. The number of abolitionists increased, the operations of the Underground Railroad became more efficient, and new personal-liberty laws were enacted in many Northern states. These state laws were among the grievances officially referred to by South Carolina in December 1860 as justification for its secession from the Union. Attempts to carry into effect the law of 1850 aroused much bitterness and probably had as much to do with inciting sectional hostility as did the controversy over slavery in the territories.

For some time during the American Civil War, the Fugitive Slave Acts were considered to still hold in the case of blacks fleeing from masters in border states that were loyal to the Union government. It was not until June 28, 1864, that the acts were repealed.

ALIEN AND SEDITION ACTS (1798)

The Alien and Sedition Acts were four internal security laws passed by the U.S. Congress in 1798 that restricted aliens and curtailed the press in anticipation of an expected war with France. After the XYZ Affair (1797), in which American ministers negotiating a treaty with France to protect U.S. shipping were asked to pay a bribe to the French foreign minister, war between the two countries appeared inevitable. Federalists, aware that French military successes in Europe had been greatly facilitated by political dissidents in invaded countries, sought to prevent such subversion in the United States and adopted the Alien and Sedition Acts as part of a series of military preparedness measures.

The three alien laws, passed in June and July, were aimed at French and Irish immigrants, who were mostly pro-French. These laws raised the waiting period for naturalization from 5 to 14 years, permitted the detention of subjects of an enemy nation, and authorized the chief executive to expel any alien he considered dangerous. The Sedition Act (July 14) banned the publishing of false or malicious writings against the government and the inciting of opposition to any act of Congress or the president—practices already forbidden in some cases by state libel statutes and the common law but not by federal law. The federal act reduced the oppressiveness of procedures in prosecuting such offenses but provided for federal enforcement.

The acts were mild compared with later wartime security measures in the United States, and they were not unpopular in some places. Jeffersonian Republicans vigorously opposed them, however, as drastic curtailments of liberty in the Virginia and Kentucky Resolutions, which the other state legislatures either ignored or denounced as subversive. Only one alien was deported, but there were 25 prosecutions, resulting in 10 convictions, under the Sedition Act. With the war threat passing and the Republicans winning control of the federal government in 1800, all the Alien and Sedition Acts expired or were repealed during the next two years.

VIRGINIA AND KENTUCKY RESOLUTIONS (1798, 1799)

The Virginia and Kentucky Resolutions were passed by the legislatures of Virginia and Kentucky as a protest against the Federalist Alien and Sedition Acts. The resolutions were written by James Madison and Thomas Jefferson (then vice president in the administration of John Adams), but the role of those statesmen remained unknown to the public for almost 25 years. Generally, the resolutions argued that because the federal government was the outcome of a compact between the states, all powers not specifically granted to the central authority were retained by the individual states or by the people. For this reason, they maintained that the states had the power to pass upon the constitutionality of federal legislation.

The Virginia and Kentucky Resolutions were primarily protests against the limitations on civil liberties contained in the Alien and Sedition Acts rather than expressions of full-blown constitutional theory. Later references to the resolutions as authority for the theories of nullification and secession were inconsistent with the limited goals sought by Jefferson and Madison in drafting their protests.

EMBARGO ACT (1807)

The Embargo Act was designed to resist British and French molestation of U.S. merchant ships carrying, or suspected of carrying, war materials and other cargoes to the European belligerents. At Thomas Jefferson's request the two houses of Congress considered and passed the act quickly in December 1807. All U.S. ports were closed to export shipping in either U.S. or foreign vessels, and restrictions were placed on imports from Great Britain. The act was a hardship on U.S. farmers as well as on New England and New York mercantile and maritime interests, especially after being buttressed by harsh enforcement measures adopted in 1808. Its effects in Europe were not what Jefferson had hoped. French and British dealers in U.S. cotton, for example, were able to raise prices at will while the stock already on hand lasted. The embargo would have had to endure until these inventories were exhausted. Napoleon is said to have justified seizure of U.S. merchant ships on the ground that he was assisting Jefferson in enforcing the act. The Federalist leader Timothy Pickering even alleged that Napoleon himself had inspired the embargo. Confronted by bitter and articulate opposition, Jefferson on March 1, 1809 (two days before the end of his second term), signed the Non-Intercourse Act, permitting U.S. trade with nations other than France and Great Britain.

MISSOURI COMPROMISE (1820)

The Missouri Compromise was a measure worked out between the North and the South and passed by the U.S. Congress that allowed for admission of Missouri as the 24th state in 1821. It marked the beginning of the prolonged sectional conflict over the extension of slavery that led to the American Civil War.

The territory of Missouri first applied for statehood in 1817, and by early 1819 Congress was considering enabling legislation that would authorize Missouri to frame a state constitution. When Rep. James Tallmadge of New York attempted to add an antislavery amendment to that legislation, however, there ensued an ugly and rancorous debate over slavery and the government's right to restrict slavery. The Tallmadge amendment prohibited the further introduction of slaves into Missouri and provided for emancipation of those already there when they reached age 25. The amendment passed the House of Representatives, controlled by the more populous North, but failed in the Senate, which was equally divided between free and slave states. Congress adjourned without resolving the Missouri question.

When it reconvened in December 1819, Congress was faced with a request for statehood from Maine. The Senate passed a bill allowing Maine to enter the Union as a free state and Missouri to be admitted without restrictions on slavery. Sen. Jesse B. Thomas of Illinois then added an amendment that allowed Missouri to become a slave state but banned slavery in the rest of the Louisiana Purchase north of latitude 36°30 . Henry Clay then skillfully led the forces of compromise, and on March 3, 1820, the decisive vote in the House admitted Maine as a free state, Missouri as a slave state, and made free soil all western territories north of Missouri's southern border.

When the Missouri constitutional convention empowered the state legislature to exclude free African Americans and mulattoes, however, a new crisis was brought on. Enough northern congressmen objected to the racial provision that Rep. Henry Clay was called upon to formulate the Second Missouri Compromise. On March 2, 1821, Congress stipulated that Missouri could not gain admission to the Union until it agreed that the exclusionary clause would never be interpreted in such a way as to abridge the privileges and immunities of U.S. citizens. Missouri so agreed and became the 24th state on Aug. 10, 1821; Maine had been admitted the previous March 15.

Although slavery had been a divisive issue in the United States for decades, never before had sectional antagonism been so overt and threatening as it was in the Missouri crisis. Thomas Jefferson described the fear it evoked as "like a firebell in the night." The compromise measures appeared to settle the slavery-extension issue, however, and the sectional conflict did not grow to the point of civil war until after the Missouri Compromise was repealed by the Kansas-Nebraska Act (1854) and was declared unconstitutional in the Dred Scott decision of 1857.

INDIAN REMOVAL ACT (1830)

The Indian Removal Act was the first major legislative departure from the U.S. policy of officially respecting the legal and political rights of the American Indians. The act authorized the president to grant Indian tribes unsettled western prairie land in exchange for their desirable territories within state borders (especially in the Southeast), from which the tribes would be removed. The rapid settlement of land east of the Mississippi River made it clear by the mid-1820s that the white man would not tolerate the presence of even peaceful Indians there. Pres. Andrew Jackson (1829–37) vigorously promoted this new policy, which became incorporated in the Indian Removal Act of 1830. Although the bill provided only for the negotiation with tribes east of the Mississippi on the basis of payment for their lands, trouble arose when the United States resorted to force to gain the Indians' compliance with its demand that they accept the land exchange and move west.

A number of northern tribes were peacefully resettled in western lands considered undesirable for the white man. The problem lay in the Southeast, where members of what were known as the Five Civilized Tribes (Chickasaw, Choctaw, Seminole, Cherokee, and Creek) refused to trade their cultivated farms for the promise of strange land in the Indian Territory with a so-called permanent title to that land. Many of these Indians had homes, representative government, children in missionary schools, and trades other than farming. Some 100,000 tribesmen were forced to march westward under U.S. military coercion in the 1830s. Up to 25 percent of the Indians, many in manacles, perished en route. The trek of the Cherokee in 1838–39 became known as the infamous Trail of Tears. Even more reluctant to leave their native lands were the Florida Indians, who fought resettlement for seven years (1835–42) in the second of the Seminole Wars.

The frontier began to be pushed aggressively westward in the years that followed, upsetting the "guaranteed" titles of the displaced tribes and further reducing their relocated holdings.

MARRIED WOMEN'S PROPERTY ACTS (1839)

The Married Women's Property Acts were a series of statutes that gradually expanded the rights of married women to act as independent agents in legal contexts.

The English common law concept of coverture, the legal subordination of a married woman to her husband, prevailed in the United States until the middle of the 19th century, when the economic realities of life in the New World demanded greater flexibility for women. Because men sometimes could be away from home for months or years at a time, a married woman's ability to maintain a household pivoted upon her freedom to execute contracts. Furthermore, real estate played a somewhat different role in the United States than it did in England, being an important and relatively more abundant trade commodity in the former. Beginning in 1839 in Mississippi, states began to enact legislation overriding the disabilities associated with coverture. They established the rights of women to enjoy the profits of their labour, to control real and personal property, to be parties to lawsuits and contracts, and to execute wills on their own behalf. Most property rights for women emerged in piecemeal fashion over the course of decades, and, because judges frequently interpreted the statutes narrowly, women often had to agitate repeatedly for more expansive and detailed legislation.

KANSAS-NEBRASKA ACT (1854)

The Kansas-Nebraska Act changed U.S. national policy concerning the expansion of slavery into the territories by affirming the concept of popular sovereignty over congressional edict. In 1820 the Missouri Compromise had excluded slavery from that part of the Louisiana Purchase (except Missouri) north of the 36°30′ parallel. The Kansas-Nebraska Act, sponsored by Democratic Sen. Stephen A. Douglas, provided for the territorial organization of Kansas and Nebraska under the principle of popular sovereignty, which had been applied to New Mexico and Utah in the Compromise of 1850.

Written in an effort to arrest the escalating sectional controversy over the extension of slavery, the Kansas-Nebraska Act ironically fanned the flame of national division. It was attacked by free-soil and antislavery factions as a capitulation to the proponents of slavery. Passage of the act was followed by the establishment of the Republican Party as a viable political organization opposed to the expansion of slavery into the territories. In the Kansas Territory a migration of proslavery and antislavery factions, seeking to win control for their respective institutions, resulted in a period of political chaos and bloodshed.

CONFISCATION ACTS (1861–64)

The Confiscation Acts were a series of laws passed by Congress during the American Civil War that were designed to liberate slaves in the seceded states. The first Confiscation Act, passed on Aug. 6, 1861, authorized Union seizure of rebel property, and it stated that all slaves who fought with or worked for the Confederate military services were freed of further obligations to their masters.

Pres. Abraham Lincoln objected to the act on the basis that it might push border states, especially Kentucky and Missouri, into secession in order to protect slavery within their boundaries. He later convinced Congress to pass a resolution providing compensation to states that initiated a system of gradual emancipation, but the border states failed to support this plan. And Lincoln repudiated the position of generals John C. Frémont and David Hunter, who proclaimed that the first Confiscation Act was tantamount to a decree of emancipation.

The second Confiscation Act, passed July 17, 1862, was virtually an emancipation proclamation. It said that slaves of civilian and military Confederate officials "shall be for-ever free," but it was enforceable only in areas of the South occupied by the Union Army. Lincoln was again concerned about the effect of an antislavery measure on the border states and again urged these states to begin gradual com-pensated emancipation.

On March 12, 1863, and July 2, 1864, the federal govern-ment passed additional measures ("Captured and Abandoned Property Acts") that defined property subject to seizure as that owned by absent individuals who sup-ported the South. The Confederate Congress also passed property confiscation acts to apply to Union adherents. But the amount of land actually confiscated during or after the war by either side was not great. Cotton constituted nearly all the Southern nonslave property confiscated.

With the issuance of the Emancipation Proclamation (1863) and passage of the Thirteenth Amendment to the Constitution, however, Southern slaveholders lost an esti-mated $2 billion worth of human property.

HOMESTEAD ACT (1862)

The Homestead Act was designed to provide land in the Midwest, Great Plains, and the West to people willing to settle on and cultivate it. The law granted 160 acres (65 hectares) of public land free of charge (except for a small filing fee) to anyone either 21 years of age or head of a fam-ily, a citizen or person who had filed for citizenship, who had lived on and cultivated the land for at least five years. The law represented the culmination of the Homestead Movement, which had gradually gathered strength since the 1830s.

From the beginning of the republic, the dominant view of the federal government was that public land should be sold to raise revenue. Seeking to change this view came petitions from western farmers asking that land in the public domain be given without charge to settlers willing to work the land.

Up until about 1830 there was little resembling a concerted drive for homestead legislation. But starting in that decade, eastern labourers and reformers of all stripes began to join the farmers in pressing for a homestead act. In 1848 the Free-Soil Party included a plank in the party platform urging distribution of public land to settlers free of charge.

Yet there was always significant opposition to the Homestead Movement. Eastern employers did not want workers to have the option of leaving low-paying jobs for a farm in the West. And eastern landowners feared the threat to land values posed by a huge public domain given away to anyone willing to settle on it. Southern slaveholders saw homesteaders as antislavery advocates, and so they too blocked homestead legislation.

In 1846, Andrew Johnson of Tennessee emerged as one of the leading spokesmen of the Homestead Movement. But bills introduced in Congress in 1846 and 1852 failed. Only when Southern participation in the federal government ceased in 1861 did homestead legislation become a genuine possibility.

The Republican Party, in control of the government, had come out in support of a homestead measure during the 1860 campaign, and on May 20, 1862, Pres. Abraham Lincoln signed the Homestead Act into law. By the turn of the 20th century, more than 80 million acres (32.3 million hectares) had been claimed by a total of 600,000 homestead farmers.

LAND-GRANT COLLEGE ACT (1862)

The Land-Grant College Act, also known as the Morrill Act (named for its sponsor, Vermont Congressman Justin

Smith Morrill), provided grants of land to states to finance the establishment of colleges specializing in "agriculture and the mechanic arts." The act granted each state 30,000 acres (12,140 hectares) for each of its congressional seats. Funds from the sale of the land were used by some states to establish new schools. Other states turned the money over to existing state or private colleges to create schools of agriculture and mechanic arts (known as "A&M" colleges). The military training required in the curriculum of all land-grant schools led to the establishment of the Reserve Officers Training Corps, an educational program for future army, navy, and air force officers. The second Morrill Act (1890) initiated regular appropriations to support land-grant colleges, which came to include 17 predominantly African American colleges and 30 American Indian colleges.

PACIFIC RAILWAY ACTS (1862, 1864)

The Pacific Railway Acts provided federal subsidies in land and loans for the construction of a transcontinental railroad across the United States.

The first Pacific Railway Act (July 1, 1862) authorized the building of the railroad and granted rights of way to the Union Pacific to build westward from Omaha, Neb., and to the Central Pacific to build eastward from Sacramento, Calif. The act also granted 10 alternate sections of public domain land per mile on both sides of the railway, and it provided loan bonds for each mile of track laid. The loans were repayable in 30 years, and the dollars per mile escalated in accord with the difficulty of the terrain.

Two years later, the railroads were still hampered in their quest for sufficient capital for the vast construction project. Congress obliged with the second Pacific Railway Act (July 2, 1864), which doubled the size of the land grants and allowed the railroads to sell their own bonds. After the transcontinental railroad was completed in 1869, congressional investigations revealed that some railroad entrepreneurs had illegally profiteered from the two Pacific Railway Acts.

TENURE OF OFFICE ACT (1867)

The Tenure of Office Act, passed in the post–Civil War period of U.S. history, was a law forbidding the president to remove civil officers without senatorial consent. It was passed over Pres. Andrew Johnson's veto by Radical Republicans in Congress in their struggle to wrest control of Reconstruction from Johnson. Vigorously opposing Johson's conciliatory policy toward the defeated South, the Radicals gained enough strength in the congressional elections of 1866 to impose their military and civil program upon the defeated territory in the spring of 1867. At the same time, to further ensure the success of Radical Reconstruction, Congress passed the Tenure of Office Act. The act was often taken to have been aimed specifically at preventing Pres. Johnson from removing from office Secretary of War Edwin Stanton, the Radicals' ally in the cabinet, although during congressional debate on the bill some Republicans declared that cabinet members would be exempt. Still, the president's attempt to thwart this law by dismissing Stanton led directly to his impeachment the following year. The Tenure of Office Act was repealed partly in 1869 and entirely in 1887 and was also declared by the U.S. Supreme Court in 1926 to have been unconstitutional.

FORCE ACTS (1871–75)

The Force Acts were a series of four laws passed by Republican Reconstruction supporters in Congress between May 31, 1870, and March 1, 1875, to protect the constitutional rights guaranteed to African Americans by the Fourteenth and Fifteenth Amendments.

The major provisions of the acts authorized federal authorities to enforce penalties upon anyone interfering with the registration, voting, officeholding, or jury service of blacks; provided for federal election supervisors; and empowered the president to use military forces to make summary arrests. Under the act of April 20, 1871, nine South Carolina counties were placed under martial law in October 1871. This act and earlier statutes resulted in more than 5,000 indictments and 1,250 convictions throughout the South. In subsequent Supreme Court decisions, various sections of the acts were declared unconstitutional.

COMSTOCK ACT (1873)

The Comstock Act was a federal statute passed by the U.S. Congress as an "Act of the Suppression of Trade in, and Circulation of, Obscene Literature and Articles of Immoral Use."

Named for Anthony Comstock, a zealous crusader against what he considered to be obscenity, the act criminalized publication, distribution, and possession of information about or devices or medications for "unlawful" abortion or contraception. Individuals convicted of violating the Comstock Act could receive up to five years of imprisonment with hard labour and a fine of up to $2,000. The act also banned distribution through the mail and import of materials from abroad, with provisions for even stronger penalties and fines.

Vestiges of the act endured as the law of the land into the 1990s. In 1971 Congress removed the language concerning contraception, and federal courts until *Roe* v. *Wade* (1973) ruled that it applied only to "unlawful" abortions. After *Roe,* laws criminalizing transportation of information about abortion remained on the books, and, although they have not been enforced, they have been expanded to ban distribution of abortion-related information on the Internet. Rep. Barney Frank of Massachusetts introduced legislation in 1997 to repeal abortion-related elements of federal obscenity law rooted in the Comstock Act.

RESUMPTION ACT (1875)

The Resumption Act was the culmination of the struggle between "soft money" forces, who advocated continued use of Civil War greenbacks, and their "hard money" opponents, who wished to redeem the paper money and resume a specie currency.

By the end of the Civil War, more than $430 million in greenbacks were in circulation, made legal tender by congressional mandate. After the Supreme Court sanctioned the constitutionality of the greenbacks as legal tender, hard money advocates in Congress pushed for early resumption of specie payments and retirement of the paper money.

On Jan. 14, 1875, Congress passed the Resumption Act, which called for the secretary of the Treasury to redeem legal-tender notes in specie beginning Jan. 1, 1879. The bill also called for reducing the greenbacks in circulation to $300 million and for replacing the fractional paper currency ("shinplasters") with silver coins as rapidly as possible.

Members of the new Greenback Party were bitterly opposed to the Resumption Act, and in 1878 they succeeded in raising the amount of paper money allowed in circulation. Specie resumption proceeded on schedule, however, and Treasury Secretary John Sherman accumulated enough gold to meet the expected demand. When the public realized that the paper money was "good as gold," there was no rush to redeem, and greenbacks continued as the accepted currency.

PRIMARY DOCUMENT: THE CHINESE EXCLUSION ACT

Whereas, in the opinion of the government of the United States the coming of Chinese laborers to this country endangers the good order of certain localities within the territory thereof; therefore,

Be it enacted by the Senate and House of Representatives of the United States of America in Congress assembled, that from and after the expiration of ninety days next after the passage of this act, and until the expiration of ten years next after the passage of this act, the coming of Chinese laborers to the United States be, and the same is hereby, suspended; and during such suspension it shall not be lawful for any Chinese laborer to come, or, having so come after the expiration of said ninety days, to remain within the United States.

Section 2. That the master of any vessel who shall knowingly bring within the United States on such vessel, and land or permit to be landed, any Chinese laborer from any foreign port or place shall be deemed guilty of a misdemeanor, and on conviction thereof shall be punished by a fine of not more than $500 for each and every such Chinese laborer so brought, and may be also imprisoned for a term not exceeding one year. ...

Section 8. That the master of any vessel arriving in the United States from any foreign port or place shall ... deliver and report to the collector of customs of the district in which such vessels shall have arrived a separate list of all Chinese passengers taken on board his vessel at any foreign port. ... Any willful refusal or neglect of any such master to comply with the provisions of this section shall incur the same penalties and forfeiture as are provided for a refusal or neglect to report and deliver a manifest of the cargo...

Section 11. That any person who shall knowingly bring into or cause to be brought into the United States by land, or who shall knowingly aid or abet the same, or aid or abet the landing in the United States from any vessel of any Chinese person not lawfully entitled to enter the United States, shall be deemed guilty of a misdemeanor, and shall, on conviction thereof, be fined in a sum not exceeding $1,000, and imprisoned for a term not exceeding one year.

Section 12. That no Chinese person shall be permitted to enter the United States by land without producing to the proper officer of customs the certificate in this act required of Chinese persons seeking to land from a vessel. And any Chinese person found unlawfully within the United States shall be caused to be removed therefrom to the country from whence he came, by direction of the President of the United States, and at the cost of the United States, after being brought before some justice, judge, or commissioner of a court of the United States and found to be one not lawfully entitled to be or remain in the United States. ...

Section 14. That hereafter no state court or court of the United States shall admit Chinese to citizenship; and all laws in conflict with this act are hereby repealed.

CHINESE EXCLUSION ACT (1882)

The Chinese Exclusion Act was a law that limited Chinese labour immigration to the United States. By the time of its passage approximately 375,000 Chinese had immigrated to the country, nearly all on the West Coast. The Burlingame Treaty of 1868 provided for unlimited immigration, but denied the Chinese the right of citizenship. During the early 1870s an economic depression and the massing of cheap Chinese labour in West Coast cities gave rise to fierce economic competition with American workers, whose demand for higher wages put them at a disadvantage. Fearing civil disorder, Congress in 1879 passed an act restricting Chinese immigration, but Pres. Rutherford B. Hayes vetoed it on the grounds that it violated the Burlingame treaty. In 1880 the treaty was revised to limit Chinese labour immigration, and on May 6, 1882, Congress passed the Chinese Exclusion Act.

PENDLETON CIVIL SERVICE ACT (1883)

The Pendleton Civil Service Act was a landmark piece of legislation establishing the tradition and mechanism of permanent federal employment based on merit rather than on political party affiliation (the spoils system).

Widespread public demand for civil service reform was stirred after the Civil War by mounting incompetence, graft, corruption, and theft in federal departments and agencies. After Pres. James A. Garfield was assassi-

nated in 1881 by a disappointed office seeker, civil service reform became a leading issue in the midterm elections of 1882. In January 1883, Congress passed a comprehensive civil service bill sponsored by Sen. George H. Pendleton of Ohio, providing for the open selection of government employees—to be administered by a Civil Service Commission—and guaranteeing the right of citizens to compete for federal appointment without regard to politics, religion, race, or national origin. Only about 10 percent of the positions in the federal government were covered by the new law, but nearly

Sen. George H. Pendleton of Ohio. Brady-Handy Photograph Collection/Library of Congress, Washington, D.C. (neg. no. LC-DIG-cwpbh-02930)

every president after Chester A. Arthur, who signed the bill into law, broadened its scope. By 1980 more than 90 percent of federal employees were protected by the act.

DAWES GENERAL ALLOTMENT ACT (1887)

The Dawes General Allotment Act provided for the distribution of Indian reservation land among individual tribesmen, with the aim of creating responsible farmers in the white man's image. It was sponsored in several sessions of Congress by Sen. Henry L. Dawes of Massachusetts and finally was enacted in February 1887. Under its terms, the president determined the suitability of the recipients and issued the grants, usually by a formula of 160 acres (65 hectares) to each head of household and 80 acres (32 hectares) to each unmarried adult, with the stipulation that no grantee could alienate his land for 25 years. The Indians who thus received land became U.S. citizens, subject to federal, state, and local laws. The original supporters of the act were genuinely interested in the welfare of the Indians, but there were not enough votes in Congress to pass it until it was amended to provide that any land remaining after the allotment to the Indians would be available for public

Henry Laurens Dawes, who sponsored the Dawes General Allotment Act. Portraits of Henry Laurens Dawes, Washington, D.C. (neg. no. LC-DIG-ppmsca-07783)

sale. The combined influence of friends of the Indians and land speculators assured passage of the act.

Under the Dawes Act, Indian life deteriorated in a manner not anticipated by its sponsors. The social structure of the tribe was weakened; many nomadic Indians were unable to adjust to an agricultural existence; others were swindled out of their property; and life on the reservation came to be characterized by disease, filth, poverty, and despondency. The act also provided that any "surplus" land be made available to whites, who by 1932 had acquired two-thirds of the 138 million acres (55.8 million hectares) the Indians had held in 1887.

INTERSTATE COMMERCE ACT (1887)

The Interstate Commerce Act inaugurated the federal policy of regulation and control of business enterprises. Public indignation over railroad policies was in part responsible for the act, but equally necessary for its passage in the Senate was the acquiescence of railroad owners and other businessmen, who saw federal regulation as the only way to stop ruinous competition between the roads. The act created a five-man commission empowered to resolve problems of transport rate discrimination, rate rebates, use of terminal facilities, and shortage of freight cars. Weaknesses of the act, coupled with debilitating rulings by the Supreme Court, made subsequent legislation necessary to strengthen the commission and enlarge its scope of activities.

SHERMAN ANTITRUST ACT (1890)

The Sherman Antitrust Act was the first legislation enacted by the U.S. Congress to curb concentrations of power that interfere with trade and reduce economic competition. It was named for Sen. John Sherman of Ohio, who was an expert on the regulation of commerce.

One of the act's main provisions outlawed all combinations that restrain trade between states or with foreign nations. This prohibition applied not only to formal cartels but also to any agreement to fix prices, limit industrial output, share markets, or exclude competition. A second key provision made illegal all attempts to monopolize any part of trade or commerce in the United States. These two provisions, which comprise the heart of the Sherman Act, were enforceable by the Department of Justice through litigation in the federal courts. Firms found in violation of the act could be ordered dissolved by the courts, and injunctions to prohibit illegal practices could be issued. Violations were punishable by fines and imprisonment. In addition, private parties injured by violations were permitted to sue for triple the amount of damages done them.

For more than a decade after its passage, the Sherman Act was invoked only rarely against industrial monopolies, and then not successfully, chiefly because of narrow judicial interpretations of what constitutes trade or commerce among states. Its only effective use was against trade unions, which were held by the courts to be illegal combinations. The first vigorous enforcement of the Sherman Act occurred during the administration of Pres. Theodore Roosevelt (1901–09). In 1914 Congress passed two legislative measures that provided support for the Sherman Act. One of these was the Clayton Antitrust Act, which elaborated on the general provisions of the Sherman Act and specified many illegal practices that either contributed to or resulted from monopolization. The other measure created the Federal Trade Commission, providing the government with an agency that had the power to investigate possible violations of antitrust legislation and issue orders forbidding unfair competition practices.

In 1920, however, the Supreme Court applied the so-called "rule of reason" interpretation of the Sherman Act, which explains that not every contract or combination restraining trade is unlawful. Only "unreasonable" restraint of trade through acquisitions, mergers, exclusionary tactics, and predatory pricing constitute a violation of the Sherman Act. This interpretation allowed large firms considerably more latitude. But in a case involving the Aluminum Company of America (1945), the court reversed its stance, declaring that the size and structure of a corporation were sufficient grounds for antitrust action. Since that ruling, the prohibition against monopoly has been periodically enforced, involving in some cases the dismemberment of the offending firm. One notable example late in the 20th century was the 1984 breakup of the American Telephone & Telegraph Company, which left the parent company, AT&T, as a provider of long-distance service while seven regional "Baby Bell" companies provided local telephone service. Many of the original Baby Bell companies have since merged. One of the largest antitrust suits since that time was brought against the Microsoft Corporation. A decision in 1999 found the company had attempted to create a monopoly position in Internet browser software, but a court-ordered breakup of Microsoft was overturned by an appeals court in 2001.

CLAYTON ANTITRUST ACT (1914)

The Clayton Antitrust Act was a law enacted by the U.S. Congress to clarify and strengthen the Sherman Antitrust Act (1890). The vague language of the latter had provided large corporations with numerous loopholes, enabling them to engage in certain restrictive business arrangements that, though not illegal per se, resulted in concentrations that had an adverse effect on competition. Thus, despite the trust-busting activities of the administrations of presidents Theodore Roosevelt and William Howard Taft under the Sherman Act, it appeared to a congressional committee in 1913 that big business had continued to grow bigger and that the control of money and credit in the country was such that a few men had the power to plunge the nation into a financial panic. When Pres. Woodrow Wilson asked for a drastic revision of existing antitrust legislation, Congress responded by passing the Clayton measure.

Whereas the Sherman Act only declared monopoly illegal, the Clayton Act defined as illegal certain business practices that are conducive to the formation of monopolies or that result from them. For example, specific forms of holding companies and interlocking directorates were forbidden, as were discriminatory freight (shipping) agreements and the distribution of sales territories among so-called natural competitors. Two sections of the Clayton Act were later amended by the Robinson-Patman Act (1936) and the Celler-Kefauver Act (1950) to fortify its provisions. The Robinson-Patman amendment made more enforceable Section 2, which relates to price and other forms of discrimination among customers. The Celler-Kefauver Act strengthened Section 7, prohibiting one firm from securing either the stocks or the physical assets (i.e., plant and equipment) of another firm when the acquisition would reduce competition; it also extended the coverage of antitrust laws to all forms of mergers whenever the effect would substantially lessen competition and tend to create a monopoly. Earlier

legislative measures had simply restricted horizontal
mergers—those involving firms that produce the same
type of goods. In contrast, the Celler-Kefauver Act went
further by restricting even mergers of companies in different industries (i.e., conglomerate mergers). The
Clayton Act and other antitrust and consumer protection
regulations are enforced by the Federal Trade Commission.

JONES ACT (1916)

In the Jones Act, formally known as the Philippine Autonomy
Act, the U.S. government announced its intention to
"withdraw their sovereignty over the Philippine Islands as
soon as a stable government can be established therein."
The U.S. had acquired the Philippines in 1898 as a result of
the Spanish-American War; and from 1901 legislative
power in the islands had been exercised through a Philippine
Commission effectively dominated by Americans. One of
the most significant sections of the Jones Act replaced the
commission with an elective senate and, with minimum
property qualifications, extended the franchise to all liter-
ate Filipino males. The law also incorporated a bill of rights.

American sovereignty was retained by provisions of
the act reserving to the governor general power to veto
any measure passed by the new Philippine legislature. The
liberal governor general Francis B. Harrison rarely used
this power and moved rapidly to appoint Filipinos in place
of Americans in the civil service. By the end of Harrison's
term in 1921, Filipinos had taken charge of the internal
affairs of the islands.

The Jones Act remained in force as a de facto constitution for the Philippines until it was superseded by the
Tydings-McDuffie Act of 1934. Its promise of eventual
absolute independence set the course for future American
policy in the islands.

SMOOT-HAWLEY TARIFF ACT (1930)

The Smoot-Hawley Tariff Act raised import duties to protect American businesses and farmers, adding considerable strain to the international economic climate of the Great Depression. The act took its name from its chief sponsors, Sen. Reed Smoot of Utah, chairman of the Senate Finance Committee, and Rep. Willis Hawley of Oregon, chairman of the House Ways and Means Committee. It was the last legislation under which the U.S. Congress set actual tariff rates.

The Smoot-Hawley Tariff Act raised the United States' already high tariff rates. In 1922 Congress had enacted the Fordney-McCumber Act, which was among the most punitive protectionist tariffs passed in the country's history, raising the average import tax to some 40 percent. The Fordney-McCumber tariff prompted retaliation from European governments but did little to dampen U.S. prosperity. Throughout the 1920s, however, as European farmers recovered from World War I and their American counterparts faced intense competition and declining prices because of overproduction, U.S. agricultural interests lobbied the federal government for protection against agricultural imports. In his 1928 campaign for the presidency, Republican candidate Herbert Hoover promised to increase tariffs on agricultural goods, but after he took office lobbyists from other economic sectors encouraged him to support a broader increase. Although an increase in tariffs was supported by most Republicans, an effort to raise import duties failed in 1929, largely because of opposition from centrist Republicans in the U.S. Senate. In response to the stock market crash of 1929, however, protectionism gained strength, and, though the tariff legislation subsequently passed only by a narrow margin (44–42) in the Senate, it passed easily in the House of

Representatives. Despite a petition from more than 1,000 economists urging him to veto the legislation, President Hoover signed the bill into law on June 17, 1930.

Smoot-Hawley contributed to the early loss of confidence on Wall Street and signaled U.S. isolationism. By raising the average tariff by some 20 percent, it also prompted retaliation from foreign governments, and many overseas banks began to fail. (Because the legislation set both specific and ad valorem tariff rates [i.e., rates based on the value of the product], determining the precise percentage increase in tariff levels is difficult and a subject of debate among economists.) Within two years some two dozen countries adopted similar "beggar-thy-neighbour" duties, making worse an already beleaguered world economy and reducing global trade. U.S. imports from and exports to Europe fell by some two-thirds between 1929 and 1932, while overall global trade declined by similar levels in the four years that the legislation was in effect.

In 1934 Pres. Franklin D. Roosevelt signed the Reciprocal Trade Agreements Act, reducing tariff levels and promoting trade liberalization and cooperation with foreign governments. Some observers have argued that by deepening the Great Depression the tariff may have contributed to the rise of political extremism, enabling leaders such as Adolf Hitler to improve their political strength and gain power.

NORRIS–LA GUARDIA ACT (1932)

The Norris–La Guardia Act removed certain legal and judicial barriers against the activities of organized labour in the United States. The act declared that the members of labour unions should have "full freedom of association" undisturbed by employers. The act also barred the federal courts from issuing injunctions to prevent strikes, picketing, or boycotts by labour groups and prohibited "yellow-dog" contracts. Previously, employers could, as a condition of employment, require employees to sign an agreement pledging that they would not join a union. If the workers did join a union after signing such a document, they were fired.

The Norris–La Guardia Act was cosponsored in Congress by George Norris and Fiorello La Guardia. It was passed during the depths of the Great Depression, when public opinion had shifted both against employers who sought to prevent workers from joining unions and against judges who used the power of the courts to limit normal union activities. The act was a precursor to the more sweeping Wagner Act of 1935.

HARE-HAWES-CUTTING ACT (1933)

The Hare-Hawes-Cutting Act was the first law to set a specific date for Philippine independence from the United States. It was passed by Congress as a result of pressure from two sources: American farmers, who, during the Great Depression, feared competition from Filipino sugar and coconut oils; and Filipino leaders, who were eager to run their own government.

The bill was passed by the Senate in December 1932 but was vetoed by Pres. Herbert Hoover. To Hoover's surprise, Congress promptly overrode his veto, and the bill became law on Jan. 17, 1933. The act, however, required approval by the Philippine Senate, and this was not forthcoming. Filipino political leader Manuel Quezon led a campaign against the bill because of provisions in it that allowed the indefinite retention of U.S. military bases in the islands. The Tydings-McDuffie Act, substantially similar to the rejected measure but incorporating minor changes, was accepted by the Philippine Senate in 1934.

INDIAN REORGANIZATION ACT (1934)

The Indian Reorganization Act was a measure enacted by the U.S. Congress aimed at decreasing federal control of American Indian affairs and increasing Indian self-government and responsibility. In gratitude for the Indians' services to the country in World War I, Congress in 1924 authorized the Meriam Survey of the state of life on the reservations. The shocking conditions under the regimen established by the Dawes General Allotment Act (1887), as detailed in the Meriam report of 1928, spurred demands for reform.

Many of the Meriam report's recommendations for reform were incorporated in the Indian Reorganization Act. The act curtailed the future allotment of tribal communal lands to individuals and provided for the return of surplus lands to the tribes rather than to homesteaders. It also encouraged written constitutions and charters giving Indians the power to manage their internal affairs. Finally, funds were authorized for the establishment of a revolving credit program for tribal land purchases, for educational assistance, and for aiding tribal organization.

About 160 tribes or villages adopted written constitutions under the act's provisions. Through the revolving credit fund, many Indians improved their economic position. With the funds for purchase of land, millions of additional acres were added to the reservations. Greatly improved staffs and services were provided in health and education, with more than half of all Indian children in public school by 1950. The act awakened a wider interest in civic affairs, and Indians began asking for the franchise, which they had been technically granted in 1924.

The act's basic aims were reinforced in the 1960s and 1970s by the further transfer of administrative responsibility for reservation services to the Indians themselves, who continued to depend on the federal government to finance those services.

TYDINGS-MCDUFFIE ACT (1934)

The Tydings-McDuffie Act was a statute that provided for Philippine independence, to take effect on July 4, 1946, after a 10-year transitional period of Commonwealth government. The bill was signed by Pres. Franklin D. Roosevelt on March 24, 1934, and was sent to the Philippine Senate for approval. Although that body had previously rejected the similar Hare-Hawes-Cutting Act, it approved the Tydings-McDuffie Act on May 1.

Following the terms of the independence act, Filipinos elected delegates for a constitutional convention on July 10, and Roosevelt approved the Philippine constitution on March 23, 1935. The Commonwealth government, under the presidency of Manuel Quezon, was inaugurated in November of that year. For the next 10 years the Philippines remained U.S. territory. Foreign affairs, defense, and monetary matters remained under U.S. jurisdiction, but all other internal matters were in the hands of Filipinos. During the Commonwealth period, duties were to be imposed on a graduated scale, but the trade provisions were subsequently amended in 1939 in favour of the Philippines.

SOCIAL SECURITY ACT (1935)

The Social Security Act established a permanent national old-age pension system through employer and employee contributions. The system was later extended to include dependents, the disabled, and other groups. Responding to the economic impact of the Great Depression, 5 million old people in the early 1930s joined nationwide Townsend clubs, promoted by Francis E. Townsend to support his program demanding a $200 monthly pension for everyone over the age of 60. In 1934 Pres. Franklin D. Roosevelt set up a committee on economic security to consider the matter. After studying its recommendations, Congress in 1935 enacted the Social Security Act, providing old-age benefits to be financed by a payroll tax on employers and employees. Railroad employees were covered separately under the Railroad Retirement Act of 1934. The Social Security Act was periodically amended, expanding the types of coverage, bringing progressively more workers into the system, and adjusting both taxes and benefits in an attempt to keep pace with inflation.

WAGNER ACT (1935)

The Wagner Act, officially known as the National Labor Relations Act, was the single most important piece of U.S. labour legislation in the 20th century. It was enacted to eliminate employers' interference with the autonomous organization of workers into unions.

Sponsored by Sen. Robert F. Wagner, a Democrat from New York, the Wagner Act established the federal government as the regulator and ultimate arbiter of labour relations. It set up a permanent, three-member National Labor Relations Board (NLRB) with the power to protect the rights of most workers (with the notable exception of agricultural and domestic labourers) to organize unions of their own choosing and to encourage collective bargaining. The act prohibited employers from engaging in such unfair labour practices as setting up a company union and firing or otherwise discriminating against workers who organized or joined unions. Under the Wagner Act, the NLRB was given the power to order elections whereby workers could choose which union they wanted to represent them. The act prohibited employers from refusing to bargain with any such union that had been certified by the NLRB as being the choice of a majority of employees.

FAIR LABOR STANDARDS ACT (1938)

The Fair Labor Standards Act was the first act in the United States prescribing nationwide compulsory federal regulation of wages and hours. It was sponsored by Sen. Robert F. Wagner of New York and signed on June 14, 1938, effective October 24. The law, applying to all industries engaged in interstate commerce, established a minimum wage of 25 cents per hour for the first year, to be increased to 40 cents within seven years. No worker was obliged to work, without compensation at overtime rates, more than 44 hours a week during the first year, 42 the second year, and 40 thereafter.

HATCH ACT (1939)

The Hatch Act was a measure enacted by the U.S. Congress aimed at eliminating corrupt practices in national elections. It was sponsored by Sen. Carl Hatch of New Mexico following disclosures that officials of the Works Progress Administration were using their positions to win votes for the Democratic Party. The Hatch Act forbade intimidation or bribery of voters and restricted political-campaign activities by federal employees. As amended in 1940, it also severely limited contributions by individuals to political campaigns and spending by campaign committees.

SMITH ACT (1940)

The Smith Act, formally known as the Alien Registration Act, made it a criminal offense to advocate violent overthrow of the government or to organize or be a member of any group or society devoted to such advocacy. After World War II this statute was made the basis of a series of prosecutions against leaders of the Communist Party and the Socialist Workers Party. The conviction of the principal officers was sustained, and the constitutionality of the "advocacy" provision upheld, by the Supreme Court in *Dennis* v. *United States* (1951); but in a later case (*Yates* v. *United States,* 1957) the court offset this position somewhat by a strict reading of the language of the Smith Act, construing "advocacy" to mean only urging that includes incitement to unlawful action.

BELL TRADE ACT (1946)

The Bell Trade Act was a law that specified the economic conditions governing the emergence of the Republic of the Philippines from U.S. rule. The act included controversial provisions that tied the Philippine economy to that of the United States.

When the Philippines became independent on July 4, 1946, its economy had been thoroughly devastated by World War II. Payment of war damage claims by the U.S. government and an influx of capital were both desperately needed. The Bell Act set quotas on Philippine exports to the U.S., pegged the Philippine peso to the U.S. dollar at a rate of 2:1, and provided for free trade between the two countries for 8 years, to be followed by gradual application of tariffs for the next 20 years. Many Filipinos objected to the so-called Parity Amendment, which required an amendment to the Philippine constitution allowing U.S. citizens equal rights with Filipinos in the exploitation of natural resources and operation of public utilities. Nonetheless, some powerful Filipinos involved in these negotiations stood to benefit from the arrangement.

A strong incentive for Philippine acquiescence was the fact that American payment of $800 million in war damage claims was made contingent upon Filipino ratification of the Bell Act. The act remained extremely unpopular in the Philippines. It was later superseded by an agreement more favourable to Filipino interests, the Laurel-Langley Agreement, which took effect in 1956.

TAFT-HARTLEY ACT (1947)

The Taft-Hartley Act—enacted by Congress over the veto of Pres. Harry S. Truman—amended much of the pro-union Wagner Act of 1935. A variety of factors, including the fear of communist infiltration of labour unions, the tremendous growth in both membership and power of unions, and a series of large-scale strikes, contributed to an anti-union climate in the United States after World War II. Republican majorities in both houses of Congress—the first since 1930—sought to remedy the union abuses seen as permitted under the Wagner Act.

Sponsored by Sen. Robert A. Taft of Ohio and Rep. Fred A. Hartley, Jr. of New Jersey, the act, while preserving the rights of labour to organize and to bargain collectively, guaranteed employees the right not to join unions (outlawing the closed shop); permitted union shops only where state law allowed and where a majority of workers voted for them; required unions to give 60 days' advance notification of a strike; authorized 80-day federal injunctions when a strike threatened to imperil national health or safety; narrowed the definition of unfair labour practices; specified unfair union practices; restricted union political contributions; and required union officers to deny under oath any communist affiliations.

The Landrum-Griffin Act of 1959 set further union restrictions, barring secondary boycotts and limiting the right to picket.

WOMEN'S ARMED SERVICES INTEGRATION ACT (1948)

The Women's Armed Services Integration Act was a law that permitted women to serve as full members of the U.S. armed forces.

During World War I many women had enlisted as volunteers in the U.S. military services; they usually served in clerical roles. When the war ended they were released from their duties. The same was true during World War II, when an even greater number of women volunteers served in the armed forces. Although the U.S. Congress in 1943 had given the Women's Army Corps (WAC) full army status during wartime, the WAC law was scheduled to expire on June 30, 1948. In anticipation of this event the leaders of the U.S. Army in 1946 requested that the WACs be made a permanent part of their personnel. Following two years of legislative debate, the bill was passed by Congress in the spring of 1948. Signed into law by Pres. Harry S. Truman on June 12, 1948, as the Women's Armed Services Integration Act, it enabled women to serve as permanent, regular members of not only the army but also the navy, marine corps, and the recently formed air force. The law limited the number of women who could serve in the military to 2 percent of the total forces in each branch.

LANDRUM-GRIFFIN ACT (1959)

The Landrum-Griffin Act was a legislative response to widespread publicity about corruption and autocratic methods in certain American labour unions during the 1950s. Even though the AFL-CIO (American Federation of Labor–Congress of Industrial Organizations) expelled three of the worst offenders (the Teamsters, the Bakery and Confectionery Workers, and the Laundry Workers Union), Pres. Dwight D. Eisenhower and the McClellan Committee, which had investigated ties between labour and organized crime, insisted on a law to put internal union affairs on a more honest and democratic basis.

Thus, the Landrum-Griffin Act instituted federal penalties for labour officials who misused union funds, who had been found guilty of specific crimes, or who had violently prevented union members from exercising their legal rights. The act contained other provisions that strengthened parts of the Taft-Hartley Act, which was detested by nearly all elements of organized labour. These provisions included a strict ban on secondary boycotts (union efforts to stop one employer from dealing with another employer who is being struck or boycotted) and greater freedom for individual states to set the terms of labour relations within their borders. The latter provision hampered labour organizing in the South, the least unionized region in the United States.

PEACE CORPS ACT (1961)

The Peace Corps Act created the Peace Corps, a government agency of volunteers. The act was passed at the

A Peace Corps volunteer teaching children in Paraguay. Courtesy of
Peace Corps

initiation of Pres. John F. Kennedy. Its first director was
Kennedy's brother-in-law R. Sargent Shriver.

The purpose of the Peace Corps was to assist other
countries in their development efforts by providing skilled
workers in the fields of education, agriculture, health,
trade, technology, and community development. Peace
Corps volunteers were assigned to specific projects on the
basis of their skills, education, and experience. Once
abroad, the volunteer was expected to function for two
years as a good neighbour in the host country, to speak its
language, and to live on a level comparable to that of the
volunteer's counterparts there.

The Peace Corps grew from 900 volunteers serving 16
countries in 1961 to a peak of 15,556 volunteers in 52 countries in 1966. By 1989 the budget had reduced the number
of volunteers to 5,100, but some increases occurred thereafter, the number of countries served having risen to about
90. The organization's global reach extended in the early

U.S. Pres. John F. Kennedy (left) and R. Sargent Shriver addressing journalists and Peace Corps volunteers at the White House, 1961. Courtesy of the Peace Corps

1990s to include eastern European countries such as Hungary and Poland in 1990 and extended to the former Soviet Union in 1992, adding China in 1993 and South Africa in 1997. By the early 21st century, 136 countries had hosted more than 170,000 Peace Corps volunteers through four decades of service.

CIVIL RIGHTS ACT (1964)

The Civil Rights Act was a comprehensive set of legislation intended to end discrimination based on race, colour, religion, or national origin. It is often called the most important U.S. law on civil rights since Reconstruction (1865–77). Title I of the act guaranteed equal voting rights by removing registration requirements and procedures biased against minorities and the underprivileged. Title II prohibited segregation or discrimination in places of public accommodation involved in interstate commerce. Title VII banned discrimination by trade unions, schools, or employers involved in interstate commerce or doing business with the federal government. The latter section also applied to discrimination on the basis of sex and established a government agency, the Equal Employment Opportunity Commission (EEOC), to enforce these provisions. The act also called for the desegregation of public schools (Title IV), broadened the duties of the Civil Rights Commission (Title V), and assured nondiscrimination in the distribution of funds under federally assisted programs (Title VI).

The Civil Rights Act was a highly controversial issue in the United States as soon as it was proposed by Pres. John F. Kennedy in 1963. Although Kennedy was unable to secure passage of the bill in Congress, a stronger version was eventually passed at the urging of his successor, Pres. Lyndon B. Johnson, who signed the bill into law on July 2, 1964, following one of the longest debates in Senate history. White groups opposed to integration with African Americans responded to the act with a significant backlash that took the form of protests, increased support for pro-segregation candidates for public office, and some racial violence. The constitutionality of the act was immediately challenged and was upheld by the Supreme Court in the test case *Heart of Atlanta Motel* v. *U.S.* (1964). The act gave federal law enforcement agencies the power to prevent racial discrimination in employment, voting, and the use of public facilities.

GULF OF TONKIN RESOLUTION (1964)

The Gulf of Tonkin Resolution was put before the U.S. Congress by Pres. Lyndon Johnson, assertedly in reaction to two allegedly unprovoked attacks by North Vietnamese torpedo boats on the destroyers *Maddox* and *C. Turner Joy* of the U.S. Seventh Fleet in the Gulf of Tonkin on August 2 and August 4, 1964 respectively. Its stated purpose was to approve and support the determination of the president, as commander in chief, in taking all necessary measures to repel any armed attack against the forces of the United States and to prevent further aggression. It also declared that the maintenance of international peace and security in Southeast Asia was vital to American interests and to world peace.

Both houses of Congress passed the resolution on August 7, the House of Representatives by 414 votes to nil, and the Senate by a vote of 88 to 2. The resolution served as the principal constitutional authorization for the subsequent vast escalation of the United States' military involvement in the Vietnam War. Several years later, as the American public became increasingly disillusioned with the Vietnam War, many congressmen came to see the resolution as giving the president a blanket power to wage war, and the resolution was repealed in 1970.

In 1995 Vo Nguyen Giap, who had been North Vietnam's military commander during the Vietnam War, acknowledged the August 2 attack on the *Maddox* but denied that the Vietnamese had launched another attack on August 4, as the Johnson administration had claimed at the time.

VOTING RIGHTS ACT (1965)

The Voting Rights Act aimed to overcome legal barriers at the state and local levels that prevented African Americans from exercising their right to vote under the Fifteenth Amendment (1870) to the Constitution of the United States. The act significantly widened the franchise and is considered among the most far-reaching pieces of civil rights legislation in U.S. history.

Shortly following the American Civil War (1861–65), the Fifteenth Amendment was ratified, guaranteeing that the right to vote would not be denied "on account of race, color, or previous condition of servitude." Soon afterward the U.S. Congress enacted legislation that made it a federal crime to interfere with an individual's right to vote and that otherwise protected the rights promised to former slaves under both the Fourteenth (1868) and Fifteenth amendments. In some states of the former Confederacy, African Americans became a majority or near majority of the eligible voting population, and African American candidates ran and were elected to office at all levels of government.

Nevertheless, there was strong opposition to the extension of the franchise to African Americans. Following the end of Reconstruction in 1877, the Supreme Court of the United States limited voting protections under federal legislation, and intimidation and fraud were employed by white leaders to reduce voter registration and turnout among African Americans. As whites came to dominate state legislatures once again, legislation was used to strictly circumscribe the right of African Americans to vote. Poll taxes, literacy tests, grandfather clauses, whites-only primaries, and other measures disproportionately disqualified African Americans from voting. The result was that by the early 20th century nearly all African Americans were disfranchised. In the first half of the 20th century, several such measures were declared unconstitutional by the U.S. Supreme Court. In 1915, for example, grandfather clauses were invalidated, and in 1944 whites-only primaries were struck down. Nevertheless, by the early 1960s voter registration rates among African Americans were negligible in much of the Deep South and well below those of whites elsewhere.

In the 1950s and early 1960s the U.S. Congress enacted laws to protect the right of African Americans to vote, but such legislation was only partially successful. In 1964 the Civil Rights Act was passed and the Twenty-fourth Amendment, abolishing poll taxes for voting for federal offices, was ratified, and the following year Pres. Lyndon B. Johnson called for the implementation of comprehensive federal legislation to protect voting rights. The resulting act, the Voting Rights Act, suspended literacy tests, provided for federal oversight of voter registration in areas that had previously used tests to determine voter eligibility (these areas were covered under Section 5 of the legislation), and directed the attorney general of the United States to challenge the use of poll taxes for state and local elections. An expansion of the law in the 1970s also protected voting rights for non-English-speaking U.S. citizens. Section 5 was extended for 5 years in 1970, 7 years in 1975, and 25 years in both 1982 and 2006.

The Voting Rights Act resulted in a marked decrease in the voter registration disparity between whites and blacks. In the mid-1960s, for example, the overall proportion of white to black registration in the South ranged from about 2 to 1 to 3 to 1 (and about 10 to 1 in Mississippi). By the late 1980s racial variations in voter registration had largely disappeared. As the number of African American voters increased, so did the number of African American elected officials. In the mid-1960s there were about 70 African American elected officials in the South, but by the turn of the 21st century there were some 5,000, and the number of African American members of the U.S. Congress had increased from 6 to about 40. In what was widely perceived as a test case, *Northwest Austin Municipal Utility District Number One* v. *Holder, et al.* (2009), the Supreme Court declined to rule on the constitutionality of the federal-oversight provision of the Voting Rights Act.

TREATY ON THE NON-PROLIFERATION OF NUCLEAR WEAPONS (1968)

The Treaty on the Non-proliferation of Nuclear Weapons, also known as the Nuclear Non-proliferation Treaty, was signed in 1968 by the United Kingdom, the United States, the Soviet Union, and 59 other states. The treaty committed the three major signatories, which possessed nuclear weapons, not to assist other states in obtaining or producing them. Ratified by the Senate in 1969, the treaty became effective in March 1970 and was to remain so for a 25-year period. Additional countries later ratified the treaty; as of 2009 only three countries (India, Israel, and Pakistan) had refused to sign the treaty, and one country (North Korea) had signed and then withdrawn. The treaty was extended indefinitely and without conditions in 1995 by a consensus vote of 174 countries at the United Nations headquarters in New York.

The Non-proliferation Treaty was uniquely unequal, as it obliged nonnuclear states to forgo development of nuclear weapons while allowing the established nuclear states to keep theirs. Nevertheless, it was accepted because, especially at the time of signing, most nonnuclear states had neither the capacity nor the inclination to follow the nuclear path, and they were well aware of the dangers of proliferation for their security. In addition, it was understood in 1968 that, in return for their special status, the nuclear states would help the nonnuclear states in the development of civilian nuclear power (although in the event the distinction between civilian and military nuclear technology was not so straightforward) and also that the nuclear states would make their best efforts to agree on measures of disarmament. In the 2005 Review Conference of the Parties to the Treaty on Non-proliferation of Nuclear Weapons, this inequality was a major complaint against the established nuclear powers.

The treaty has continued to play an important role in sustaining the international norm against proliferation, but it has been challenged by a number of events, including (1) North Korea's withdrawal from the treaty in 2003 as it sought to acquire nuclear weapons, (2) evidence of the progress Iraq made in the 1980s on its nuclear program despite being a signatory to the treaty, and (3) allegations about uranium enrichment facilities in Iran, yet another signatory to the treaty. The credibility of the nonproliferation norm has also been undermined by the ability of India and Pakistan to become declared nuclear powers in 1998 without any serious international penalty—and indeed by India establishing its own special arrangements as part of a bilateral deal with the United States in 2008.

ENDANGERED SPECIES ACT (1973)

The Endangered Species Act is a law that obligates federal and state governments to protect all species threatened with extinction that fall within the borders of the United States and its outlying territories. The U.S. Fish and Wildlife Service (USFWS) of the Department of the Interior and the National Oceanic and Atmospheric Administration (NOAA) of the Department of Commerce are responsible for the conservation and management of fish and wildlife resources and their habitats, including endangered species. The Endangered Species Act allowes authorities to determine whether a given species qualifies for endangered or threatened status. It also barres the unauthorized harvest, custody, trade, and transport of endangered plants, animals, and other at-risk organisms and allowes for the application of civil and criminal penalties upon those who violate this law. Among other powers, the law gives the federal government the authority to establish cooperative agreements with and award monetary grants to the states to provide protection for at-risk organisms within their borders. In addition, this legislation is aided by a regularly updated endangered species list.

Because the "species" definition extends to subspecies or any distinct population segment capable of interbreeding, threatened subsets of species can also be singled out for protection. In addition, provisions for threatened species—that is, any species expected to become endangered in the future within a substantial portion of its geographic home range—are also included in the law. The Endangered Species Act also promotes the protection of critical habitats (that is, areas designated as essential to the survival of a given species).

The Endangered Species Act is being credited with the protection and recovery of several prominent species, such as the bald eagle (*Haliaeetus leucocephalus*), the American alligator (*Alligator mississippiensis*), and the gray wolf (*Canis lupus*).

WAR POWERS ACT (1973)

The War Powers Act, enacted by Congress over the veto of Pres. Richard Nixon, was intended to restrain the president's ability to commit U.S. forces overseas by requiring the executive branch to consult with and report to Congress before involving U.S. forces in foreign hostilities. In passing the legislation, members of Congress believed that they were restoring to Congress some of the constitutional war-making authority that had been effectively surrendered to the president in the Gulf of Tonkin Resolution (1964), which precipitated a massive increase in U.S. involvement in the Vietnam War. Although widely considered a measure for preventing "future Vietnams," the War Powers Act was nonetheless resisted or ignored by subsequent presidents, most of whom regarded it as an unconstitutional usurpation of their executive authority.

AMERICANS WITH DISABILITIES ACT (1990)

The Americans with Disabilities Act provides civil rights protections to individuals with disabilities and guarantees them equal opportunity in public accommodations, employment, transportation, state and local government services, and telecommunications. Some 43 million disabled people are affected by the law. The employment provisions applies to employers with 25 or more employees beginning July 26, 1992; those with 15 to 24 employees have to be in compliance starting on July 26, 1994. The public accommodations provisions generally became effective beginning Jan. 26, 1992. They required that necessary changes be made to afford access by persons with disabilities to all public facilities, including restaurants, theatres, day-care centres, parks, institutional buildings, and hotels.

In assessing their difficulties with compliance, many business leaders pointed to the confusion caused by vague language and definitions used in the act. For instance, employers are required to make "reasonable accommodation" for disabled job applicants or employees at the workplace, yet an accommodation need not be made if it would bring "undue hardship" to the employer's business. Discrimination is prohibited against "qualified" individuals with disabilities. A disabled person need only be able to handle the "essential functions" of a job with or without "reasonable accommodation."

Employers also quarreled with the broad definition of *disability*, which would include, for instance, alcoholics as long as they could perform the essential functions of the job. Such prospects sent employers scrambling to rewrite job descriptions in a way that clearly defined what was essential and what was not.

NORTH AMERICAN FREE TRADE AGREEMENT (1992)

The North American Free Trade Agreement (NAFTA) was a treaty designed to gradually eliminate most tariffs and other trade barriers on products and services passing between the United States, Canada, and Mexico. The pact effectively created a free-trade bloc among the three largest countries of North America.

NAFTA was inspired by the success of the European Community in eliminating tariffs in order to stimulate trade among its members. A Canadian-U.S. free-trade agreement was concluded in 1988, and NAFTA basically extended this agreement's provisions to Mexico. NAFTA was negotiated by the administrations of U.S. President George H. W. Bush, Canadian Prime Minister Brian Mulroney, and Mexican Pres. Carlos Salinas de Gortari. Preliminary agreement on the pact was reached in August 1992, and it was signed by the three leaders on Dec. 17, 1992. NAFTA was ratified by the three countries' national legislatures in 1993 and went into effect on Jan. 1, 1994.

NAFTA's main provisions called for the gradual reduction of tariffs, customs duties, and other trade barriers between the three members, with some tariffs being removed immediately and others over periods of as long as 15 years. NAFTA ensured eventual duty-free access for a vast range of manufactured goods and commodities traded between the signatories. Other provisions were designed to give U.S. and Canadian companies greater access to Mexican markets in banking, insurance, advertising, tele-communications, and trucking.

DON'T ASK, DON'T TELL (1993)

Don't Ask, Don't Tell is a byname for the official U.S. policy regarding the service of homosexuals in the military. The term was coined after Pres. Bill Clinton in 1993 signed a law (consisting of statute, regulations, and policy memo-randa) that directed military personnel to implement a policy characterized by the formula, "don't ask, don't tell, don't pursue, and don't harass."

In the period between winning election as president in November 1992 and his inauguration in January 1993, Clinton announced his intention to fulfill a campaign pledge by quickly seeking to end the U.S. military's long-standing ban on homosexuals in the ranks. His effort, however, met with strong opposition, including from Sen. Sam Nunn, the Democrat head of the Senate Armed Services Committee. Indeed, Clinton's declaration put him at odds with top military leaders and with a number of key civilians who had oversight responsibilities for the armed forces. After heated debate in Congress and the media, Clinton managed to gain support for a compromise measure under which homosexual servicemen and servicewomen could remain in the military if they did not openly declare their sexual orientation. Yet military officers were overwhelmingly opposed to that approach, fearing that the mere presence of homosexuals in the armed forces would undermine morale. The policy was further subverted by discrimination suits that upheld the right of gays to serve in the military without fear of discrimination.

Under the terms of the law, homosexuals serving in the military were not allowed to talk about their sexual orientation or to engage in sexual activity, and commanding officers were not allowed to question service members about their sexual orientation. Although Clinton introduced "don't ask, don't tell" as a liberalization of existing policy, saying it was a way for gays to serve in the military after decades of exclusion, many gay rights activists objected to the law because it forced homosexual military personnel to be secretive about their sexual orientation and because it fell far short of a policy of complete acceptance. For a variety of reasons, the policy did little to change the behaviour of commanders; gay and lesbian soldiers continued to be discharged. The policy came under further scrutiny during the Iraq War (2003), when the military discharged many gay linguists specializing in Arabic. By the 15-year anniversary of the law in 2008, more than 12,000 officers had been discharged for refusing to hide their homosexuality. When Barack Obama campaigned for the presidency in 2008, he pledged to overturn "don't ask, don't tell" and to allow gays to serve openly in the military (a stance that was, according to public opinion polls, backed by a large majority of the public). During Obama's transition his press secretary unequivocally reiterated that position.

MEGAN'S LAW (1996)

Megan's Law was a statute that required law-enforcement officials to notify local schools, day-care centres, and residents of the presence of convicted sex offenders in their communities. The law was named after Megan Kanka, a seven-year-old New Jersey girl who was brutally raped and murdered in 1994 by a twice-convicted sexual offender who had been living across the street from her home. In various forms such statutes were passed by many U.S. states in the mid-1990s. In 1996 it was adopted as a federal law in the United States.

Concern about sexually related child abuse, and especially pedophilia, became intense during the 1980s, chiefly in the United States but also in Europe and elsewhere. Although the main threat to children continued to come from members of the victim's family, by about 1990 attention had come to be focused on sexual molestation committed by non-family members and strangers, and it was widely believed that offenders in such cases typically attacked many children before they were apprehended. In response, many U.S. states passed stringent sexual-predator laws. Under a law passed in Washington state in 1990, for example, convicted sex offenders whom prosecutors considered still dangerous were required to register with local police when they changed residence.

Following the attack on Megan Kanka, New Jersey enacted a law that created a three-tiered classification of offenders based on prosecutors' assessments of how likely it was that the offender would repeat his crime, and it required that police notify local residents of the presence of high-risk offenders. The law was soon imitated in other U.S. states and in Europe.

One unintended side effect of these laws has been the increase in the psychological trauma to which some victims were exposed. Traditionally, prosecutors attempted to arrange plea bargains with defendants in child-abuse cases in order to spare the child the ordeal of testifying in court. Some versions of Megan's Law, however, require all persons convicted of a sexual offense against a minor, and not just those considered to be high-risk, to register with police. Thus, in the hope of avoiding the necessity of registration, which normally has devastating effects on the defendant's employment prospects, some defendants choose to go to trial rather than plead guilty. Megan's Law has been criticized on other grounds by civil libertarians, who argue that the stigmatization and ostracism that inevitably result from registration constitute a second punishment for the same crime and make rehabilitation of the offender more difficult.

TELECOMMUNICATIONS ACT (1996)

The Telecommunications Act, signed into law by Pres. Bill Clinton in 1996, was essentially a long-awaited update to the Communications Act of 1934.

In the nearly sixty-two years since that first bill went into effect, methods of communication in America had changed radically, particularly at the end of the century with the adoption of new digital forms of connection. It was also a milestone for deregulation, and it created a flurry of mergers, acquisitions, and divestitures among the giants of the telecommunications industry, as well as the rapid rise and fall of many small entrepreneurs. In essence the Telecommunications Act allowed for greater competition among local telephone, long-distance telephone, and cable television markets, which existed for the most part as regulated monopolies. Beyond these base industries, however, the act had far-reaching effects on such businesses as traditional radio stations and other radio spectrum users, Internet providers and broadcasters, computer hardware manufacturers, and software developers. It also opened new doors for emerging technologies, such as digital television, wireless and satellite services, and subscription programming.

DIGITAL MILLENNIUM COPYRIGHT ACT (1998)

The Digital Millennium Copyright Act was designed to adapt copyright laws to the rise of the Internet in the 1990s. Traditionally, copyright laws focused on published material, but the Internet made possible the electronic reproduction of virtually any document. The inadequacy of existing laws particularly alarmed businesses that needed copyright protection, such as book publishers, music recording companies, software publishers, and film-makers. In response to these concerns, Congress passed the Digital Millennium Copyright Act in 1998. The act, among other provisions, banned the use of software that circumvented copyright protections in computer programs. Although many hailed the act as a wise step in protecting fundamental copyrights, some critics charged that it suppressed free speech and unfairly limited the freedom of computer scientists and researchers. Others warned that the act would ultimately backfire, claiming that it would deter research to study flaws in computer security programs.

NO CHILD LEFT BEHIND ACT (2001)

The No Child Left Behind Act (NCLB) was a U.S. federal law aimed at improving public primary and secondary schools, and thus student performance, via increased accountability for schools, school districts, and states. The act was passed by Congress with bipartisan support in December 2001 and signed into law by Pres. George W. Bush in January 2002.

NCLB introduced significant changes in the curriculum of public primary and secondary schools in the

United States and dramatically increased federal regulation of state school systems. Under the law, states were required to administer yearly tests of the reading and mathematics skills of public school students and to demonstrate adequate progress toward raising the scores of all students to a level defined as "proficient" or higher. Teachers were also required to meet higher standards for certification. Schools that failed to meet their goals would be subject to gradually increasing sanctions, eventually including replacement of staff or closure.

Supporters of NCLB cited its initial success in increasing the test scores of minority students, who historically performed at lower levels than white students. Indeed, in the 2000 presidential campaign Bush touted the proposed law as a remedy for what he called "the soft bigotry of low expectations" faced by the children of minorities. Critics, however, complained that the federal government was not providing enough funding to implement the law's requirements and that it had usurped the states' traditional control of education as provided for in the Constitution. Moreover, they charged that the law was actually eroding the quality of education by forcing schools to "teach to the test" while neglecting other parts of the curriculum, such as history, social science, and art.

USA PATRIOT ACT (2001)

The USA PATRIOT Act, formally called the Uniting and Strengthening America by Providing Appropriate Tools Required to Intercept and Obstruct Terrorism Act, was enacted in October 2001 in the wake of the September 11 terrorist attacks. Designed to enable law-enforcement authorities to move more nimbly against terrorist threats, it relaxed legal checks on surveillance and granted the Central Intelligence Agency (CIA) and the Federal

Bureau of Investigation (FBI) a freer hand to gather data electronically on citizens and resident foreigners. The legislation, approved by a sweeping majority in Congress, reduced the need for subpoenas, court orders, or warrants for eavesdropping on Internet communications, monitoring financial transactions, and obtaining individuals' electronic records. As part of criminal investigations, law-enforcement and intelligence agencies were authorized to track the Web sites that suspects visited and identify those to whom they sent e-mail. Internet service providers were required to turn over data on customers' Web-surfing habits to authorities on demand.

Many of these provisions were hailed as necessary revisions of surveillance laws to keep increasingly sophisticated and determined terrorists at bay. Civil liberties advocates, however, worried that the PATRIOT Act's easing of judicial oversight and vague definition of legitimate subjects for electronic surveillance opened it to abuse and could cast the legal dragnet too wide in the search for incriminating evidence. Most of the law's provisions, however, were made permanent in 2006 by the USA PATRIOT Improvement and Reauthorization Act.

The USA PATRIOT Act paved the way for wider deployment of the controversial FBI program formerly known as Carnivore—renamed, less menacingly, DCS 1000—which sifted e-mail for particular addresses or specific text strings (sequences of characters). In December 2001 it was reported that the FBI had developed "Magic Lantern," a so-called Trojan horse program designed to crack encrypted files and e-mails. The program could implant itself surreptitiously in a suspect's computer via an e-mail message and then record keystrokes to obtain the user's passwords. In mid-2002 the Department of Justice (DOJ) announced Operation TIPS (Terrorism Information and Prevention System), a plan to recruit workers such as mail carriers and utility meter readers as informants to spot and report "suspicious activity."

EMERGENCY ECONOMIC STABILIZATION ACT (2008)

The Emergency Economic Stabilization Act (EESA) was designed to prevent the collapse of the U.S. financial system during the subprime mortgage crisis (2007–08), a severe contraction of liquidity in credit markets worldwide brought about by widespread losses in the subprime mortgage sector. The EESA sought to restore liquidity to credit markets by authorizing the secretary of the treasury to purchase up to $700 billion in mortgage-backed securities and other troubled assets from the country's banks, as well as any other financial instrument the secretary deemed necessary "to promote financial market stability." The act also included provisions to minimize foreclosures on federally owned mortgages, to recover possible future losses on the government's mortgage investments, to prevent windfalls for executives of banks that benefit from the act, and to monitor the investments of the Treasury Department through reports to Congress and a specially created oversight board.

Pres. George W. Bush and Secretary of the Treasury Henry Paulson first proposed the EESA in September 2008, and the measure was introduced in the House of Representatives as an amendment to a bill to provide tax relief to members of the uniformed services. Despite intense lobbying by the White House and support by leaders of both the Democratic and Republican parties and by Barack Obama and John McCain, the presidential nominees of the two parties, the House rejected the plan

228–205 (two-thirds of Democrats and one-third of Republicans voted in favour of the measure) on Sept. 29, 2008. The measure was opposed in part because many in Congress—and in the public—considered the plan an unfair subsidy by taxpayers to Wall Street bankers. Three days later the Senate amended a bill to provide parity for mental-health insurance coverage with the EESA and other bills, including measures to create tax incentives for energy investments and to extend various exemptions for middle-class taxpayers. The new legislation, though $150 billion more expensive than the original House version, was passed by the Senate and the House after many representatives who had opposed the EESA changed their minds, in part because of continuing deterioration of the financial markets and shifting public opinion. The legislation was signed into law by Bush on Oct. 3, 2008.

The EESA authorized the treasury secretary to establish a Troubled Asset Relief Program (TARP) to protect the ability of consumers and businesses to secure credit. The Treasury Department's purchases of illiquid assets under the TARP would make it easier for banks to extend credit and would thereby increase confidence in the credit markets. The EESA featured a graduated release of funds to the Treasury Department. The treasury secretary was immediately authorized to spend up to $250 billion; an additional $100 billion would become available if the president confirmed that the funds were needed, and a further $350 billion would be authorized upon confirmation by the president and approval by Congress. The EESA also directed the treasury secretary to create a program to allow banks to insure their troubled assets with the government.

The EESA required the Treasury Department to modify distressed loans when possible to prevent home foreclosures. Many of these subprime loans were extended to individuals who were unable to qualify for normal loans or unwilling to provide certain financial information. The EESA also directed other federal agencies to make similar adjustments to the loans they owned or controlled, and it made various improvements in the Hope for Homeowners program, which allowed certain homeowners to refinance their mortgages with fixed rates for terms of up to 30 years.

The EESA mandated that banks that sell troubled assets to the government under the TARP provide warrants to ensure that taxpayers benefit from any future growth the banks may enjoy as a result of their participation in the program. Furthermore, the act required the president to submit legislation to recoup from the financial industry any net loss to taxpayers that had occurred after a five-year period.

The EESA also included provisions designed to prevent executives of participating banks from unjustly enriching themselves. Under the act, the banks would lose certain tax benefits and, in some cases, would be forced to limit executive pay. The EESA imposed limits on so-called "golden parachutes" by requiring that unearned bonuses of departing executives be returned. Finally, the EESA established an oversight board to ensure that the treasury secretary did not act in an "arbitrary" or "capricious" manner, as well as an inspector general to protect against waste, fraud, and abuse. The Treasury Department was required to report to Congress on its use of the funds as well as on its progress in addressing the crisis.

Paulson at first intended to limit his purchases under the EESA to mortgage-backed securities and other troubled assets. In the days immediately following the law's passage, however, it became increasingly apparent that this approach alone would not restore liquidity to the credit market soon enough to avert additional bank failures and further damage to the economy. After meetings in Washington with finance ministers from other member countries of the World Bank and the International Monetary Fund, Paulson and Bush announced plans to use $250 billion immediately to buy stock in troubled banks, a move designed to expand their capital bases directly so that they could begin lending again as quickly as possible.

Supporters of the EESA argued that the act was necessary to extend immediate assistance to homeowners and restore confidence in the financial markets, thereby preventing the collapse of the financial system and a deep recession. Opponents maintained that the EESA was vaguely formulated, that it gave the treasury secretary too much power, that it was too costly, and that it unfairly benefited investors while failing to address the immediate crisis or the potential long-term effects on the economy.

THE LEGISLATIVE BRANCH IN TRANSITION

It is often said that, since the early 20th century, legislatures have gradually lost power to chief executives in most countries of the world. Certainly, chief executives have assumed an increasingly large role in the making of law, through the initiation of legislation that comes before parliaments, assemblies, and congresses; through the exercise of various rule-making functions; and as a result of the growth of different types of delegated legislation. In some jurisdictions, the chief executive has acquired enhanced power to veto bills passed by the legislature. In the United States, for example, many governors now use a "line-item veto" to strike particular provisions of a bill passed by the state legislature, thereby effectively remaking the bill instead of simply enacting or killing it. At the federal level, presidents who believe that a certain provision of a bill is unconstitutional or improper intrusion on executive power have sometimes issued informal "signing statements" to declare their intention to ignore the provision or to apply it only in certain cases. Although presidents have issued signing statements since the early 19th century to comment on legislation, it is only since the late 20th century that they have been used to reinterpret legislation to the president's liking.

It is also true that chief executives have come to predominate in the sphere of foreign affairs. By devices such as executive agreements, which are frequently used in place of treaties, chief executives have freed themselves from dependence upon legislative approval as the executive budget and the rise of specialized budgetary agencies in the executive division have threatened the traditional fiscal controls of legislatures.

In some countries, legislative powers have been effectively ceded to the chief executive because the legislature does not insist upon exercising them itself. Since the end of the Franklin D. Roosevelt administration in 1945, for example, most U.S. presidents have committed the country's armed forces to major hostilities abroad, but none have asked for or received a formal declaration of war from Congress. Nevertheless, Congress has sometimes checked executive war making by refusing to pass necessary appropriations bills or by passing legislation to prevent the chief executive from spending already appropriated funds for certain purposes. In other respects, too, Congress retains a substantial measure of power with respect to the executive through its oversight of the executive bureaucracy, through its investigative powers, and through its control over legislative programs of foreign aid.

Appendix:
Table of Speakers of the House of Representatives

		SPEAKERS OF THE HOUSE OF REPRESENTATIVES			
NO.	NAME	PARTY OR FACTION	STATE	CONGRESS	TERM OF SERVICE
1	Frederick Augustus Muhlenberg	Pro-Administration	Pa.	1st	1789–91
2	Jonathan Trumbull, Jr.	Federalist	Ct.	2nd	1791–93
3	Frederick Augustus Muhlenberg	Anti-Administration	Pa.	3rd	1793–95
4	Jonathan Dayton	Federalist	N.J.	4th and 5th	1795–99
5	Theodore Sedgwick	Federalist	Mass.	6th	1799–1801
6	Nathaniel Macon	Democratic-Republican	N.C.	7th, 8th, and 9th	1801–07
7	Joseph Bradley Varnum	Democratic-Republican	Mass.	10th and 11th	1807–11
8	Henry Clay	Democratic-Republican	Ky.	12th and 13th	1811–14
9	Langdon Chevesn	Republican	S.C.	13th	1814–15
10	Henry Clay	Democratic-Republican	Ky.	14th, 15th, and 16th	1815–20
11	John W. Taylor	Republican	N.Y.	16th	1820–21
12	Philip Barbour	Republican	Va.	17th	1821–23

No.	Name	Party or Faction	State	Congress	Term of Service
13	Henry Clay	Democratic-Republican	Ky.	18th	1823–25
14	John W. Taylor	Republican	N.Y.	19th	1825–27
15	Andrew Stevenson	Jacksonian/Democratic	Va.	20th, 21st, 22nd and 23rd	1827–34
16	John Bell	Jacksonian	Tn.	23rd	1834–35
17	James Polk	Jacksonian/Democratic	Tn.	24th and 25th	1835–39
18	Robert M.T. Hunter	Democratic	Va.	26th	1839–41
19	John White	Whig	Ky.	27th	1841–43
20	John Winston Jones	Democratic	Va.	28th	1843–45
21	John Wesley Davis	Democratic	Ind.	29th	1845–47
22	Robert Charles Winthrop	American	Mass.	30th	1847–49
23	Howell Cobb	Democratic	Ga.	31st	1849–51
24	Linn Boyd	Republican	Ky.	32nd and 33rd	1851–55
25	Nathaniel Banks	Republican	Mass.	34th	1855–57
26	James Lawrence Orr	Republican	S.C.	35th	1857–59
27	William Pennington	Republican	N.J.	36th	1859–61
28	Galusha A. Grow	Republican	Pa.	37th	1861–63

NO.	NAME	PARTY OR FACTION	STATE	CONGRESS	TERM OF SERVICE
29	Schuyler Colfax	Republican	Ind.	38th, 39th, and 40th	1863–9
30	Theodore Medad Pomeroy	Republican	N.Y.	40th	1869
31	James G. Blainey	Republican	Maine	41st, 42nd, and 43rd	1869–75
32	Michael Crawford Kerr	Democratic	Ind.	44th	1875–76
33	Samuel Jackson Randall	Democratic	Pa.	44th, 45th, and 46th	1876–81
34	Joseph Warren Keifer	Republican	Ohio	47th	1881–83
35	John Griffin Carlisle	Democratic	Ky.	48th, 49th, and 50th	1883–89
36	Thomas Brackett Reed	Republican	Maine	51st	1889–91
37	Charles Crisp	Democratic	Ga.	52nd and 53rd	1891–95
38	Thomas Brackett Reed	Republican	Maine	54th and 55th	1895–99
39	David B. Henderson	Republican	Iowa	56th and 57th	1899–1903
40	Joseph Gurney Cannon	Republican	Ill.	58th, 59th, 60th, and 61st	1903–11
41	James Beauchamp Clark	Democratic	Mo.	62nd, 63, 64th, 65th, and 66th	1911–19
42	Frederick Gillett	Republican	Mass.	66th, 67th, and 68th	1919–25
43	Nicholas Longworth	Republican	Ohio	69, 70th, and 71st	1925–31
44	John Nance Garner	Democratic	Texas	72nd	1931–33

NO.	NAME	PARTY OR FACTION	STATE	CONGRESS	TERM OF SERVICE
45	Henry T. Rainey	Democratic	Ill.	73rd	1933–35
46	Joseph Wellington Byrns	Democratic	Tn.	74th	1935–36
47	William Brockman Bankhead	Democratic	Ala.	74th, 75th, and 76th	1936–40
48	Samuel T. Rayburn	Democratic	Texas	76th, 77th, 78th, and 79th	1940–47
49	Joseph W. Martin, Jr.	Republican	Mass.	80th	1947–49
50	Samuel T. Rayburn	Democratic	Texas	81st and 82nd	1949–53
51	Joseph W. Martin, Jr.	Republican	Mass.	83rd	1953–55
52	Samuel T. Rayburn	Democratic	Texas	84th, 85th, 86th, and 87th	1955–61
53	John W. McCormack	Democratic	Mass.	87th, 88th, 89th, 90th, and 91st	1962–71
54	Carl B. Albert	Democratic	Okla.	92nd, 93rd, and 94th	1971–77
55	Thomas P. O'Neill, Jr.	Democratic	Mass.	95th, 96th, 97th, 98th, and 99th	1977–87
56	James C. Wright, Jr.	Democratic	Texas	100th and 101st	1987–89
57	Thomas S. Foley	Democratic	Wash.	101st, 102nd, and 103rd	1989–95
58	Newt Gingrich	Republican	Ga.	104th and 105th	1995–99
59	J. Dennis Hastert	Republican	Ill.	106th, 107th, 108th, and 109th	1999–2007
60	Nancy Pelosi	Democratic	Calif.	110th and 111th	2007–

Glossary

acquiescence The act of agreeing passively or without objection.

aggrandizement An increase in size, degree, or number.

agrarian Agricultural.

annexation The incorporation of a territory into an existing nation or state.

antebellum Existing prior to the war (usually in reference to the Civil War).

apportionment The proportional distribution of members of the U.S. House of Representatives on the basis of each state's population.

appropriation The act of a legislature authorizing money to be paid from the treasury for a specific use.

arbitration The settling of a dispute between parties.

archetype A model after which similar things are made.

bigot One who is intolerant of other groups, races, or religions.

bivouac To assemble in an improvised military camp.

bureaucracy The layered and subdivided administration of a government or other complex organization.

caucus A group within a legislative body that pursues its interests through the legislative process.

codification The process of reducing to a code, as in law, or the process of arranging something in a systematic form.

demagogue A leader who gains power by exploiting popular prejudices, often using lies and distortions.

dignitary A person who holds high rank.

emancipation The act of freeing from restraint.

filibuster To prevent legislation by using obstructive tactics, most commonly by making very long speeches to retain control of the floor.

flamboyant Showy, extravagant.

gubernatorial Relating to a governor.

incumbent Currently holding an official position.

insurgent One who forcefully opposes a civil authority or established government.

jurisdiction The extent or territory within which judicial authority may be exercised.

laxity Looseness.

lobbyist A person who tries to influence legislation on behalf of a special interest.

magnanimity Generosity in forgiveness of insult or injury.

monopolize To obtain exclusive possession or control; to dominate completely.

obloquy Abusive language aimed at a person or thing.

populist A supporter of the rights and power of the people.

proliferation Rapid growth, as if by producing new parts or offspring.

prolix long and wordy.

prototype The original model on which something is based.

proxy An authorized substitute.

quorum The minimum number of members of a legislative body that must be present for business to officially be conducted.

ratify To confirm by approval or formal sanction.

roil To stir up, agitate, or anger.

secession The withdrawal of a state from a larger political body.

sedition An act intended to incite rebellion against an established government.

semantics The study of meaning in language.

sobriquet A nickname.

sovereignty An autonomous state.

statute A law enacted by a legislature.

tactician One skilled at employing available means to accomplish an end.

trenchant Incisive, keen.

truculent Fierce, cruel.

veto The power to prevent the enactment of measures passed by a legislature.

whip A person in the legislature whose job is to ensure party members turn up for important votes.

For
Further
Reading

Abraham, Henry J. *Justices, Presidents, and Senators: A History of the U.S. Supreme Court Appointments from Washington to Bush II.* New York, NY: Rowman & Littlefield Publishers, 2007.

Baker, Ross K. *House & Senate.* New York, NY: W. W. Norton, 2008.

Beeman, Richard. *Plain, Honest Men: The Making of the American Constitution.* New York, NY: Random House, 2009.

Carey, John M. *Legislative Voting and Accountability.* New York, NY: Cambridge University Press, 2008.

Davidson, Roger H., Walter J. Oleszek, and Frances E. Lee. *Congress and Its Members.* Washington, DC: CQ Press, 2007.

Fisher, Louis. *Constitutional Conflicts Between Congress and the President.* Lawrence, KS: University Press of Kansas, 2007.

Gold, Martin B. *Senate Procedure and Practice.* New York, NY: Rowman & Littlefield Publishers, 2008.

Gould, Lewis. *The Most Exclusive Club: A History of the Modern United States Senate.* New York, NY: Basic Books, 2006.

Greenburg, Jan. *Supreme Conflict: The Inside Story of the Struggle for Control of the United States Supreme Court.* New York, NY: Penguin, 2008.

Mayhew, David R. *Congress: The Electoral Connection*. New Haven, CT: Yale University Press, 2004.

Oleszek, Walter J., *Congressional Procedures and the Policy Process*. Washington, DC: CQ Press, 2007.

Quirk, Paul J. and Sarah A. Binder, eds. *Institutions of American Democracy: The Legislative Branch*. New York, NY: Oxford University Press, 2006.

Remini, Robert V. *The House: The History of the House of Representatives*. New York, NY: HarperCollins, 2007.

Rosen, Jeffrey. *The Supreme Court: The Personalities and Rivalries That Defined America*. New York, NY: Macmillan, 2007.

Sinclair, Barbara. *Unorthodox Lawmaking: New Legislative Processes in the U.S. Congress*. Washington, DC: CQ Press, 2007.

Toobin, Jeffrey. *The Nine: Inside the Secret World of the Supreme Court*. New York, NY: Random House, 2008.

Index